HANDFULS ON PURPOSE

SERIES X

BY
Pastor JAMES SMITH

Author of "A Survey of the Wondrous Cross,"
"Spiritual Patterns" etc.

WM. B. EERDMANS PUBLISHING COMPANY

Grand Rapids   **Michigan**

American Edition

———

Published in 1947, by

WM. B. EERDMANS PUBLISHING CO.
by
Special Arrangement with

PICKERING & INGLIS, LTD.
14 Paternoster Row, London, E.C.4
229 Bothwell St., Glasgow, C.2
Manchester—Newcastle—Liverpool—Edinburgh

PHOTOLITHOPRINTED BY CUSHING - MALLOY, INC.
ANN ARBOR, MICHIGAN, UNITED STATES OF AMERICA
1962

Guide to Series 1 to 12

SERIES 1 to 10 .. By Pastor JAMES SMITH
SERIES 11 and 12, .. By ROBERT LEE
SERIES 13, .. COMPLETE INDEX TO SERIES

PREFACE.

"HANDFULS ON PURPOSE, Volume IX, was written before I left Scotland, fifteen years ago. I am thankful that after the lapse of these years I have been permitted to add one more to the number. In my own manner I was hoping to get through the Wonderful Book with this volume; but while I have managed to get to Malachi in the Old Testament Section, I have only got, with 51 Separate Studies, from Corinthians to Titus in the New Testament Series. I felt compelled to halt at the gate of "HEBREWS," partly for lack of space.

It is now about 25 years since these "Handfuls" first appeared, and from the fact that they still have the freshness of youth in their face is ample proof that while men's words and thoughts may in time grow stale and loose their vitality, the living and life-sustaining truth unveiled in God's Word, like the living Christ Himself, is the "same yesterday, to-day, and for ever."

In these "Expository Outlines" we have diligently and prayerfully sought to honour the Lord, by first *receiving*, and then endeavouring to make known the discoveries made "in the volume of *The Book.*"

May the blessing of the Lord that maketh rich, attend all who are pleased to make use of these "Notes" for their own spiritual growth in grace, as well as in their more public service for the Master. I am now in my 80th year, and can praise Him that I still know something of the holy *heart-burn* that comes while "He talks with us by the way, and while He opens to us the Scriptures" (Luke 24. 32). I am thankful to the "Giver of All" to know that in His great goodness, through His Holy Spirit, He has been making these "Outline Studies" helpful to many. I wish also to thank the many friends who have been doing good service in making these books known to needy and weary workers, and especially do I offer my sincere thanks to the Publishers, who have been so faithful, so considerate, and generous in their dealings with the Author.

It is a God-honouring work to "minister seed to the sower, and bread for eating, that *their giving* may yield a plentiful harvest" (2 Cor. 9. 10).

Yours in the Eternal Fellowship.

JAMES SMITH.

NHILL, VICTORIA,
AUSTRALIA.

INDEX OF SUBJECTS.

INDEX OF TEXTS.

Handfuls on Purpose

Old Testament Outlines

GOD'S GRACIOUS AND ETERNAL PURPOSE
HOSEA 2. 14-18.

HOSEA is reckoned the first of the minor prophets, a contemporary of Isaiah, in the eventful days of Uzziah and Hezekiah, Kings of Judah. "The Word of the Lord came to him," and by his vital relationship with a morally depraved and faithless wife, he symbolically revealed Israel's treacherous relationship with her longsuffering God. Here let us try and see something of the abounding grace of this God with whom we have to do.

I. **His Gracious Method.** "I will *allure* her into the wilderness" (v. 14). He does not say, "I will *drive* her," but "I will allure her" into a condition where her old evil associations and habits will not have the same bewitching influence over her. Thus the first act of grace is seen in a merciful alluring. Why are we so slow to recognise and believe in this blessed work of the Holy Spirit, and to imagine that when the pleasures of material things begin to wither and die in our experience, that life has lost its value? It is always a seeming barren wilderness to the worldly-minded to be brought into a position where they having nothing left but God.

II. **His Merciful Purpose.** "I will speak comfortably unto her." God knows what our deep needs are, and how best to meet them, for "as a mother comforteth, so the

Lord." Oh, the bliss that dawns upon our souls when in our bewilderment the peace of God breaks in upon our troubled hearts. His comforting words and ways bring us out of the darkness of doubt and fearfulness, into His marvellous light and restfulness. Why is it that we need so much alluring to bring us into that condition where God can give us His most precious gifts? Surely this is the blindness and the stubbornness of our natural minds. Still, "He *giveth* us the victory."

III. The Wonderful Results.

1. "I WILL GIVE her *vineyards from thence*" (v. 15). What! vineyards from the *wilderness*, where we could see nothing but barrenness and desolation? Yes, out of our experiences, of weariness, and seeming failure God can make, even these, fresh sources of refreshing and strength. By this we are assured that the Divine leading is never contrary to our highest good. Our Father's *hand* is never out of harmony with our Father's *heart*. His wisdom never contradicts His love. Therefore, let us confidently and joyfully trust, even when we have been disappointed and brought low. *"Where* He leads I will follow." The Holy Spirit is still alluring into new and deeper experiences.

2. "I WILL GIVE HER THE VALLEY OF ACHOR (trouble or trembling) *for a door of hope.*" In the dark and fearsome valley of trouble He can and will open a new door into fresh hopefulness and larger liberty (Josh. 7. 26) to every humble believer. We dread the experience of "trouble," it may be because it brings to us such a deep sense of our weakness and helplessness. Don't let us imagine that we are only making spiritual progress when we are climbing. Our wonder-working God can make our valley of trouble a place to lie down in (Isa. 65. 10).

3. "I WILL GIVE HER THE JOY OF YOUTH" (v. 15).

"She shall sing as in the days of her youth," when, as a nation, she was delivered out of Egypt. She had restored to her the freshness of his happy, youthful days. The God of Israel is the God of our salvation, still ready to renew and restore. Every answered prayer gives occasion for a new song. Every fresh manifestation of His wisdom and power brings additional victory into our spiritual being. In this sense, that which is truly Christian never grows old. "Even youths may faint, and young men utterly fail, but they that wait on the Lord shall change strength." When God satisfies the craving of our spiritual nature with "good things" the youth is "renewed like the eagle's" (Psa. 103. 5).

4. NEW RELATIONSHIP. "In that day thou shalt call me, My Husband" (v. 16). Blessed day for Israel when their "Deliverer shall come out of Zion, turning away captivity," and when "all Israel shall be saved" (Rom. 11. 26). "My husband." This is something deeper and sweeter than the mere formal designation, "My lord." "My wife" means much more to me than "my servant." What marvellous grace is here revealed. God pledging Himself to act for His people the part of a "Husband." Think of all that is involved in such a promise. Taking the responsibility of supplying our every need, and bringing us and keeping us in closest fellowship with Himself. "Call ME *Husband*, and trust Me to be loving and faithful as long as you do live." How sweet is this assurance to the weary, trembling heart. "Let not your heart be troubled, ye believe in God" (John 14. 1).

THE DIVINE BETROTHAL.
HOSEA 2. 19-23.

GOD did not love Israel because of her loveliness. She had been guilty of spiritual adultery; even her mother had played the harlot (v. 5). "Herein is love, not that we loved God, but that He loved us. " Even "while we were yet sinners, Christ died for us. " Note—

I. The Manner of this Betrothal. Betrothing is always a delicate business, and should be done on just and sacred principles; and so it is with our God.

1. In Righteousness. In a manner consistent with His character and our real need. He must be *just* to be a trustworthy Saviour (Isa. 45. 21). This betrothal is in perfect accord with all the holiness of Heaven, and will be faultless through the ages of eternity. But it must also be—

2. In Judgment. The betrothed is presently guilty, unclean, and deep in debt. How is she to be cleansed from sin and her great debt cancelled? This is the great problem of Divine grace. The wages of her sin is death. Sin and guilt must be judged. Glory and honour be to His Holy Name. Jesus Christ. God's Eternal Son, in seeking to betroth humanity to Himself, took our nature, bore our sins, shed His Blood to cleanse us, and became a propitiation for the whole world (1 John 2. 2).

3. In Lovingkindness. Yes, in that *love* that delighted to manifest itself in *kindness* toward us. This expressive word was used by the Psalmist over twenty times. Is it not marvellous to find it used here in connection with an adultrous nation? Behold the triumph of redeeming love. In *righteousness* and in *judgment*, these are the banks of the channel through which the stream of His *lovingkindness* flow, "that He might show the exceeding riches of His grace, in His kindness towards us, through Jesus Christ. For *by grace* are ye saved" (Eph. 2. 7, 8).

4. In Mercies. His mercies, Oh, how manifold! These are the gifts of His love to the betrothed. The apostle calls them "the riches of His grace" freely be-

stowed. When Rebekah decided to "go with this man," she doubtless received many mercies by the way. When the prodigal came home the mercies the father bestowed were many. The mercies of God constitute a powerful incentive to yield ourselves unto Him. Paul fully realised this, for in writing to the Romans, he says: "I beseech you by the *mercies of God*, that ye present your bodies a living sacrifice unto God...your reasonable service" (Rom. 12. 1).

5. IN FAITHFULNESS. This proposed union is all in faithfulness on His part. "My covenant will I not break." Faithful is He that hath promised. "I am the God of *Jacob*, that changing and doubtful one, but "I change not." He abideth faithful. What a comforting promise this is, when weakness, failure, and defeat overtake us in our work for Him.

II. **The Purpose of this Betrothal.** It is in prospect of marriage—Eternal union.

1. That we might KNOW Him. "Thou shalt know the Lord" (v. 20). Know Him sufficiently to love, serve, adore, and praise Him. This means *heart* knowledge, and His promise still is: "I will give them a heart to know Me" (Jer. 24. 7). This new God-given heart is what men need to know God. "This is life eternal to know...Jesus Christ whom He hath sent" (John 17. 3).

2. That we might BELONG to Him. "Thou shalt not be for another. So will I also be for thee" (chap. 3. 3). This is a searching truth. He is wholehearted for us; we must be wholehearted for Him, or play the harlot with our affections. Christ did not purchase us with His Blood that we might belong to *any other*. "ONE is your Master, even Christ." Ye are not your own. Do we desire as sincerely and fully to be His as He desires to be wholly ours?

3. That we might CONFESS Him. "They shall say,

Thou art my God" (v. 23). What harmony could there
be in a home where the wife was ashamed to say, "Thou
art my husband?" There are many who drink greatly
at the stream of God's mercies who never look up and say,
"Thou art my God." There is a present and eternal
honour for all who confess Jesus Christ *before men* (Luke
12. 8), for Christ will confess such *before the angels of God.*
Open thy mouth wide for Him and He shall fill it.

4. That we might be CO-WORKERS with Him. The
wife is to be the husband's *helpmate.* The members of
the body are co-workers with the head. We who have
been allowed into the family of God, by His merciful
and persistent grace, must surely feel our responsibility
to seek the furtherance of His kingdom. The cause of
God is a *family* business. Are you in His family? Then
are you in His business? "Lord, what wilt Thou have
me to do?"

THE PERIL OF SPIRITUAL IGNORANCE.
HOSEA 4. 6-11.

THIS chapter deals further with this sinful people, and
God's exposure of their character and judgment against
them, for "the Lord hath a controversy with them"
(v. 1). Here they are charged with the lack of knowledge.

I. **Ignorance of God is Common.** Israel had many
manifestations of God's wisdom and power in their past
history. Many messages from the lips and lives of His
prophets; yet in practical life they knew Him not. The
same is true to-day of multitudes in this so-called "Christian age." There are many that try to justify such
ignorance by saying, "God is unknowable," which is a
denial of the "testimony of Jesus," who is "the *image* of
the invisible God." "He that hath seen ME," He said,
"*hath seen* the Father." How sayest thou then, "God is
unknowable?" (John 14. 7-10).

II. Ignorance of God is often Wilful. "Thou hast *rejected* knowledge" (v. 6). Paul, writing to the same nation, says: "Being ignorant of God's righteousness, have *not submitted themselves*" (Rom. 10. 3). Those who have "left off to take heed to the Lord" (v. 10) are surely guilty of wilful blindness, because they love the darkness rather than the light. The darkness being better suited for the working out of their selfish and evil deeds. We reject the highest wisdom and knowledge when we reject Christ, who is the wisdom of God. Now to be willingly ignorant of God in the presence of His glorious Gospel is to be a voluntary criminal. "How shall we escape if we neglect?"

III. Wilful Ignorance of God is Fatal. "My people are destroyed (cut off) for lack of knowledge" (v. 6). It is fatal to spiritual life and fruitfulness as a branch cut off from the vine. God is not mocked. Such ignorance leads to—

1. DIVINE REJECTION. "Because thou hast rejected knowledge, I will also reject thee" (v. 6). There can be no real fellowship with God where the light of His Word is despised or ignored. The darkness of the unbelieving heart *cuts off* the vision of the face of God in Jesus Christ. Think of it. To reject the pleadings of His sacrificial love is to be finally rejected.

2. GLORY TURNED INTO SHAME. "I will change their glory into shame" (v. 7). Were they glorying in their false gods, in their growing numbers, in their material prosperity, or in their freedom from Divine restraint? They were not glorying in their God, so He would change all into a burning shame. Our God is "a jealous God." His love is so great and tender that He will not suffer any rival for our affections and devotion. Beware, for whatever takes His place in the heart's affections will certainly be changed into shame and confusion.

3. FRUITLESS EFFORT. "They shall eat and not have enough" (v. 10). No matter how much of material things they seek to cram into their greedy lives, they never have enough. Such is the experience of many a worldly man and woman. Frantic, fruitless effort to gain soul satisfaction, but they never have enough. They don't know the depth of the hunger of their own souls. Christ said: "I am the Bread of Life." Eat, O beloved, there is enough here and to spare. He satisfieth the hungry soul with good. "I am the Living Bread which came down from Heaven: if any man eat this Bread *he shall live for ever.*" Surely this is *enough.* "All fulness dwells in Him." Herein is God's ocean, to fill that little cup of yours, called *the heart.*

———

THE WITHDRAWAL OF GOD'S FACE.
HOSEA 5.

THIS simply means the withdrawal of His favour. Here is—

I. A Sad and Solemn Possibility. "He hath withdrawn Himself from them" (v. 6). The *face* of God stands for Divine presence and approval: guidance, comfort, and help. How miserable and hopeless must that nation or that soul be when this face is withdrawn from them. "The face of the Lord is against them that do evil" (Psa. 34. 16). How can we pray, "Make *Thy face* to shine upon us" (Psa. 31. 16) if in our service we are secretly seeking self-glory or the praise of men? He will not give His countenance to that which is displeasing to His heart. But, blessed be God, we can now behold His glory in the face of Jesus Christ (2 Cor. 4. 6). That face which is ever turned to those who love Him and faithfully follow on to know. "My presence (lit. face) shall go with you" (Exod. 33. 14). Beware. Grieve not the Holy Spirit, lest His face be hidden. Thou hast said, "Seek ye My face. " My heart would answer · "Thy face, Lord, will I seek. "

II. **The Reasons for His Withdrawal.** There must be a cause for this a cause that is painful to a loving heart.

1. THEY HAD BECOME A SNARE (v. 1). Instead of being a light and example, encouraging others to trust and serve the Lord, they had been as a snare and a net, trapping unwary feet into their ungodly ways. Do you wonder that God turns away His face and favour from those whose life and example encourages others to dishonour His Name and His message? "He that is not for Me is against Me. "

2. "THEY WOULD NOT FRAME THEIR DOINGS *to turn unto their God*" (v. 4). Or, "Their doings would not suffer them to honour their God. " Is it not so with many in our own day? Their daily *doings* are such that they will not suffer them to take time to pray, or even to think of the merciful God they are so persistently ignoring. Christian workers, take time to look up. Don't let the multitude of your engagements hinder the act of worship, lest He hide His face from you.

3. "THEY HAD DEALT TREACHEROUSLY with the Lord" (v. 7). Treachery is a violation of allegiance, a breach of faith. We are traitors to the Captain of our Salvation when we identify ourselves with the ranks of the enemy. To be unfaithful to our Lord is to miss the shining of His face. "Be not deceived, God is not mocked. " Now let us note some of—

III. **The Results of His Withdrawn Face.** On their part there was—

1. VAIN SACRIFICES. "They shall go with their flocks and herds,...but they shall not find Him" (v. 6). No number of sacrifices will atone for the hidden face of God as long as the heart is not right towards Him. Not any

number of works, nor any amount of fleshly energy
expended in His service will make up for the absence of
the Holy Spirit of power. Out of fellowship with God
means to us vain and fruitless testimony. They were—

2. OPPRESSED AND BROKEN (v. 11). Because they had
lost the vision of the face of their God, they sought help
from the gods made by hands. Disobeying the Word of
the Lord, they became obedient to the commandment of a
worldly-wise man (see Kings 12. 28). Distressed by the
powers of the world, and broken like a potter's vessel.
This becomes the destiny of the soul that has deliberately
grieved away the saving presence of its God. Then they—

3. SEEK FOR ANOTHER REMEDY (v. 13). But they
found no healing for their sickness, no balm for their
wound. Lord, to whom can we go when the true fountain
of our life has been dried up? All other sources are but
"broken cisterns" that can hold nothing that a sinful
soul needs. When faith in God has failed, then life is but
a desperate and hopeless struggle. "Without Me ye can
do nothing."

4. GOD WAITS TILL THEY SEEK HIS FACE. "I will
return to my place till they acknowledge their guilt and
seek My face" (v. 15, *margin*). Although His face may
be hidden because of their sin, yet in love He longs for
fellowship with the prodigal nation. *Confession* is needed,
and the search of the backslider should be not only for
healing, but for the brightness of the face of the Healer.
"Ye shall find Me when ye shall seek Me with *all your
heart.*" "He restoreth my soul." When the prodigal in
penitence saw the face of his father, he immediately
received of the riches of his grace. Those who refuse the
favour of God now, as revealed in the face of Jesus, may
have to say: "Hide me from the face of Him that sitteth
upon the throne, and from the wrath of the Lamb"
(Rev. 6. 16).

A CALL TO REPENTANCE.
HOSEA 6. 1-3.

THIS call evidently came through the lips of the prophet. And from all that follows it appears that they repented not, but the time will come when as a nation these words will be literally fulfilled (Jer. 30. 17). Let us think of these wonderful words in the light of New Testament teaching.

I. **The Need for Repentance.** They were "torn" and "smitten" (v. 1). Torn and tortured with their own wretchedness, and smitten with defeat and failure, and all this as the result of the Divine Providence, because of their unbelief. There is need for repentance on our part when we are torn with anxieties and smitten with shameful defeat in our work for the Lord. He knows how much there is in us that needs to be *torn* up and *smitten* down. Such as selfishness and pride.

II. **The Manner of this Repentance.** "Return unto the Lord." To return implies a backsliding condition. The repentance that does not bring us right back into the Lord is a repentance that needs to be repented of. The proof of the prodigal's repentance was in the fact that he arose and *came to his father.* Repentance is a "saving grace" only when it brings us to God in humility of heart, and it may be, with a trembling trust. The Divine arms are ever extended in loving welcome to the truly penitent soul. It is *with Him* we have to do at such a time, not with any earthly priest.

III. **The Results of Such Repentance.**

1. There will be "HEALING AND BINDING." "He will heal and He will bind us up" (v. 1). Our diseased hearts and torn hopes will be healed and bound up. "He healeth all our diseases" and "bindeth up the broken in heart." They have repented deeply who live in the joy of this spiritual health and wholeness.

2. There will be QUICKENING. "He will revive us"
(v. 2). After the "healing" and the "binding" there
comes the energising powers of a new life. When the
sinner has been pardoned and reconciled to God there will,
or should be, a revitalizing of the soul by the Holy Spirit.
"It is the Spirit that quickeneth." He can make all things
in our daily lives new.

3. There will be a "LIVING IN THE LIGHT OF GOD."
"We shall live in His light" (v. 2). The man of the world
may be all alive in the light of his fellowmen, but it is a
very different thing to be really alive in the light of God.
Not merely living under His eye, as all are, but to have the
life that is life indeed in God's reckoning. "I am come,"
said Jesus Christ, "that ye might have life." "He that
hath the Son hath life," and may have it in abundance.
This is the real life as God sees it. The world's estimate
is very different; but what does it matter as long as we
are *living* in God's sight that life that is eternal.

4. There shall be a GROWING EXPERIENCE. "Then shall
we know if we follow on to know the Lord" (v. 3). It is
the nature of every living thing to *grow*. The new spiritual
life is not to be like a stagnant pool, but an ever deepening
stream. We are to "grow in *grace* and in the *knowledge*"
of Him who is the source and force of the new life. This
we shall do if we faithfully follow on. "My son, if thou
wilt receive My words...and hide them with thee, then
thou wilt understand righteousness and judgment and
equity, yea every good path" (Prov. 2. 1, 9).

5. There will be TIMES OF REFRESHING. "He shall go
forth as the morning...and He shall come unto us as the
rain" (v. 3). What a bright, cheerful experience to have
His presence breathing upon us like the dawning of the
day, and to have our drooping and fainting hearts refreshed
like the rain upon the mown grass. The *Presence* of God,

by His Spirit, always brings times of refreshing   We áre taught to pray: "Give us this day our daily bread." May we not also pray: "Give us this day a fresh dawning of Thy glorious presence upon the whole landscape of our lives?"

THE DIVINE REVIEW.
HOSEA 11. 1-11.

HERE Jehovah tenderly reminds His wayward people of what He had done for them.   Oh, how ready we are to forget the past mercies of our God.   "Son, remember." The sin of discouragement may often be the sin of forgetfulness.   "Bless the Lord, O my soul, and forget not all His benefits" (Psa. 103. 1-5).   He reminds them of—

I. What He Did for Them.

1. HE LOVED.   "When Israel was a child, then I loved him" (v. 1).   When Israel was a child then he had no wisdom or strength to glory in.   But the child's ignorance and weakness did not hinder the love of God.   Let us never forget that God loved us even "while we were yet sinners."

2. HE DELIVERED.   "I called My Son out of Egypt" (v. 1).   Out of the land of darkness, sorrow, and bondage. He hath delivered us out of the kingdom of darkness and the slavery of ignorance, into the glorious light and liberty of the children of God.   Delivered that we might be a separated people unto His Name.

3. HE TAUGHT.   "I taught Ephraim also to go, taking them by the arms" (v. 3).   What a picture this is of Divine patience and carefulness.   Like a father taking his child by the arms and teaching him to walk.   God means us "to go," and although we may feel shaky in our feet, He will "perfect His strength in our weakness."

4. HE DRAWS.   "I drew them with cords of a *man,*

with bands of love" (v. 4). Not with cords of a *beast*, following in ignorance of its master's will. Not with the iron bonds of compulsion, dragging against the will; but with that tender and most effective of all ties—LOVE. "The love of Christ constraineth us." "O Love, that wilt not let me go, I yield my willing heart to Thee."

5. HE ENCOURAGED. "How shall I give thee up?" (v. 8). What comfort we may draw from language like this, as if He said: "I have done great things for thee; I have had long patience with thee. How shall I give thee up?" Let us hear these words as coming from the lips of our Redeemer: "I have ransomed thee with My own Blood, endowed thee with My own life, called thee by My own Name, given thee My own Spirit, and promised thee Eternal Life and a place in My own Home. How shall I give thee up?"

6. HE ASSURED. "I am God, the Holy One, in the midst of thee" (v. 9). The assurance of His Presence is the fortaste of victory (Exod. 33. 15). "Greater is He that is with us, and in us, than all that can be against us." "*He hath said*, I will never leave thee nor forsake thee. So that *we may boldly say*, The Lord is My Helper, and I will not fear" (Heb. 13. 5, 6). We may well have *boldness* in His service with such an all-sufficient and unfailing promise. For "in His presence there is fulness of joy" (Psa. 16. 11). He also reminds them of—

II. How they had Requited His Goodness.

1. They had LISTENED TO OTHER VOICES. "They called them, so they went" (v. 2). How unstable are the human affections. The worshippers of other gods called them, so they sacrificed unto Baalim. Before we pass judgment on their shameful faithlessness, let us ask: Are there no voices of the world, the flesh, our social relationships or sceptical acquaintances to which we have listened

and turned aside from our ardent service of God? Satan is an adept in this alluring art. "Be ye faithful unto death."

2. They did not RECOGNISE HIS GOOD HAND as they should. "They knew not that I healed them" (v. 3). What? Recipients of His great mercies, and blind to the Giver? Is there any sin more common than this? The world is crowded with such sinners, and the so-called Church is by no means destitute of such wilful ingrates. They receive with open heart and willing arms all the mercies God may pour into their earthly lot, but never recognise the Giver with even an upward look. God has given His Son to the death of the Cross to save them, but they have never said: "Thanks be unto God for His unspeakable gift."

3. They had A TENDENCY TO BACKSLIDE. "My people are bent on backsliding from Me" (v. 7). Alas, this *bent* is only too common among the Lord's professing people. How much we need to pray: "Uphold Thou my goings, that I slip not." The temptations of the world to turn aside always press heavily upon the Christian pilgrim. Yet in midst of all these tendencies to go out of His way, we are assured that He is faithful who hath promised. "Cleanse Thou me from *secret* faults."

THE FINAL APPEAL.

HOSEA 14.

AGAIN we hear the pathetic voice of that inextinguishable love that "suffers long and is kind." They had fallen by their iniquity, but here is hope.

I. **The Urgent Call.** We may regard this call as four-fold.

1. TO RETURN. "O Israel, return unto the Lord *thy* God" (v. 1.) He is still *thy* God, even when you have

lusted after other gods and caused Him to hide His face
from thee. There is no remedy for Israel's sin, nor for
ours, but to return to the Lord, and in humility and faith
own Him as "My Lord and my God," even as Thomas
did (John 20. 28).

2. To PRAYER. "Take with you words,...and say
unto Him, Take away all iniquity, and receive us
graciously" (v. 2). The separating causes are in their
"iniquity;" the uniting elements are all in the graciousness of our God. This kind of praying is very definite
business. There are many who hope their sins may be
forgiven, but who have never *said a word* to God about
them. Here is a simple but God-given formula for such:
"Take with you words and say: Take away my iniquity,
and receive me graciously, for Jesus' sake."

3. To PRAISE. "So will we render the calves of our
lips." The calves of the lips are more precious to God
than the calves of the stall. The true priestly offering in
this age is, "The sacrifices of praise unto God continually."
That is the richest and ripest fruit of lips, "giving thanks
to His Name" (Heb. 13. 15). "Oh that men would
praise the Lord for His goodness and wonderful works"
(Psa. 107. 8, 15, 21, 31).

4. To OPEN CONFESSION. Verse 3 is very emphatic,
which simply means: No mighty *nation* shall save us.
No material instruments of battle can deliver us (horses
and chariots). No works of our own hands can inspire us.
But we will trust in the eternal love of our Father God,
with whom such orphans find mercy. "Believe in thine
heart, and confess with thy mouth the Lord Jesus," and
prove in your own daily experience His mightiness to
save. Now note—

II. The Divine Promises.

1. "I will HEAL their backsliding" (v. 4). To *heal*

a wound is something better than merely *binding* it up. To Israel, backsliding was a festering sore; but in answer to their pleading He will heal them. There is no disease so deeply rooted in our moral nature that our Great Physician cannot heal. He can "heal all our diseases." This disease of backsliding—a wilful desertion from the Word and Will of God—is perhaps one of the most inveterate.

2. "I will LOVE THEM FREELY" (v. 3). This is the love that is not restrained because of our unworthiness. To the pardoned and restored soul His love flows as fully and as freely as if they had never sinned. What an encouragement this is to the ministers of the Gospel of our Lord Jesus Christ. To him that cometh He says, "I will in no wise cast out."

3. "I will be AS THE DEW unto Israel" (v. 5). The *dew* falls gently, silently, and effectively *in the night*. The Lord will yet be to the nation of Israel as refreshing dew in the long night of their drought and affliction. Meanwhile, all who turn unto Him in the night of their sorrow and need will find His Presence as the dew, a real though invisible something gently falling upon their thirsty souls. If we had eyes to see nature as God sees it, we would doubtless behold many symbols of His wonderful works toward the children of men.

4. "FROM ME IS THY FRUIT FOUND" (vv. 6-8). Fruit is always the result of favourable conditions, and a manifestation of the *character* of the tree. Jehovah reminds them that the many rich mercies to be enjoyed would not be as a reward of merit, or a product of mere chance, but as an outcome of Divine activity in them and through them. We are reminded here of the parable of the vine (John 15). "The branch cannot bear fruit of *itself*. No more can ye." The vine might say to the branch: "From

me is thy fruit found, for without me ye can do nothing
by way of fruitfulness. " If we abide in Him as a branch,
and He abideth in us as the Source of our supply, then
from Him shall "much fruit be found" (Gal. 5. 22-24).

THE SEVERITY AND THE GOODNESS OF GOD.
JOEL 2 and 3.

IT has been said that Joel is the prophet of the Holy Spirit,
as Isaiah is of the Messiah. Yet he gives us one of the
darkest pictures ever drawn by a prophetic pen, and also
one of the brightest (chap. 2. 28). Here we note THEIR
UTTER BANKRUPTCY. Their failure and desolation was—

I. **Complete.** "What the palmerworm left the locust
hath eaten; what the locust left hath the cankerworm
eaten; what the cankerworm left hath the caterpillar
eaten. A nation is come up upon My land whose teeth
are the teeth of a lion. My vine is waste; my figtree is
barked; my people like a virgin girded with sackcloth.
Offerings cut off from the house of the Lord. The Lord's
ministers mourn. The fields wasted, land mourneth,
harvest perished, all the trees of the field are withered,
and joy is withered away from the sons of men" (vv. 4-12).
Yet we know that "He doth not afflict willingly, but for
our profit. " As with this nation, so is it with our souls;
we need to be stripped naked and our earthly pleasures
withered before we feel our need of God.

II. This bankruptcy was **Humanly Incurable.** What
could this nation do to arrest all those adverse forces that
were warring against them? In themselves they had no
power to resist such a mighty host. Lord, teach us to
know our own helplessness, while we war "not against
flesh and blood, but against principalities, against powers,
against the rulers of the darkness of this world, against

spiritual wickedness in heavenly places" (Eph. 6. 12).
God has declared the bankruptcy of our sinful nature
with regard to spiritual power. It is also humanly
incurable. "In my flesh dwelleth no good thing."

III. This desolation reveals the **Many Instruments** at
God's disposal. The "worm," the "locust," the "waste,"
the "blight," the "drought," and the "ungodly." All
these He can turn into irresistible weapons of judgment.
Surely we have need to "Behold the goodness and *the
severity* of God" (Rom. 11. 22). He can use for our help
or hindrance the most *insignificant* things on the earth.
Great is our God, who can "make *all things* work together
for good to them that *love* God, to them who are the *called
according to His purpose*" (Rom. 8. 28).

IV. **The Divine Purpose.** The reason of God's
severity with them was to awaken in them a deep sense
of their need of *dependence* upon Him. "*Now*, saith the
Lord, turn ye to ME with all your heart. Rend your
hearts and not your garments" (vv. 11, 12, 13). The
called of God are called *for* God. It was easier for them to
rend their garments as a sign of sorrow in the sight of men,
than to rend their hearts as a proof of their humility before
God. "A broken and contrite heart He will not despise."
It may be easier for some of us to offer a gift for God's
cause than to offer *ourselves* to Him for His service. His
purpose for us is that we should present our bodies a *living*
sacrifice, and this is but "your *reasonable* service," and
the evidence of a "*renewed mind*" (Rom. 12. 1, 2).

V. **The Divine Encouragement.** "Fear not, be glad
and rejoice: for the Lord will do great things. I will
restore to you the years that the locust hath eaten, and ye
shall praise the Name of the Lord your God. My people
shall never be ashamed" (chap. 2. 21-27). What an
inspiring message for trembling hearts. Though His

hand is strong to smite, 'tis also strong to save.   Why
should we doubt in the cloudy and dark day, when we are
assured that God is light and that God is love?   "I am
the Lord, I change not" (Mal. 3. 6).   Our trials and
troubles are no proof that the *character* of our God has in
any way changed.   God, in Christ, is "the same yesterday,
to-day, and for ever."   Approach with joy "the Mercy
Seat," for He is waiting *there* to show "the kindness of
God" to every penitent soul that comes, and to restore
unto them the joy of His salvation.

THE PROPHETIC OUTLOOK.
JOEL 2. 28-32.

"AND it shall come to pass AFTERWARD."   This "afterward" is interpreted by Peter on the Day of Pentecost, as
"the last days" (Acts 2. 17).   This "afterward" seems to
embrace this whole dispensation and the one that is to
follow.   We must not overlook the fact that all these
words were spoken by Jehovah Himself, as the "I wills"
prove.   We have here then—

I. A Wonderful Promise.   "I will *pour out* My
Spirit" (v. 28).   The Holy Spirit is the mysterious
personal energy of God.   In the past age He came again
and again, and filled or clothed His chosen servants for
their God-appointed work.   But at Pentecost He was
"poured out."   As Jesus Christ poured out Himself for
our redemption, so God hath poured out His Spirit for
our guidance and enduement for service.

1. THE EXTENT OF THIS GIFT.   "Upon all flesh."   All
types of humanity—white, black, brown, red, and
yellow.   There is no respect of persons with God; but
everywhere all who believe in Christ, and desire to honour
His Holy Name, may, if they will, receive their share of
this holy unction.   "The promise is to you and to your

children, and to as many as the Lord our God shall call"
(Acts 2. 39). To your "sons and your daughters, old men
and young men, servants and handmaids." "Have ye
received the Holy Ghost since ye believed?" (Acts 19. 2);
or in believing, *did you* receive?

2. THE RESULTS PREDICTED. These results must be
such as cannot be gained without the operation of the
Holy Spirit of Promise.

(a) *"Your sons and your daughters shall prophesy."*
This may not mean the foretelling of events, but it does
mean uttering words and thought by *Divine inspiration*,
whether they are in a pulpit or a coal-pit; whether they are
in the "ministry" or the factory, in the home or in the
street. The true Christian life is a forthtelling of the
Holy Spirit's presence.

(b) *"Your old men shall dream dreams."* We sometimes
speak of a man as a dreamer, who is given to reverie, to
deep, serious thought. But the Spirit of God, who taught
Joseph and Jacob by dreams, can even while we sleep
speak to the heart. The *old men* may not be so able now
to take their part as formerly in the front of public spiritual
warfare, but God has other ways that the world knows
nothing of in bringing refreshing to their weary hearts.
In this ministry of the Holy Spirit the "old man" is not
cast off because of his age. Blessed be His Name.

(c) *"Your young men shall see visions."* *Youth* is the
time of new visions, but with many these visions are as
illusive as the mirage. *"Your* young men," or let us say,
young men who have embraced the Christian faith, yielded
to the call of Christ, and received the Holy Spirit. What
marvellous visions of possibilities you will see in the
world-wide field of labour and in the potentiality of your
own redeemed character.

(d) *"And upon the servants and the handmaids will I*

pour out My Spirit." The slaves and the kitchen maids
are not to be exempt from this spiritual endowment,
which means increased efficiency in every sphere of life.
The Holy Spirit comes to put a new and higher value into
all our activities.

II. **A Solemn Warning.** "I will shew wonders in the
heavens and in the earth...before the great and terrible
day of the Lord come." The "Day of the Lord" will be
very different from this present day of grace. Then shall
the lawless one be revealed, whom the Lord shall destroy
with the *"brightness of His Coming"* (2 Thess. 2. 8). For
"the Lord Jesus shall be revealed from Heaven with His
mighty angels, *in flaming fire,* taking vengeance on them
that know not God, and that *obey not the Gospel of our
Lord Jesus Christ"* (1 Thess. 1. 7, 8). This is the *merciful*
Day of the Lord. Then will come "the *terrible* Day of the
Lord" (v. 31). "How shall we escape if we neglect so
great salvation." Sound aloud the trumpet of His Gospel
call.

III. **A Precious Opportunity.** "And it shall come to
pass, that whosoever shall call in the Name of the Lord
shall be delivered" (v. 32). In the midst of such terrible
judgments God has not forgotten to be gracious, for yet
"in Zion and in Jerusalem shall be deliverance." Meanwhile this door of opportunity stands wide open, for
"whosoever will" (John 3. 16). Christ, by the sacrifice
of Himself, hath "put away sins" as a barrier in the way
of our approach. The responsibility of the sinner is now
great, because he is thus without excuse. It is ours to
"call on the Name." It is His *to deliver.* "Salvation is of
the Lord." "The grace of God that bringeth salvation to
all men *hath appeared"* (Titus 2. 11-14).

AN AWFUL CHALLENGE.
AMOS 4. 6-13.

IT is an awful act when God Almighty challenges a crippled nation to a final combat. "PREPARE TO MEET THY GOD, O Israel." This is a declaration of war. All negotiations had failed, a rupture had come. Now, after the manner of men, God challenges them to battle. It is quite apparent that in their past this would be a hopeless struggle. And to this end doubtless was it made.

I. Why was this Challenge Given? Because Jehovah had been trying to subdue them in other more merciful ways; and when the last of these failed, behold a challenge came. God gives His reasons before He utters this ultimatum.

1. "I have given you cleanness of teeth (starvation) in all your cities, yet ye HAVE NOT RETURNED UNTO ME" (verse 6).

2. "I caused it to rain in one city and not in another." Thus MAKING DISTINCTIONS that should have awakened anxiety, "yet have ye not returned unto Me" (v. 8).

3. "I HAVE SENT AMONG YOU THE PESTILENCE. Your young men have I slain with the sword. Yet have ye not returned unto Me" (v. 10).

4. "I have OVERTHROWN SOME OF YOU, like Sodom and Gomorrah, and ye were as a firebrand plucked out of the burning. Yet ye have not returned unto Me" (v. 11). The purpose of all these chastenings was to bring them to Himself, but they would not. "I have called, and ye refused." Now then, "Prepare to meet thy God!" Are we hearing His voice and seeing His warning hand in His providential dealings with us? It is a miserable thing to be carrying on, it may be silently, a daily controversy with the God whose merciful purpose is that we should *return* unto Him. "I will arise and go to my Father."

II. This Challenge Must be Accepted. "Ye must meet God." But how? Is it to be in battle or in peace? As an enemy or as a friend? If it is a question of our own strength against the might of our God, who shall be able to stand? Though one man could be *prepared* by being endowed with all the best resources inherent in the human race, he could not dare with any hope of success to face and defy the "wrath of God." To meet God in our own moral strength and virtue, all preparation is utterly vain and presumptive. Yet meet Him we must, and meet Him we can, but never with hope as an antagonist. Then how can we meet Him in peace who have deliberately rebelled against His law and insulted His forbearance? Ah, herein lies the mystery and the majesty of grace through Jesus Christ, His own Beloved Son, who on our and on God's behalf gave His life a ransom for our sins, that through faith in His conquering Name we are *reconciled* to God, so can come with boldness before His throne, and find grace to help in our every time of need (Heb. 4. 16). Christ, for us, hath met all the just demands of God's holy law, and all the claims of His holiness. Hence our preparation to meet God in joy and peace lies in our acceptance and trust in the finished work and victorious Name of Jesus. Thanks be unto God for His unspeakable Gift.

FAITHFUL WITNESSING.
Amos 7. 7-17.

THE Lord hath never left Himself without a witness (Heb. 11). The very "Heavens declare His glory." The personal testimony of Amos, as here recorded, leads us to meditate on some characteristics of true witness-bearing.

I. He Had a Message from God. "Thus He showed me...the Lord with a plumbline in His hand," who said

unto him, "What seest thou? and I said, A plumbline"
(vv. 7-9). A "plumbline" is an instrument for *testing*.
Being in the hand of the Lord, it was the symbol of His
righteousness and judgment. He had come, through His
prophet, to measure the "high places" and the "sanc-
tuaries of Israel," and to expose their delinquency. But
the point is, Amos *had* a message; something definite to
say, in the Name of the Lord; something that was not
manufactured to please the people, or to show forth his
own gifts, but something that burned in his own heart
like a tongue of fire (Jer. 20. 9). The early apostles, after
the Resurrection, had such a vision of the power of Christ
and of the blessed Gospel, associated with it, that their
hearts became inflamed as with a Divine passion to speak
out the "Good News." As Peter and John testified: "We
cannot but speak the things which we have seen and heard"
(Acts 4. 20). Truly they *had a message*. A message that
came to them with such commanding authority that their
whole "spirit, soul and body" were brought into subjection to it. Have we lost the vision? Are our ears dull of
hearing or our hearts become hardened through the
familiarity of words that we have so largely lost the
spiritual thrill of this holy compulsion? We have the
same message, the same promise of power, but, alas,
where is our faith?

II. **He Suffered Opposition.** "Amaziah the *priest
of Bethel*" misrepresented both Amos and his message to
the king, and then hypocritically asked him to "Go, flee
into the land of Judah" (vv. 10-13). Even modern
priests of Bethels often misunderstand and misrepresent
the man of God who boldly "declares the whole counsel
of God." Opposition may be expected in the ministry of
God's Word, when we remember the enmity of the human
heart to spiritual things. "If any man will live godly,
he must suffer persecution." "Beloved, think it not

strange concerning the fiery trials which is *to try you*;
but rejoice, inasmuch as ye are partakers of Christ's
sufferings. If ye be reproached for the Name of Christ,
happy are ye, for the Spirit of glory and of God *resteth
upon you*" (1 Peter 4. 12-14). "I will glory in my affliction
that the favour of Christ may rest upon me. " If we are
speaking God's Word, in God's Name, then leave it to
God to care for His own.

III. **He Gave his Personal Experience.**   "Then
Amos said, I was no prophet, neither a prophet's son, but
I was an herdman and a gatherer of wild figs" (v. 11,
margin), "and the Lord took me as I followed the flock,
and said unto me, Go" (vv. 14, 15).   There is no reference
made of his inexperience or "lack of education. "   One
need not depend on the help of "the schools" to receive
the *call of God*.   We are not chosen because we are wise
and strong, but because we are fit instruments for the
exhibition of His wisdom and power.   "God hath chosen
the *foolish* things of the world to confound the wise; and
weak things to confound the mighty; and *base* and *despised*
things to bring to naught things that are: that no flesh
should glory *in His Presence*" (1 Cor. 1. 25-28).   Paul's
bodily presence was "weak, and his speech contemptible,
but his letters were weighty and powerful" (2 Cor. 10. 10).
It is of vital importance for the success of our ministry
that we should be able to give a *personal testimony* as to
what God *hath done for us*.   Out of *the heart* are issues of
life.   Apart from this there may be plenty of "sound and
fury, " but the significance of it in His sight is "nothing. "
We are to speak what we *do know*, and testify what we
have seen.   It is little honour to Him that we should
prophesy beyond the measure of our own faith.   Isaiah
saw the Lord seated on a Throne, before he heard Him say,
"Go" (Isa. 6. 1-9).   The apostles were "eyewitnesses of
His Majesty" before they were sent to preach.

JONAH THE RUNAWAY.
Jonah 1. 1-3.

This is one of the most romantic of all the books of the Bible. To those who can read between the lines, it is more fascinating than the most popular novel.

I. **Who was Jonah?** From 2 Kings 14. 25, we learn that he was the servant and prophet of the Lord—no mean title. His name means "Dove." If it was an expression of his nature, then perhaps this is one reason why he fled from great and wicked Nineveh. He was the son of Amittai, but his father's name is shrouded in obscurity. All great men don't spring from great parents. Although the world has never missed your father, that is no reason why it should not miss you when you are gone. A tinker may die without much ado, but the name of Bunyan will be held in everlasting remembrance. Don't trifle with the days of your youth. Jonah was the author of this book which bears his name. Oh, what a revelation he himself gives us of his own faults and follies. Don't condemn him too severely for being a runaway prophet, for we never would have known about it had he himself not told us. Write down your own faults as Jonah did, and see if your record is not infinitely blacker than his. Would you dare to do it? At anyrate the recording angel is doing it for you. It is clear that in writing this book, Jonah does not seek his own glory. No man can be a prophet of God who does. Self-seeking is the spirit of Antichrist, and with him must be cast into the bottomless pit.

II. **His Commission.** The Lord said to Jonah: "Arise, go to Nineveh, that great city, and cry against it." This was a sudden and startling call, but all God's calls are sudden. Look at the city to which he was sent. It had been founded by Nimrod shortly after the confusion of tongues at Babel, and was therefore one thousand years old. It was the greatest city in the mightiest monarchy in the world. It was sixty miles in circumference, and contained streets and avenues twenty miles long; its walls were a hundred feet high, and so wide that three chariots could be drawn abreast on the top. Its population must have been over 600,000. But, moreover, it was *great in wickedness,* and that wickedness had climbed up to the very throne of God. Little did those wealthy and voluptuous Ninevites think that their *secret* sins were committed in the face of Jehovah. But so it was, and so it is now. The secret sins of our modern cities cry louder in the ears of God than the roar and rattle of the traffic in the streets. If we had the ears of God, nothing would strike us more, I think, than the longsuffering patience of our God. Friend, think of it, every sin unforgiven is a voice crying to Heaven for vengeance. Nothing can silence that cry but the precious Blood of Jesus. Now look at the purpose for which Jonah was sent to Nineveh. He was to "cry against" it. What a task. One little pebble in the bed of a mighty madly rushing river crying against it. But the prophet was not to be concerned about success, he was simply to obey the call, and leave the consequences in the hands of Him who called him. Ye are my witnesses, saith the Lord. Every witness for God must "cry against" the wickedness of their day and generation. The present generation is cursed with dumb dogs which cannot bark. Think of the murderous drink traffic, licensed and protected by law, to make and to bury 100,000 drunkards every year, and men professing to be witnesses for God, refusing to cry against it. Think of the gambling fever that's flushing the faces of so many of our young men, and hurrying them headlong to eternal ruin. Think of the infidelity and indifference that's settling down among the people, like a deadly malaria. Oh, that all God's prophets would "cry against it." But, say you, they only mock. Well, better be mocked for your faithfulness than your cowardliness.

III. **His Disobedience.** Instead of going to Nineveh, Jonah fled to Tarshish, at least he tried to. He arose like a pigeon let loose in a strange place, performed the circle of indecision, then darted off in the wrong direction. Perhaps you have treated the call of God in the same way. You have heard His Word, and knew that you ought to believe it, and be saved, but you turned away from it, and fled from the Lord. Jonah was displeased, and, as it were, sent in his resignation as a prophet. It is much easier to resign than to face a stern difficulty. Any craven-hearted fool can refuse to obey. Yes, it is easy to flee from the will of God, when the heart is not in sympathy with Him and His work. It is easy to refuse hearing the Word of God on a Sunday, when the heart and mind are occupied only with worldly things. Jonah was on the "down grade" to shame and confusion when he went *down to Joppa*, then *down into the ship*. If we are seeking to shake ourselves clear of God's call to repentance and faith, we are as surely on the down grade to spiritual desolation. Think of the sin of it, "fleeing from the presence of the Lord." Why? Because the presence of the Lord is intolerable to a rebellious will. It is because of this that men will one day cry on the rocks to fall on them and hide them from His presence. Just now God is calling men to arise and flee to Christ, but instead of doing that, they are fleeing to Nineveh, seeking to drown conviction in the pleasures of the world. Jonah having fled, the next thing he had to do was to "pay the fare." So he "paid the fare and went down." Ah, but Jonah had more to pay than he expected. The fare is not all paid in advance. Young man, have you ever considered what the fare is, from the presence of the Lord to the land of godlessness? Look at that shattered frame, that bloached face, that blasted character, that man fled to strong drink, and he is now paying the fare.   See that miserable miser with greed stamped on his face, and a heart as cold and callous as the gold he hoards; he fled to money, and had to pay the fare of becoming its slave.   That young woman who once thought of becoming a Christian, but was hindered through the fear of man, and who has fled from the presence of Christ, is now paying the fare, in a seared conscience and a hopeless life.   Truly the way of transgressors is hard.   The prodigal in the far country, in rags and wretchedness, staring with hungry eyes at the swine troughs, was just paying the fare to get away from his father.   What is the meaning of that weeping and wailing in eternity?   It is this: The souls who have fled from the presence of the Lord Jesus Christ paying the fare.   What a price.   Are you prepared to pay your own fare, or will you trust the price Jesus has paid on your behalf? (1 Peter 1. 18, 19).

JONAH FOUND OUT.
JONAH 1. 4-7.

THE disobedient prophet fled with all speed to Joppa, Disobedient feet are sure to run quickly.   It is always easy running down hill.   But God's messengers are swifter than the feet of any runaway.   He sent out the storm as His detective to apprehend His guilty servant.   The seamen are dreadfully alarmed, and take to lighting the ship; the wares are cast into the sea.   It is the old story. "All that a man hath will he give for his life."   Many who have led godless lives take to lighting the ship when death is staring them in the face.   But wares cannot appease the storm of God's wrath against sin.   Let us look at—

I. **The Sleeping Prophet.**   He had a journey of about three days, but being in such a hurry to get away from the presence of God he may have done it in less than two. Being weary with his flight, and having paid the fare, he is soon fast asleep in the ship. How sad. *Weary* fleeing from God. Truly the way of the transgressor is hard. If the way to Hell is paved with good intentions, it is also sprinkled with many tears. It is full of sighs and heartaches. Sleep is what *runaway souls* are seeking. They long for complete insensibility to their sins. How many convictions have been drowned in drink, and smothered in the haunts of sinful pleasure. Remember, insensibility is not security. A man may never be more in danger than when he is dreaming of ease. Jonah slept, while his companions on board were in desperation about their lives. I am afraid a good many professing Christians are playing the Jonah here, enjoying selfish ease, instead of seeking to help perishing souls. A sleeping Christian is not only helpless and useless, but is a positive hindrance to others. What was the cause of this great tempest that so oppressed the ship that it was "like to be broken." It was the disobedience of the servant of God. Think of the solemn responsibility resting upon us as the servants of Christ. It is possible to endanger the souls of others by our uncharitable behaviour towards God. Gospel hardened saints make Gospel hardened sinners.

II. **The Arousing Call.** "What meanest thou, O sleeper; arise, call upon thy God." This is the language of the skipper, heathen as he was, he believed in prayer. Our country is crammed with such heathen; men who believe in prayer when the waves of death are wildly dashing about them. Those who think prayer best becomes foul weather. An infidel who scoffed at a minister of Christ on board ship when the wind was fair, prayed: "O God, if there be a God, have mercy on me," when the storm came. Such fair-weather sailors are common. The drowsy prophet awakened to find that the God he sought

to flee from is on his track, and has blocked his way. The
seamen thinking the storm has come because some one of
them is guilty, cast lots, that he may be found out, and
the lot *"fell upon Jonah."*

III. **Found Out.** The runaway is found out. What a
great awakening this must have been to him. Be sure
your sins will find you out. We see here the proof of an
overruling Providence. The lot fell on Jonah. God always
puts the cap on the right head. When God comes to dis-
pose of the lot that has been cast into the lap of time, every
one will receive their due. "I'll take my chance," said
a reckless sinner, when urged to accept Christ and be
saved. What chance? The chance of escaping detection
at the judgment? Remember, the lot *"fell on Jonah."*
Let us remember that one transgressor may be a great
stumbling block to others. One Christian, whose life is
not in harmony with the will of God may hinder the cause
of Christ. Achan's sin hindered the whole army of Israel
(Josh. 7. 8-18). Learn also the folly of attempting to flee
from God. As a sinner, you may be permitted to flee into
the wilderness of eternal ruin, but as a servant, God is
sure to pull you up as it were, with bit and bridle. Judas
sold our Lord, committed suicide, and went to his own
place. Peter denied our Lord, but through the prayer of
his Master, he wept, and was restored. In hiding from
God we are tempting Him to shut us out from His presence
—which is life for evermore.

IV. **Disobedience Leads to Confusion.** What a
weakling Jonah was in presence of these heathen sailors.
Instead of being a lighthouse and a tower of strength to
help them, he was a source of sorrow and perplexity. It
is sad to see the prophet of God confused and confounded
in the presence of the ungodly. A *powerless* Christian is
a very pitiable object. Salt without savour is a worthless

thing. Samson in the power of the Spirit of God is more
mighty than a host of Philistines, but as a runaway from
his God, he becomes a miserable laughing-stock. A
Christian ought to be a man of fearless courage and irresistible power. He would be so if he were not like Jonah,
cowardly and disobedient. In the lap of Delilah, Samson
was smuggled of his strength. In the lap of the pleasures
and gaiety of the world the Church herself is being shorn
of her power. The inconsistency of a Christian will not
hide any more than Jonah's. It is impossible to be out of
fellowship with God and yet have the influence and
authority of an *obedient servant*. Our strength lies in our
nearness to God. The nearer the fire we keep the more
will its warmth possess us. Moses knew this when he
prayed: "If Thy presence go not with us, carry us not up
hence." If we have His presence, nothing shall be
impossible; if we have not His presence, we have nothing
worth having. Jonah fled from God. David fled to God.
Whither fleest thou?

JONAH OVERBOARD.
JONAH 1. 8-15.

Now that the skipper has got Jonah thoroughly awake,
he is besieged with questions of the seamen. There is
something very sad in a prophet of the Lord being asked:
"What is thine occupation?" Like a soldier, the proof
of his calling should be always manifest. Men did not
need to say to Elijah, "What is thine occupation?" or
to Peter or Paul? His connection with God was stamped
upon his every action. If men have to ask us if we are
Christians, after being in our company for a time, it is
surely proof enough that we are backsliders.

I. **Jonah Makes Confession.** "I am an Hebrew and
fear the Lord God of Heaven." If he fears Jehovah, why
does he not call upon Him? Others have been calling

upon their Gods, why is he silent? Perhaps the reason is
here, Jonah had sinned, and had not yet confessed his sin
to God. Unconfessed sin shuts the mouth of prayer. This
is why many give up praying. Sin is in their conscience,
they will not confess it, so they cannot pray. "He that
covereth his sin shall not prosper." Prayers, once uttered
at a mother's knee, are now choked by a guilty conscience.
Another heart-searching question is put to Jonah: "Why
hast thou done this?"

To this he was speechless. We can always give good
reasons for fleeing to God, but who can give a reasonable
answer for fleeing from God? Are you a backslider?
Have you turned aside from following Christ? Why hast
thou done this? What answer can you give to this question? Alas, that the lives of so many should bare the
mark of Cain, the mark of those who have gone out from
the presence of the Lord, those who once professed to be
Christians, but who now deny Him by their wicked works.
What wilt thou say when God Himself shall put this
question to thee: "Why has thou done this?" Another
question is put to Jonah that must have been like a dagger
to his soul. "What shall we do unto thee that the sea
may be calm unto us?" These men believed in the doctrine
of substitution. Why do the heathen practice it? Where
did they learn it? It was the first lesson that God taught
fallen man in clothing him with coats of skins. But now,
in these days, this Divine truth is despised, because of
the pride of intellect. We are not now to speak about
"the fall of man," it is "the ascent of man." We are not
now to teach that God made man in His own image, but
that he sprung up from a drop of dirty water, called pro-
toplasm. The apostasy of the last days is among us.
Jonah's answer implies—

II. A Noble Surrender. "Take me up, and cast me
forth into the sea; so shall it be calm unto you." He feels

his guilt, and sees in the storm the hand of Divine vengeance. Every child of God can read Providence as none other can. He is willing to offer himself a sacrifice to the God of the tempest that his companions in trial might be saved. It seems that self-sacrifice is the way to true service. Are we willing to be cast out for God that we might be a blessing to others? Jonah confessed that for his sake the tempest was upon them. If we are guilty of bringing others into trouble by our lack of faithfulness to God, don't let us add sin to sin by denying it. But the sailors were, as yet, unwilling to fling the culprit overboard, they were a crew of noble-hearted men, and displayed a magnanimous reluctance.

"Nevertheless the men rowed hard to bring it to the land." Yes, but their hard rowing will not suffice, where sacrifice is demanded. All the strivings of men will not avert the tempest of God's wrath against sin, there must be a sacrifice. We would rather give to God the work of our hands than the sacrifice of a broken heart. "They rowed hard to bring it to land, but they *could not.*" It is an utter impossibility for us to succeed in the teeth of God's purpose. You, who are seeking by dint of effort to pull your soul to Heaven, will need to give up in despair. If you wish to work out your own salvation you must see that it is God who worketh in you. Finding their efforts useless, they cry unto the Lord that this man's life may not be laid to their charge

III. **Divinely Thwarted.** "Then they took up Jonah and cast him into the sea, and the sea ceased from her raging." It must have been with heavy hearts they heaved him overboard. As a passenger he had paid the fare from Joppa to Tarshish, and now he is thrown out of the ship. See how God can thwart our self-made plans. It is sad to bury the dead at sea, but much more sad to bury the living. The terrible plunge would scarcely be

heard amidst the rush and roar of the tempest. The
sacrifice was made. God accepted the offering, and
immediately "the sea ceased from her raging." The key
to all this is found in Christ's own words. "The Jews
require a sign, there shall be no sign given, but the sign
of Jonah, the prophet." Jonah then is a sign. A sign
of what? Of death and resurrection. What a picture we
have here of a greater than Jonah, who willingly offered
Himself a sacrifice that others through Him might be
saved. In the storm and the tempest we see the judgment
of God, because of sin. The sin was that of disobedience,
by one man's disobedience many were made sinners. The
remedy was the sacrifice of a prophet. What a striking
illustration of Christ, the great Prophet, who took the
place of the disobedient, and allowed Himself to be cast
out that the storm of judgment may be averted, and many
precious souls saved. "Then the men feared the Lord and
made vows." They made their vows after the storm was
over. Many vow to God in the time of affliction, but deny
Him when deliverance comes. The vows of the unconverted are usually vows that need to be converted. If
you have been saved through Christ plunging into the sea
of God's wrath on your behalf, then make your covenant
vows to God, and keep them.

JONAH PRAYING IN HIS GRAVE.
JONAH 2. 1-10.

GOD has many ways of working. The truant prophet was
caught by a storm, swallowed by a fish, and landed safely
on shore. What encouragement to those who may be
praying for disobedient sons and daughters. You have
had no letter for a long time, but trust the God of Jonah.
With the rod of affliction He may hook them out of their
disobedience and sin, and yet cheer your heart with

unexpected tidings of gladness. But did a whale swallow Jonah? Scientific men say that the throat of a whale is too small to swallow a man, and loud mouthed infidelity has been quick to magnify the difficulty. Jonah does not say it was a whale, he says: "The Lord prepared a great fish." Where the word is used, in Matthew 12. 40, it simply means "monster." In the year 1758, a man went about exhibiting a shark that had swallowed himself. The story is that he left the ship to bathe, and was swallowed by the shark. The captain shot it, the man was vomited up and rescued little the worse of his double dip. The shark was taken and presented to the man who had been swallowed by it. If a shark could swallow and vomit a sailor, what is to hinder it from doing the same with a prophet? Jonah is—

I. A Sign of Christ. The Jews require a sign. Jesus said: "There shall be no sign given but the sign of the prophet Jonah." They had had many signs. One yet remained to be given—the sign of His resurrection. Jonah is a sign of Christ—

1. IN HIS BURIAL. He was cast forth; so was Christ cast out by His brethren. They led Him outside the gate and then put Him to death. Jonah was buried in the heart of the sea; Christ in the heart of the earth. Notice that the purpose for which they both were cast forth was the same— to make peace. "Cast me forth," said Jonah, "and it shall be calm for you." Christ hath made peace through the Blood of His Cross. The sin was *in* Jonah; the sin was *on* Jesus. Jonah was also a type of Jesus—

2. IN HIS CONSCIOUS ACTIVITY in the place of death. The seamen buried Jonah in the sea, and doubtless mourned over him as one dead, but he was—

II. Alive After he was Buried. A living, conscious, active soul in the deep. We are not to suppose, as com-

monly believed, that the great fish devoured the man the
moment he was flung overboard. He himself tells us that
"the depths closed him round about, that the weeds were
wrapped about his head, and that he went down to the
bottom of the mountains. " When Christ was buried, His
friends mourned Him as dead; but while they were pre-
paring the spices for His body, He was preaching to the
spirits in prison, those—we believe—who had died in the
faith of His Coming, and who waited His resurrection.
When Samuel was brought back from the other world, he
was disquieted, because he was in a place of happiness.
If the rich man, mentioned in Luke 16, had been raised, he
would not have talked about being troubled at the change,
he would have been more than thankful. If we could see
now the joys or sorrows of our departed dead, it would unfit
us for this present life.   Jonah was also a type of Jesus—

1. IN HIS RESURRECTION.   "The Lord spake unto the
fish and it vomited Jonah out upon the dry land. He came
out of the depths with the same individuality with which
he was cast in. It was the same Jesus that rose from the
dead, that was buried in the tomb. Neither of them saw
corruption. The casting of Jonah upon the dry land is but
the earnest of that time when both earth and sea shall
vomit out the dead that are in them; some to the sunshine
of eternal life, some to the darkness of eternal shame and
contempt. Here we might see also—

III. **The History of a Soul.** The inner experience of
Jonah has to some extent been the experience of all who
have passed from death unto life, all who have been brought
from the bondage of sin into the liberty of the sons of God.
Will you notice seven steps in the experience of Jonah.

1. DISOBEDIENCE. He deliberately refused to obey
what he knew to be the will of God. Who among us has
not taken that step?

2. CONVICTION. His soul is now encompassed with the horrors of Hell. The weeds are wrapped about the heart as well as his head. Disobedience to God is the straight way into the abyss of despair.

3. CONFESSION. He acknowledges the hand of God in arresting him. "Thou hast cast me into the deep." A man is not in a state to be saved until he is prepared to acknowledge the justice of God in punishing transgressors. We must confess our sins if we would hope for His mercy to forgive.

4. CONTRITION. "When his soul fainted within him he remembered the Lord." At the remembrance of His goodness the heart is melted. Truth lodged in the mind in early years often proves effectual in later life. If men would only remember the Lord Jesus Christ, how soon would they be delivered from the bitterness of their lives.

5. PRAYER. "He cried unto the Lord." Where there is true sorrow for sin it must gush out in prayer to God. A prayerless soul is like a sealed vessel. It took great faith to cry to God from the belly of a sea-monster. There is nothing like the jaws of death for opening the mouth of prayer. Many tempt God by their rebellion to plunge them into the belly of Hell, that they might learn to pray. Better pray in the sunshine than wait till you sink into the depths of despair, and death comes like Jonah's fish to swallow you up.

6. DELIVERANCE. Jonah was vomited out upon the dry land. It was to him as it is to every one saved by the Lord—a resurrection from the dead. "A passing from death into life." Some think that nobody can know when they are saved. Did Jonah not know? He shouted: "Salvation is of the Lord." Yes, Jonah had to pay the fare to get away from the presence of the Lord, but he got a *free passage back*. The Lord was at all the expense of

his home coming   It is always so, if you run from God,
you must pay your own fare; if you come to God there is
nothing to pay.   "Him that cometh unto Me I will in no
wise cast out."

7. THANKSGIVING.   He said when he got out of the
belly of death into the light of Heaven: "I will sacrifice
unto Thee with the voice of thanksgiving," and so well
he may.   Thanksgiving becomes a reality when salvation
is enjoyed.   If there were more saved souls in our churches
there would be less need for musical instruments.   There
are three states that may include us all.

(*a*) Those who are *indifferent* about salvation.

(*b*) Those who are *praying* to be saved.

(*c*) Those who *thank God* because they *are saved*.   Which
is yours?   "Thanks be unto God for His unspeakable
Gift" (Psa. 40. 1-5).

———

JONAH OBEDIENT.
JONAH 3. 1-10.

THERE are many questions one would like to ask here,
but who can answer them?   What did the sailors do after
the storm, when their cargo had been pitched overboard?
Did they return to Joppa to get it renewed?   If so, the
story of the storm being hushed by casting a prophet into
the sea would doubtless be rapidly circulated, and perhaps
reached Nineveh before Jonah did.

I. **The Repeated Call.**   "The Word of the Lord came
unto Jonah a *second time*."   How gracious God is, to give
a man a *second chance* of serving Him.   He might have
left him in his disobedience to perish.   What hope there
is in the Second Man, the Lord from Heaven.   Is there one
of us who have not had a second call?   Yea, a sixth, a
seventh, and a seventieth, and perhaps as yet there has
been no response.   God's right to take vengeance is often
denied, but dare you deny His patience and longsuffering?

The *Law* was given, that failed through our disobedience; now humanity's *second* chance is in His call of *grace*. Note the changed commission: "Go and preach unto it, the preaching that I bid thee." At the first Jonah was to "Cry against it," now he is just to speak what he is told. The call is repeated, but the commission is altered. Do you notice that the Word of the Lord came to Jonah before he was asked to preach it? Preachers must have a revelation from God. If they have seen no vision, then they have no message. Paul could say: "I have received of the Lord that which I have delivered unto you." We testify of what we have seen, else we are not witnesses. In these days a bold attempt is being made to discredit everything that savours of the miraculous. If there be no miracle, then there can be no mercy.

II. **The Ready Obedience.** "Jonah arose and went." What a task is before him; a journey of over 800 miles, and then to preach in the streets of the mightiest, the gayest, and the guiltiest of cities. But his forty days' journey is much easier than his three days' run to Joppa, because his heart is now right with God. It is easier doing great things for God than little things for the Devil. It was easier for Daniel to go to the lions' den than deny his God. It was easier for our faithful Scottish martyrs to go to the fires than to deny the faith. But where did Jonah learn this obedience? He learned it where most of us have had to learn it—in the depths, when the floods compassed him about, when the waves and billows passed over him, and the weeds were wrapped about his head. We would not always pity the afflicted if we understood the purpose of God. May God plunge many more into the belly of Hell, if so be that it will bring them to repentance. When God by the hand of death snatched your bright-eyed child from the home, did you understand that He was seeking to bring you into the faith that saves?

III. The Startling Proclamation. "Yet forty days,
and Nineveh shall be overthrown." A strange message
from a strange man. Jonah, footsore and weary, enters
the great and mighty city, probably clad in a coat of
camel's hair, girded with a leathern girdle. He may seem
very small and insignificant in the presence of those
haughty gentry, clothed in their gaudy robes, and those
high flying chariots, rushing along on the top of the wall,
but he has a dignity superior to the King of Assyria. He
has *a message from God* that will bring the guilty and
conceited Ninevites to their knees. The mightiest men
in the world are those who know God's will, and are
courageous as lions in declaring it. Sometimes sermons
are characterised as being as destitute of grace as Jonah's.
"Yet forty days and Nineveh shall be overthrown."
Jonah's message was one of mercy and judgment. Yet
forty days—*forty days' grace* to be followed with judgment
if these days were neglected. Grace has been reigning
now these 1928 years, and will assuredly be followed with
judgment in the case of those who despise the mercy
offered.

IV. The Confirming Sign. From the Lord Jesus
Christ Himself we learn that Jonah was a sign to the
Ninevites (Luke 11. 30). How could he be a sign to them
if they did not know his character and history? This is
indeed significant. The Ninevites not only heard the
Divine message at his lips, but they saw in himself a
proof of God's mighty saving power. Jonah wrought no
miracle, but he himself was a miracle. He was as one
raised from the dead. Three things the subtle infidelity
of to-day seek to deny. Incarnation, Regeneration,
Inspiration. But every regenerated soul is in itself a
sign, and an evidence of the Divine and the supernatural.
What we are will tell more powerfully than what we say.
Signs are needed. Men and women who have themselves

been saved and taught by God. Is there no such sign beside you or in your own home? To see a true Christian is to see a sign from Heaven.

V. The Grand Result. "Nineveh repented at the preaching of Jonah." If he had gone with the Gospel of the "higher critics," and hobnobbed with the gentry, he might have got on for chaplain to the king, but Nineveh would never have repented. "By their fruits ye shall know them." The preaching that does not bring sinners face to face with their sins and with God will never produce repentance. There were no sleepers under Jonah's preaching. There are scores who go to our churches for no other purpose than to see and to be seen, and to get a nap. It is interesting to observe the process of their repentance.

1. THEY BELIEVED GOD. It is not said that they believed Jonah, but that they believed God. This ought to be the aim and end of all preaching, to lift the hearts of the people right up to the Lord Himself. What will it avail you although you believe in the kirk and in the minister, if you have no faith in God? I would rather die a heathen Hottentot than an unconverted Church member. Then they humbled themselves, "and put on sackcloth." This is always the result of believing God; faith is accompanied with the sackcloth of confession. Sackcloth is never very fashionable, sealskin is more in vogue. There is nothing like a deep conviction of sin for stripping one of their gaudy garments of pride. Oh, man, if you saw yourself in the light of God's judgment, you would as quickly as Ninevites, put on the sackcloth of a broken spirit. A haughty sinner is the imp of Hell. Never say that you believe in God if you have never been on your face before Him. Then—

2. THEY CRIED TO GOD. Every one was to "cry mightily

to God." There is no use telling an awakened soul that
God has so bound Himself with fixed laws that he cannot
answer prayer. It is as natural for such to cry as the new-
born babe. Only those encased in their own conceit can
talk so lightly about prayer. No prayer book will suffice
when the soul is alive to its true need. Such are like dead
men's grave clothes. But they did more than pray, they
"Turned every one from his evil ways." No prayer is in
earnest as long as sin is indulged. If we are not prepared
to forsake our sins, then all our prayers are a mockery
(Psa. 66. 18). A man once told me that he always said
his prayers except when he was drunk. Poor man, he was
afflicted with two devils. A drinking one and a self-
righteous one. Both are alike unclean. *Their* prayer
was sincere. The result was—

3. THEY FOUND MERCY. "God saw their works and
repented, and did it not. What! Does God repent?
Yes, I am thankful that He does. In His Character as
holy, just, and good, He is unchangeable, and without
shadow of turning; but in mercy He turns His face to every
penitent seeking sinner. "Draw nigh unto Me," God says,
"and I will draw nigh unto you." "Seek, and ye shall
find."

———

JONAH DISPLEASED.
JONAH 4. 1-6.

THERE is a great difference between mere obedience and
sympathy. Every parent sees it when the one child has to
be driven to obey, and when the other delights in it,
because in full sympathy with the parents' plans and
purposes. The elder brother in the parable (Luke 15) had
been obedient, but he had no sympathy with the father in
making such an ado over the returning prodigal. There
are many Christians like this, they obey from sheer
necessity, but they have no joy in the will and purposes

of God. Such seems to have been the character of Jonah. He obeyed from a powerful sense of duty, but had not entered joyfully into all the mind of the Lord.

I. His Complaint. "It displeased Jonah exceedingly, and he was very angry," or, as it might be rendered, he was very hot, greatly perplexed and excited. He saw now what perhaps he did not expect to see—Nineveh in sackcloth and prayer. The Assyrians, being the enemies of Israel, he probably was secretly rejoicing in the prospect of their downfall. It is so easy to mix our own selfish motives with the purposes of God, and bring confusion to our own souls. It is here where thousands are making shipwreck, they set up then own opinions and think that God is bound by His honour to conform to their plans. Perhaps Jonah was thinking of his own honour as a prophet when he got so excited. He had been crying, "Yet forty days and Nineveh shall be overthrown." Now that God was going to spare the city, what would they think of him as a prophet? We are not much use in the Lord's service until we are willing to become fools for Christ. It is ours to obey and to trust. Opinions formed apart from the light of God's Word will sooner or later bring the blush of confusion to your face.

II. His Prayer. "He prayed unto the Lord." If Jonah's heart had been filled with anger against the Lord, how could he pray? No one can pray with anger in their heart. This is the remedy for all unholy passion—get to your knees. It is wonderful how our creeds get corrected in our prayers. Open up your heart to God, and your crooked things will be made straight. In Jonah's prayer there is a revelation. Here we get the reason why he fled from God at the first. He says: "I fled, for I knew that thou art a gracious God." This is the very reason why some of us have fled to Him. What does he mean? Perhaps this: "I knew that Thou art such a merciful God, that although I prophesied its destruction, Thou would forgive them, so my preaching would be in vain, and I would be mocked for my trouble." There was much of both good and evil in Jonah, but something more might be learned from this—

III. His Testimony. His description of God's character is simply grand. "Gracious, merciful, slow to anger, of great kindness, and ready to turn from judgment." How could he be angry at such a God? He is gracious to consider the sinner's need, and merciful to forgive their iniquities. My friend, can you say, like Jonah, "I know Him." He is slow to anger. What a mercy. This is an age of hurry and excitement and "Go." The Devil knows that his days are short, and he is driving this world—"that lieth in the wicked one"—at express speed. The Devil is always in a hurry   "The wheels of God grind slow, but they grind exceeding small." God is slow to anger, but He *is quick* to forgive. "There is life for a look." This is the reason why some of you are spared till to-day, who have been wasting your time in selfishness and sin. "God is slow to anger." Why despise such great kindness, and weary out the patience of God? Oh, remember, that although God is slow to anger, when He does strike, it will be the blow of the Almighty.

IV. His Foolish Request. "O Lord, take my life from me, it is better for me to die than to live" Is it? How do you know? Here again is another manifestation of self. "Better for me." Oh, yes, it is the old story: "Suffer *me first.*" This is the fly in the ointment of much of our Christian service—"Self-seeking." But there is some faith mingled with his faults. If he knew it would be better for him to die, then he had a good hope for the world to come. Would it be better for you? Paul said, "to depart and be with Christ is far better." It takes faith to die in gladness, alone in the midst of heathen.

V. His Watchfulness. "So Jonah went out of the city, and made him a booth." He might have shared the hospitality of the king, but he preferred a booth outside the city. "Moses chose rather to suffer affliction with the people of God, than enjoy the pleasures of sin for a season." Those who testify against the world aught not to live as the world. "Come out from among them lest ye perish with them." The command to Lot was, "Flee to the mountains, tarry not in all the plain." He sat under his booth till he might see what would become of the city. Do you know anything about calmly waiting *to see what God will do*? It is a solemn time. The doctor has given up that child, the mother has committed it to God, and is waiting in silence to see what God will do. There are times in Christian work when we know not what to do; we have to sit down like Jonah till we might see what the Lord will do. God is worth waiting on. Beloved friends, have patience with God. "They that wait upon the Lord shall renew their strength" (Isa. 40. 31).

VI. His Great Joy. "The Lord prepared a gourd, and made it come up over Jonah, so Jonah was exceeding glad." How quickly God can turn our sadness into gladness. This gourd is supposed to be the palm-christ, a plant like the running ivy, with broad leaves the shape of a man's hand. Every leaf might remind him of the hand of the Almighty. What a shelter—to be covered with Jehovah's hands—no wonder he was glad. This sheltering gourd was the gift of God—a *handful on purpose* for a weary, downcast pilgrim. How often has God raised a gourd for us in our day of trouble. It was given for a twofold purpose. (1) To be a shadow over his head. (2) To deliver him from his grief. Is not this what you need—shelter from danger, and deliverance from inward grief. This gourd raised by the Lord seems to be a passing chadow of the Cross. Here sinners find a refuge from the piercing rays of Divine vengeance and deliverance from their sins and sorrows. This double salvation every one of us need. Christian, in the day of your trial, sit under its shadow, and wait and see what God will do. Unsaved one, here is a resting place for you, here is deliverance from your grief. No matter how deep your need, sit here and see what God will do for you. "Come unto Me all ye that labour and are heavy laden, and I will give you rest." He is "mighty to save."

JONAH SILENCED.

JONAH 4. 7-11.

EVERY visible thing is stamped with uncertainty. All our earthly comforts will, sooner or later, wither and die. The countenance of nature herself, although governed by unerring law, is continually changing. Kingdoms and nations change. What changes have taken place in our homes, and among our friends. How many old faces are gone, how many new faces have come.

> "Change on all around I see,
> Oh, Thou who changeth not,
> Abide with me."

When all earthly things shall wax old and pass away like a garment, the unchanging Saviour still remains. "Blessed are all they that trust in Him." We have here—

I. **A Short Lived Pleasure.** "God prepared a worm the next day, and it smote the gourd that it withered." God can prepare the *worm* as well as the *gourd*. While we are enjoying our gourd of pleasure, we are apt to forget that there may be a worm at the root. How many little unseen things may be at work in the night. Receive your mercies with humble thankful hearts. Are there not many whose gourd has suddenly withered. That child which used to be the delight of your eye—God prepared the worm of disease, and it has withered away. That husband that used to cast over you his protecting hands has suddenly withered away. That mother who used to be your gourd, in delivering you from your grief, has been cut down by the worm of death. Oh, this world is strewed all over with withered gourds. Each ruin says to us, "Set not your heart on the things which are seen, for they are temporal." Every earthly thing has its worm. The worm of time is already working at the root of your present worldly pleasures. That gourd of false profession will turn out a lifeless mass on the day of God's fierce anger. God has prepared a worm that will bring to ruin every refuge of lies. What an awful discovery to awaken on the resurrection morning, to find our hopes, like Herod's body, eaten up of worms. The incorruptible Christ has paid an incorruptible price for your incorruptible soul.

"Here everlasting springs abide,
And never-withering flowers."

The heart that has laid hold on Christ has received a portion that can never fade away.

II. An Overcoming Trial. "And it came to pass, when the sun did rise, that God prepared a vehement east wind, and the sun beat upon the head of Jonah that he fainted." Alas, for you, if your joys are bound up in your circumstances, instead of in your God. It is so easy and natural to be more anxious about the gift than the Giver. It does seem strange at first sight, how God dealt with Jonah. He prepared a gourd to cover him, then a worm to vex him, then a wind to smite him. We may find fault, but we cannot mend it. The Divine Teacher is not obliged to explain Himself to His stupid pupils. A great and

merciful purpose is here.   This piercing east wind upon
Jonah's defenceless head was a sore trial.   It has been said
that "When the wind is in the east, 'tis neither good for
man nor beast," but this does not tally with our own good
Scottish proverb: "It is an ill wind that blaws naebody
guid."   The winds are in His fists, and are flung out, not
at random, but for a definite purpose.   It was by a strong
east wind that the Lord divided the Red Sea.   The cutting,
biting, withering winds of affliction are all for some
gracious purpose.   I once made the remark to a farmer,
that these cold winds would hinder the growth.   "Yes,"
he said, "they hinder the growth upwards, but they help
the growth downwards; they make the roots take a firmer
hold."   Then welcome affliction that drives the root of our
being deeper into the things of the unseen world, and makes
us more fit to stand in the time of tempest.   Jonah fainted.
Poor fellow, he was like the seed that had no depth of earth,
and withered away when the scorching sun fell upon it.
David said, "I had fainted, unless I had believed."   If we
have no faith in God we have nothing to save us from
fainting in the time of trial.   To you who are growing faint
thinking there is no salvation for you, "Only believe."
Weary workers, remember that "He giveth power to the
faint."

III. **A Pointed Question.**   God said to Jonah, "Doest
thou well to be angry?"   Jonah's answer was that of a
man who is perfectly honest, but whose heart was likely
to deceive him.   "I do well to be angry, even unto death."
The great lesson seemingly that God wished to teach Jonah
was that "Sin worketh death," both in the nation and
individual.   Israel had turned away from God.   Idolatry,
like the worm at Jonah's gourd, was eating the life out of
the nation.   Righteousness exalteth a nation.   Now that
Nineveh was on its knees seeking mercy and righteousness,
God would lift it up.   The same principle reigns to-day;

the Divine word is, "Them that honour Me, I will honour." God looketh on the heart. Jonah was more concerned about the gourd of his own comfort than the salvation of the heathen city. Such are certain signs of a staggering faith. Faith in God is the death-blow to all this miserable self-interest.

IV. A Silencing Argument. "Thou hast had pity on the gourd, and should not I spare Nineveh, wherein are more than six-score thousand persons that cannot discern between their right hand and their left hand?" What a wonder, that God should condescend to reason with a man. There is much in God's dealings with us that we can never understand, and must be received by faith. God uses two powerful arguments to silence the doubts and fears of His servant.

1. THE ARGUMENT OF SOVEREIGNTY. God has a right to do as He will with His own. Proud man would even question this right and show displeasure at God's dealings, because he cannot comprehend His meaning. It is awful presumption to suppose that the purposes of God are to be subordinated to the reasonings of men. Paul's argument is conclusive. Nay, Oh man, who art thou that repliest against God? Shall the thing formed say to Him that formed it: "Why hast thou made me thus?" Then there is—

2. THE ARGUMENT OF PITY. The Lord reminds Jonah that there are sixty thousand persons in Nineveh that cannot discern between the right hand and the left— 60,000 babies. What a place the children have in the heart of God; what a claim their utter helplessness makes upon Divine mercy. Nineveh was spared, partly through the mute intercession of these 60,000 infant priests. You cannot tell how much your home has been blessed because of these helpless children. Mothers, make room for the children; **every baby is a blessing**, a priest that maketh

intercession for you. These arguments seem to have silenced Jonah, for we hear his voice no more. He quietly allows God to have the last word. Has God settled all your difficulties and silenced all your arguments? Don't keep up a controversy with the Almighty. Yield your will to Him, and what you cannot grasp with the intellect, believe with the heart. There is a story in ancient history of a monarch who, when some of his subjects rebelled against him, subdued them, then loaded them with precious gifts. One of his nobles asked why he was so kind to his enemies. He said, "I subdued them by my power, I must now win them by my love." It is thus that Jesus Christ, the greater than Jonah, would win us to Himself. By the power of his convicting Spirit He would show us the blackness of our evil hearts, that He might bring us to repentance and confession. Then He lavishly bestows upon us the great gifts of His grace, love, peace, joy, rest, and eternal life. He blesses all he conquers. Has He conquered you?

THE COMING KINGDOM.
MICAH 4. 1-8.

THERE is a "kingdom" coming, as predicted by the prophets and foretold by our Lord and His apostles; a kingdom such as this world has never known. This kingdom will come when the KING HIMSELF appears. He who died for the world will yet assert His "right to reign" over it. When He comes to rule the nations, then that prayer He taught us in the days of His flesh, "Thy kingdom come, Thy will be done *on earth as it is in Heaven*," will be abundantly fulfilled. "His kingdom is *not of* this world." It can never come out of present world conditions. It will come from God, and with "God our Saviour," who shall appear in "power and great glory" (1 Thess. 4. 14-17).

I. **Jesus as King is Coming Again.** As a *Prophet* He has appeared; as a *Priest* He *now* appears in the presence of God for us; as KING He *shall* yet appear, and perfect His great work by bringing the world into subjection to His will; and when His redeemed people who have suffered for Him here shall share His honour and glory (1 Cor. 6. 2; Rev. 5. 10). This is something of *the grace* that is to be brought unto us at the *Revelation of Jesus Christ* (1 Peter 1. 13). He is coming; yes, coming in Person as a Glorious Victor, just as He was seen to go (Acts 1. 11).

II. **When is this Kingdom Coming?** Micah says: "In the *last days* it shall come to pass" (v. 1). The "last days," not of the world's history, but of this present age. The day or the hour of His appearing no man can know; but the *signs* of the "last days" are something given us whereby we *might know* that the day of His appearing is drawing nigh. We are assured that *in the last days* PERILOUS times will come (2 Tim. 3. 1). These last *times* will be dangerous, hazardous, involving terrible risk: "Distress of nations with perplexity, men's hearts failing them for fear, while they are looking after those things which are coming on the earth." *Then*, while all such conditions are with us, "shall they see the SON OF MAN coming in a cloud with power and great glory" (Luke 21. 25-28). Are these "signs" with us now or not? Many of these sorrows have always been with mankind, but in these "*last* days" they become "signs," as the world has no remedy for its own diseases. These signs are danger signals.

III. **The Characteristics of His Kingdom**, as revealed by this prophecy.

1. It will be CENTRED AT JERUSALEM. "The *mountain* of the *House of the Lord* shall be established in the top of

the mountains.. and exalted above the hills and *peoples* shall flow into it" (v 1, R.V.). Where else could this heavenly kingdom find its capital but in His own City. Even *there* where He Himself was crucified for the world's sin. Blessed thought, where His Cross of suffering and shame was lifted up, there will be *His Throne* of dominion, the symbol of power and victory over *all His enemies.* "The House of the Lord" will then be worthy of His Holy Name, when *all peoples* shall flow into it, and every tongue confess that He is Lord, Jerusalem will again become a praise on the earth.

2. IT WILL BE UNIVERSAL. "Many nations shall come... He will teach us of *His ways*, and *we will walk in His paths.* and the Word of the Lord shall go forth from Jerusalem" (v. 2). The heathen shall be given Him for His inheritance, and the uttermost parts of the earth for His possession (Psa. 2. 8). He who hung on a Cross will yet have a world bowing before Him. Worthy is the Lamb that was slain, to receive this honour and glory and *dominion* (Isa. 9. 7).

3. IT WILL BE PEACEFUL. *"He shall* judge...and rebuke... *they shall* beat their swords into plowshares... and shall learn war no more" (v. 3). What a deliverance for a world now lying in wickedness! His Name shall be PRINCE OF PEACE, and the government shall be *upon His shoulders* (Isa. 9. 6). In that day the "prince of this world," now working in the children of disobedience, will be utterly overthrown. Meanwhile, let us hear and rest in His own comforting words: "Let not your heart be troubled... ye believe in Me ... *I will come again*" (John 14. 1-3).

4. IT WILL BE ABUNDANTLY PROSPEROUS. "They shall sit every man under his vine, and under his fig tree, and none shall make them *afraid*" (v. 4). No fear of raiders,

or pestilence, or drought, for the wilderness and the desert
shall blossom as the rose.   It shall blossom abundantly.
The parched ground shall become a pool, and the thirsty
land springs of water.   There shall be joy and gladness,
"and sorrow and sighing shall flee away" (Isa. 35).   No
more anxious scanning of the sky, sighing for the refreshing
rain; all the elements in earth, air, and sea under His
control, and made subservient to the good of His people
(Isa. 12).

5. IT WILL BE A TIME OF GREAT JOY.   To His ancient
people it will be a national resurrection, for "The ransomed of the Lord shall return, and come to Zion with songs
and *everlasting joy* upon their heads" (Isa. 35. 10).   Micah
tells us: "In that day, saith the Lord, will I assemble her
that *halteth*, and gather her that is *driven out*, and the
afflicted; and I will make her a *strong nation*, and the
Lord shall reign over them in Mount Zion...for ever"
(vv. 6, 7).   What a reunion for this halting, scattered, and
afflicted people.   Truly their restoration will be as "life
from the dead."   A saved and happy nation!   What a
mighty influence they will have on the peoples of the
earth.   But what about the Church?   Those who belong
to Christ now?   Ah, "Christ the *firstfruits.*"   Afterward,
"they that are Christ's at His Coming.   For He must
reign till He hath put *all enemies* under His feet"
(1 Cor. 15. 23-25).

THE LORD'S CONTROVERSY.
MICAH 6. 1-8.

"HEAR ye, O mountains, the *Lord's* controversy" (v. 2)
After all that He hath done for His people, why should
there still be a "controversy" between them?   Even
God's *chosen* ones are often stubborn.   God has had a
controversy with humanity since Adam's fall.   The

great mission of the Lord Jesus Christ was that of reconciliation. Hear His—

I. **Sorrowful Questions**. What pathos is in them, revealing His heart agony.

1. "O My people, WHAT HAVE I DONE UNTO THEE?" (v. 3). Think of what I have done for thee! Think of how thou hast requited My longsuffering patience, and kindness toward thee. O My people, redeemed by the precious Blood of Christ, what have I done unto thee, that your heart is so cold toward Me, and your service so formal and fruitless?

2. "WHEREIN HAVE I WEARIED THEE? *testify against Me*" (v. 3). Is it possible to get wearied of God? We may possibly get wearied *in* His service. Surely never *of* it. If *spiritual things* are becoming wearisome to your soul, would you dare to "testify against Him," that His dealings with you are not in harmony with His revealed will? It is a small thing for you to weary men, but will ye weary my God also? (Isa. 7. 13).

II. **Mercies Recalled**. "O My people, *remember*" (v. 5). How grievous it must be to our Heavenly Father when we grow weary of Him through *forgetfulness* of His benefits. Remember He says—

1. That "I BROUGHT THEE UP out of Egypt" (v. 4). Remember that I broke the power of your oppressors, and led you forth into joyful freedom. Brethren, let us never forget that it was the loving *grace of God* that delivered us from the power of sin, the bondage of the world, and the delusions of the Devil, into the blessed liberty of "sons of God."

2. That "I REDEEMED THEE." The price Jehovah paid to redeem Israel out of Egypt was His terrible judgments upon her enemies. But the price He paid to redeem us from guilt and sin was the life and Blood of His own

Beloved Son. "He gave Himself a ransom for us." Remember, ye are *not your own*, ye have been bought with a price. Therefore glorify God in your body and spirit, *which are His*.

3. That "I SENT BEFORE THEE MOSES, AARON, AND MIRIAM" (vv. 4, 5). These three leaders are typical of a threefold blessing: Moses, the legislator; Aaron, the intercessor; Miriam, the song leader (Exod. 15. 20, 21). The word, the worship, and the praise. Has He not also given us *His Word*, like Moses; *liberty of access*, like Aaron; and the *song of victory*, like Miriam. Thanks be unto God who giveth us the victory.

4. That "I TURNED BALAAM'S INTENDED CURSE INTO A BLESSING (v. 5; see Num. 23. 11, 12). What a wonderful proof this is of the overruling power of God on behalf of His people. Take no anxious thought for your life. He careth for you.

III. **Personal Perplexities.** In verses 6, 7, we have language that might well become an anxious sin-smitten soul, seeking the favour of God. *"Wherewith shall I come before the Lord"* (v. 6). With *what* shall I come, that I might find acceptance in His eyes? This old question is ever and anon burrowing its way into Spirit-awakened minds and hearts. There is a deep conviction that *something* is needed. But what that *something* is remains a mystery to those who know not Jesus Christ as their Redeemer. "Shall I come with burnt-offerings? Will the Lord *be pleased* with thousands of rams, or with ten thousands of rivers of oil? Shall I give the fruit of my body for the sin of my soul?" (v. 7). Abraham was willing to give his only son Isaac, but God provided Himself with an offering. "Behold the *Lamb of God*, that taketh away the sin of the world." It is *not possible* that the blood of bulls and of goats should take away sins

(Heb. 10. 4).   There is absolutely nothing man can offer
God that can in any way take the place He has given the
Christ, who *Himself* bore our sins to the accursed tree.
Anything we can offer, apart from Him, is but an insult
to His Cross.   In that Cross there is the *"wherewith"* we
can come boldly before the Lord.

IV. The Way Revealed. "He hath showed thee, O
man, what doth the Lord require of thee.   To do justly,
to love mercy, and walk humbly *with thy God*" (v. 8).
Many proud and worldly people quote these words to
justify themselves before God and men.   They say, "I do
justly; I love mercy and walk humbly." Yes, but no
experience of truly *walking with God*!   It is easy for us to
talk of justice, mercy, and humility, while we may know
nothing experimentally of the *reconciling Blood* of His
Cross.   "How can two walk together except they be
agreed?" How can we be agreed with God if we are
persistently ignoring the redemptive work of Jesus Christ
on our behalf?   We may do justly and love mercy, but to
humbly walk with thy God is impossible without a new
birth, a new spirit, and an entire *surrender of ourselves
to Him* in the daily life.

REJOICE IN THE LORD.
MICAH 7. 7-20

"THE joy of the Lord is your strength." The closing
words of this prophet give us abundant cause for this joy,
for his God *is our God*.   See here—

I. His Joyful Confidence. The following utterances
in view of very depressing conditions, seem to be the
spontaneous expressions of a satisfied and joyful heart

1. "I WILL LOOK UNTO THE LORD" (v. 7).   The *upward*
look to the believing soul is always a clear one, even when

the outward and the inward look is dark, cloudy, and foreboding. "Look unto Me, and be ye saved. "

2. "I WILL WAIT FOR THE GOD OF MY SALVATION" (v. 7). The *look* may be like a flash, but we must also *quietly wait* for Him   The waiting time may be the testing time; but if we are waiting for God's salvation it will surely come.

3. "WHEN I FALL I SHALL ARISE. " So that the joy of the enemy over the fall shall be quickly spoiled (v. 8). "Falls" are *not* to be expected, for *"He is able to keep you from falling. "* When you do fall, either openly or secretly, arise before the enemy gets time to rejoice.

4. "WHEN I SIT IN DARKNESS, THE LORD SHALL BE A LIGHT UNTO ME" (v. 8). Blessed darkness, when all the light we have is in His Holy *Presence.* "Yea though I walk through the valley of the shadow I will fear no evil, for Thou art with me" (Psa. 23).

5. "I WILL BEAR THE INDIGNATION.. UNTIL HE PLEAD MY CAUSE" (v. 9). When stricken by the chastening hand of God it is good just to *bear* the stroke *until* He plead my cause, as Job did, and God did plead his cause and reward his patience.

6. "HE SHALL BRING ME TO THE LIGHT, and I shall BEHOLD HIS RIGHTEOUSNESS" (v. 9). The patient, trustful sufferers He shall bring into the light, and cause such to behold his *righteousness* in all His dealings with them, for He doeth all things well. And at last, when He brings us into the glorious light of our Redeemer's face, and behold His righteousness in all His dealings with us while pilgrims and strangers on the earth, what a revelation, what joy, what cause for praise!

II. **Joyful Reasons for Such Confidence.** In these verses (18-20) we have what has been recognised as an unparalleled expression of the *gracious* character of our

God. "Who is a God like unto Thee?" Here are seven
things He does for His people.

1 HE PARDONETH INIQUITY. What a comfort to know
that His pardon can extend to our lack of rectitude, or
moral principle, in our dealings with our fellow-men.
Such sins may not always be apparent to others, but they
are naked in his eyes.

2. HE PASSETH BY THE TRANSGRESSION. He is willing
to overlook our trespasses against His holy law and our
presumptuous intruding into the holy domain of His
Presence, as when we come before Him in our pride and
self-confidence.

3. HE RETAINETH NOT HIS ANGER FOR EVER. His
anger is as just and as holy as His love. But in grace He
retaineth *not* His anger, because love has triumphed.
We may well rejoice as we see the proof of this in the gift
of His Son (John 3. 16).

4. HE DELIGHTETH IN MERCY. We do not read that He
delighteth in judgment. "As I live, saith the Lord, I
have *no pleasure* in the death of the wicked, but that he
should turn from *his* way, " for "He delighteth in mercy. "
Herein lies the hope of sinful men.

5. HE WILL HAVE COMPASSION AND SUBDUE OUR
INIQUITIES. To conquer and subdue is something deeper
than merely to forgive. This he does for us by the incoming
of His mighty Spirit into the citadel of the soul

6. HE CASTS ALL OUR SINS INTO THE DEPTHS OF THE
SEA. This is, of course, figurative language. They are
buried where there can be no resurrection, into the depths
of His eternal forgetfulness. "Behind His back, " where
His holy eyes can see them no more (Isa. 38. 17).

7. HE WILL PERFORM HIS PROMISES to His believing
children. "He *is faithful* that hath promised. " All these
gracious features constitute a true likeness of the Father.

as revealed to us in the face of Jesus Christ, who appeared as the *image* of the invisible God, and who said, "Him that cometh unto Me I will *in no wise* cast out." Rejoice in the Lord.

GREAT IS OUR GOD.
NAHUM 1. 1-8.

THE prophet is here *burdened* with a terrible sentence. But while the judgments recorded were against old Nineveh, they are a very solemn revelation to us of the great and terrible God with whom impenitent sinners will have to do.

I. **God is Jealous** (v. 2). Jealousy may be defined as an uneasy state of mind, under fear that *another* has engaged the affections of one you love. God is jealous of any rival for our affections and trust, just because *His love* is so good and true. "Love not the world, nor the things of the world," that you provoke Him not to jealousy. The world and self are His rivals.

II. **The Lord's Revenge is Furious** (v. 2). When God is for us His power is Almighty; when against us it is equally Almighty. When He avengeth *His adversaries* it will be with a fury that is overwhelming. O proud man, think of the God with whom ye have to do.

III. **The Lord is Slow to Anger** (v. 3). He is not what we say of some people, "quiet tempered." All past history is proof of this. In the days before the Flood God gave them 120 years' notice (Gen. 6. 3). This long-suffering patience of God is often misconstrued as utter indifference. While His *anger* comes slowly, bless His Name, His love comes quickly.

IV. **The Lord is Great in Power**, and will *not at all acquit the wicked*" (v. 3) How shall we escape if we neglect His great salvation? Here is the answer. "*Not* *at all.*" What a solemn and urgent truth this is for those who deny His love and ignore His proffered mercy in the Gospel of His grace. "He that believeth not is condemned *already*" (John 3. 18). But the final execution of this sentence awaits the day of His great power (v. 6).

V. **The Lord has His Way** in the *whirlwind*, in the *storm*, the *clouds*, the *rivers*, the *sea*, and the *fire* (v. 6). We cannot imagine any of the natural forces He has created *rebelling* against His will. They are all weapons at His disposal. He has *His way in them all.* We are assured that every atom in the universe is under law. The winds are in His fist, the clouds are the dust of His feet. It is man and fallen angels who are the rebels. But "who shall stand before His indignation?" (v. 6).

VI. **"The Lord is Good, a Strong Hold in the Day of Trouble"** (v. 7). The Lord is *great* in *power*, but also in *goodness*. His goodness is a *strong hold* for us in the day of our trouble because of sin, or weakness, or failure. "God is our refuge and strength, a *very present* help in trouble" (Psa. 46. 1). "By grace are ye saved" (Eph. 2. 8)

VII. **The Lord Knoweth Them that Trust in Him** (v. 7). We are known unto God, not by our wisdom, not by our many works, or popularity in the eyes of men, but by our *trust in Him*. The Lord knoweth such, although the world knows nothing of them. Have faith in God, and rest assured that He *knoweth* them that *trust* in Him, and will surely satisfy them with His goodness. Blessed are all they that put their trust in Him.

ON THE WATCH TOWER.

Habakkuk 2.

WE need not imagine the prophet climbing to some hill top to get this expected vision, but that in his own heart he would take the attitude of being on the outlook, and

wait for God's message. The message given can be easily
applied to the present times, as all Scripture is given by
inspiration of God, and is profitable for doctrine, for
reproof (2 Tim. 3. 16). This message is chiefly for reproof
and instruction *in righteousness*. Here are—

I. **Words of Warning**. Expressed in five solemn
"woes."—

1. WOE TO THE DISHONEST. "To him that increaseth
that which is not his own" (v. 6). This applies to the
unscrupulous master, the dishonest servant, the unsym-
pathetic miser, and to all religious hypocrites, who claim
that which is not their own.

2. WOE TO THE COVETOUS. "Him that coveteth...that
he *may set his nest on high*" (v. 9). This is coveting for
self-display and social aggrandisement. Although such
may never gain what their vanity craves for, their sin lies
in their covetous spirit. Some may even covet the gifts
and power of a Christian brother; not that they might
bring more honour to God, but that they themselves might
get more honour from men. Beware of this woe. "Pride
goeth before a fall." It is lawful and wise "to covet
earnestly the best gifts" (1 Cor. 12. 31), just as a wise
workman might covet the best tools, that he might be
able to do better work for his master.

3. WOE TO THE OPPRESSOR. "To him that buildeth
with blood and establisheth by iniquity" (v. 12). Thank
God, the old slavery has been abolished, when verily,
cruel men built fortunes on the blood of others, and
established their stronghold by iniquity. Every nation,
every cause that is built on this policy will certainly be
smitten with the *woe* of the Almighty, as all past history
attests. The footsteps of every industry and every *individual life* that is being built up by iniquity will be
followed by the unerring and overwhelming woe of God.
"*Be sure* your sin will find you out."

4. WOE TO THE DECEIVER. "To him that giveth his neighbour drink, that *they might look on their shame*" (v. 15). This attempt to drug a neighbour, that advantage may be taken of them is a kind of deception that has many practitioners in our own day. Not only in giving men drink that they might laugh at their folly, but in giving such teaching that stupify and bring such dullness and insensibility over the mind that the precious things of God's Gospel become of no vital value　And all that they might be classed as followers with us.

5. WOE TO THE IDOLATER. "Woe unto him that saith unto the wood, Awake, and to the dumb stone, Arise" (v. 19). We pity the poor blinded heathen, bowing down to the workmanship of their own hands, and worshipping the devices of their own hearts　What better are the worshippers of fashion, of fiction, of sport, and of purely selfish interests?　Whatever takes the place of God in our thoughts and lives is our *dumb* idol in the day of our real need.

II. **Words of Encouragement.** Here is a brilliant star gleaming in a cloudy sky.　It is the Morning Star of Promise heralding the new day of universal blessing. "The earth shall be *filled* with the *knowledge of the glory* of the Lord, as the waters cover the sea" (v. 14; also Isa. 11. 9).　When our Lord comes again in power and great glory, when *every eye* shall see Him, and *all shall know Him,* from the least unto the greatest, then shall be fulfilled the promise given at His birth: "He shall be great.　To Him shall be given *the throne* of His father David, and *He shall reign,* and of His kingdom there shall be no end" (Luke 1. 30-33).　Be of good cheer.　As sure as the world's Redeemer *has* come, so surely will the world's Kingly Deliverer appear, when *all power* shall be given Him *on the earth,* and when the kingdoms of this world shall become *the Kingdom* of our God and of His Anointed.

The closing verse of this part of the prophecy gives us another peace-assuring statement. "The Lord is in His Holy Temple; let all the earth *keep silence* before Him." The conditions of the world when the KING of *kings* appears will be tumult and uproar. Here is His call for SILENCE. "Let *all* the earth keep silence before Him." What a solemn, holy hush, when *all the earth* is silent *before Him*. The noise of battle, the war of traffic, the strife of tongues, the clamour of scepticism: every discordant note in His ear silenced. Peace on earth, goodwill among men, and glory to God.

THE SECRET OF ABIDING JOY.
HABAKKUK 3. 17, 18.

THIS old prophet with the crooked name had the secret of a happy life. And here it is for you: "Although the fig tree shall not blossom," etc., "yet I will rejoice in the Lord." The meaning is: Although the Chaldeans invade the land and burn up the vineyards and oliveyards, hinder the harvest, steal the flocks, and rob me of every earthly possession; yet I will rejoice in the Lord. Will you and I say that in the day of calamity?

I. **The Christian has Joy.** "I will rejoice." Christianity is not a system of melancholy. Many Christians may have long faces, but every true believer in God has a joyful heart. The joy of the Christian is not that superficial kind of mirth that finds expression only in "roars of laughter." It is more like the calm of the settled water in the deep sea, undisturbed by those elements that constantly affect the surface. "The peace of God that passeth all understanding."

II. **This Joy is in the Lord.** "I will rejoice in the Lord." This joy implies knowledge. You cannot rejoice in the Lord unless you know Him. If you knew Him you

VOL. X. 6

would love Him. If you loved Him you would rejoice in
Him. We cannot rejoice in God as we ought until we have
found in Him that which satisfies every desire of the heart,
and fills up every longing of the new-born life. See that
little dog creeping over to that sunny spot of the carpet.
How it rejoices in the sunshine. The reason why so many
Christians are not filled with joy is because they don't
abide in the bright warmth of the Holy Spirit. Friends,
the Cross of Christ is the only bright spot on earth where
guilty men can share the joy and happiness of Heaven.

III. **This Joy is the Joy of Salvation.** Habakkuk
says here, "I will joy in the God of my salvation." "How
is it that you are always so happy, Annie?" asked a
visitor who had called and marked the little girl's brightness. "Oh!" she said, "I am happy because I am forgiven." After the Israelites had passed through the Red
Sea, they struck up the Song of Salvation (Exod. 15. 1).
How can they help from singing who have been saved.
Jonah was in a sore plight when swallowed by the great
fish, with the weeds of the deep wrapt round his head—the
picture of a lost man. But he cried unto God out of the
belly of this Hell. The Lord heard and saved him. Then
how gladly he sang "Salvation is of the Lord." Salvation
has two sides—the manward and the Godward. Your
side is to *repent and believe.* God's side is to regenerate
and restore (John 3. 7-16). You cannot regenerate your
own soul, but God will if you believe. You are commanded to repent and believe the Gospel. This you can
do if you will, and you will perish if you don't. Let me
say further that—

IV. **This is the Joy of Anticipation.** In verse 19
we read: "He will make my feet like hind's feet, to walk
upon mine high places." The Christian life is not only
one of happiness, but also of progress. A climbing from
one high place of grace to another. It is not a grasping

at gaudy bubbles that vanish with the touch, but the laying hold of spiritual certainties. For this feet like the hind's feet are needed. I understand that the peculiarity of the hind's feet is that they not only rest on the rocks, but cling to them, so that they can easily stand on high places. Such represent the feet of faith that rests on and cling to the great and precious promises of God. The Christian's prospects are mountains high. The hope of the wicked shall perish.

V. This Joy is Independent of Earthly Possessions. "Although the fig tree shall not blossom," etc., "yet will I rejoice in the Lord." Although I am stripped naked of every earthly thing, yet will I joy in the God of my salvation. You see, beloved brethren, that the joys of the believer are not in the things of this world, but independent of them. Old Job could say, "Though He slay me, yet will I trust in Him."

JOHN BRADFORD, while in Newgate prison, the night before he was burned at Smithfield, swung himself on his bedpost with great glee, saying to his brother martyr: "Fine shining we shall make to-morrow when the flame is kindled." Was he mad? No. He was rejoicing in the Lord.

Do you know the Lord like that? Have you found in Him your all, your everything? A poor negro slave, who was once asked if he was never unhappy, said: "When all de world are saying, 'Dis is my house,' 'Dat is my cottonfield,' I just look up and say, 'Dare is my house, and dare is my Saviour,' and when I own de Lord me tinks I own eberyting." He rejoiced in the God of his salvation. If you are an unhappy Christian it is because you know so little of your Lord. The joys of the worldling are like the flash of a rocket that glares for a moment and is gone. The joy of the true believer is like a star in the Heavens— it abides for life; it abides for ever. "The joy of the Lord is your strength."

THE BLESSINGS OF THE LORD.
ZEPHANIAH 3. 10-20.

THE blessings here promised are, of course, for Israel, and will be completely fulfilled when the Lord will bring full deliverance to His waiting people at His Second Coming. But the spiritual import is for God's people in every age. Shall we look at—

I. **What He hath Done.** In the light of our own experience as Christians.

1. HE HATH TAKEN AWAY THY JUDGMENTS (v. 15). The judgment hanging over us like a thick cloud, because of sin, He hath taken away because of the Cross. "There is therefore *now* no condemnation to them who are in Christ Jesus" (Rom. 8. 1). The judgment is past, and the true light now shineth upon the forgiven soul.

2. HE HATH CAST OUT THINE ENEMY (v. 15). He hath dislodged that wicked spirit that still worketh in the children of disobedience. Satan's sphere of operation is now outside the citadel of the *justified* soul. Therefore keep thy gates closed against him, and yield not to temptation.

3. HE IS IN THE MIDST OF THEE (v. 15). The Mightier Spirit has come to take possession. He shall be with you and *in* you (John 14. 17). Greater is He that is *in you* than he that is *in the world.* Ye are more than conquerors through Him. "God is in the midst of her, she shall not be moved." "Lo, I am with you alway, even unto the end of the age."

II. **What He Will Do.** God is in the midst of thee.

1. HE WILL SAVE (v. 17). The salvation of God is a past, present, and future deliverance. One great whole in His eternal purpose. Don't we need a daily salvation from sin and folly, from doubting and fearfulness, from spiritual apathy and ignorance, from self-assertiveness

and fruitless testimony? He will save. There is none other Name under Heaven whereby we can be so saved.

2. HE WILL REJOICE OVER THEE WITH JOY (v. 17). Yes, those who are daily being fully saved bring gladness to the Saviour's heart. The Lord will not rejoice over a spoiled thing, or a *marred vessel*, or a professedly Christian life that is failing to fulfil His high and holy purpose. If your life is a sacrifice of joy unto the Lord you may rest assured that "He will rejoice over thee." "We joy in God through our Lord Jesus Christ" (Rom. 5. 11).

3. HE WILL REST IN HIS LOVE (v. 17). Oh, the sweetness of this thought, that our God can find *rest* in the greatness of *His love* for us: that love that never faileth, and is stronger than death. He will, and does, rest in that love that gave His beloved Son to the death for us all. Rest in His love as seen in the *willing* sacrifice offered by His Son. Rest in the triumph of that love that bringeth salvation to all men. What a resting place this is for our own hearts, now and ever. Rest in HIS LOVE, not in our own.

III. **What We Should Do.**

1. PRAISE HIS BLESSED NAME. "Sing, O daughter of Zion. Shout O Israel. Be glad and *rejoice with all the heart*" (v. 14). "Oh that men would praise the Lord for His *goodness*, and for His *wonderful works* to the children of men" (Psa. 107. 15). In that day Israel will be "made a praise among all people of the earth" (v. 20). For many generations they have been a "sneer and a byword" among the nations, but their "crowning day is coming," when their King and the Church's Redeemer shall take unto Himself *His right* and reign over the whole earth. O Christian, be glad and rejoice with all *your heart*, for He hath done great things for thee. For he *hath* delivered in the past, He *doth* deliver in the present, and *will yet* deliver (2 Cor. 1. 10). Thanks be unto God.

2. FEAR NOT. "Fear thou not" (v. 16). There is no place for fearfulness and uncertainty in the Economy of Divine Grace. He who planned the Heavens, and the whole scheme of man's salvation, and the movements of an atom, will not fail His own trusting children. *"He hath said*, I will never leave thee nor forsake thee. So that *we may boldly say*, The Lord is my Helper, I will not fear" (Heb. 13. 5-6).

3. BE DILIGENT IN SERVICE. "Let not thine hands be slack" (v. 16). Slack hands are an evidence of slack hearts. Slackness in God's work is a prevailing weakness among His people. The "go slow" policy is largely practised in the ranks of Christian workers. Whatsoever thy hand finds to do, *do it heartily* as unto the Lord. Let us seek to serve our gracious Master just as if He were standing by our side looking on, and waiting to receive the finished article.

CONSIDER YOUR WAYS.
HAGGAI 1. 3-10.

THUS saith the Lord of hosts, "Consider your ways" (v. 5). This call comes to His thoughtless, dilatory, procrastinating people Let us hear it as coming to ourselves. Is there not a tendency with us to be slack, and backward in facing facts. Consider your ways—

I. In Relation to God's Cause.

1. They said, "THE TIME IS NOT COME to build the Lord's house" (v. 2). How ready we are at times to postpone the things we should do for the cause of Christ. We feel we should consecrate ourselves to God, but "the time is not come," or that we should make an offering to some missionary enterprise but "the time is not come." The time to help on God's work is an ever present opportunity. "Consider your ways."

2. "They dwelt in THEIR OWN CEILED HOUSES, while HIS HOUSE LAY WASTE" (v. 4). They were content that their own personal interests were prosperous, while the house of the Lord was in ruins. Just as there are many professing Christians to-day satisfied with material things, while the cause of Christ languisheth for lack of faith and personal effort. "Is it nothing to you, all ye that pass by?" "Seek ye FIRST the Kingdom of God." "Consider your ways"—

II. In View of the Results of your Labours.

1. "Ye have SOWN MUCH, and bring in LITTLE" (v. 6). We who are ministers of His Word have much need to lay this reminder to heart. There is something sadly wrong where there is much sowing and little reaping. Is it the sower or the seed that is to be blamed? Or is the cause of failure the blighting breath of God's disapproval? For it is "God who giveth the increase." Those who sow much of the seed of the Word of God, and bring in little, have need to "consider their ways," for such results are not in harmony with God's purpose.

2. YE "EAT AND HAVE NOT ENOUGH" (v. 6). This is the *spiritual* condition of multitudes. They have a keen appetite for the things of this life—wealth, position, honour, and the praise of men. They are constantly eating, but never satisfied. They cannot say, like Esau, "I have enough." Hungry souls, but will not take the true "Bread of Life" that they may have *the life* which is for ever (John 6. 51).

3. YE "CLOTHE YOU, BUT THERE IS NONE WARM" (v. 6). They wrap themselves up in the flimsy garments of their own righteousness, and complain of the cold. There is nothing like the "Righteousness of God, which is unto all and *upon all them that believe*," for keeping the heart warm in the cold season of adverse circumstances. Put

ye on the Lord Jesus Christ, and His righteousness, and
the glow of His Presence will keep you warm.

4. YE PUT YOUR "WAGES IN A BAG WITH HOLES" (v. 6).
The wages you have earned by the efforts of your pride
and self-seeking become of no practical value to your soul.
"The wages of sin is death." Death is a bag with tremendous holes in it. Every ungodly thing will fall
through it. "Consider your ways"—

III. In View of the Work to be Done.

1. THE WORK. "Build the house, and I will take
pleasure in it, and I will be glorified, saith the Lord"
(v. 8). The house of the Lord was the *Temple* at Jerusalem
which stood for worship and testimony. The Church of
God, which is the "Body of Christ," stands for worship
and witnessing. It is a spiritual temple, built with
spiritual stones. That building is now going on, and we
are called to be fellow-workmen *together with Him* (2 Cor.
6. 1, *margin*). Our work then is to build this holy temple
of the Lord in which He will *take pleasure* and *be glorified*.
If we have been in any way indifferent to this Divine
purpose, let us "consider our ways."

2. THE MATERIAL. "Go up to the mountain and bring
wood" (v. 8). The temple at Jerusalem could not be
built with high and noble thoughts or eloquent speakers,
they must have timber. "Go, bring wood." The great
spiritual temple of which Christ is the Foundation, cannot
be built with mere formal prayers, or powerless sermons,
or social activities. A spiritual building needs spiritual
stones, souls quickened by the Holy Spirit of God, "built
upon the foundation of the apostles, fitly framed together,
growing unto an holy temple of the Lord" (Eph. 2. 19-22).
But where are these living stones to come from? "*Go up
to the mountains*" and bring them. They had to go up,
probably to Mount Lebanon, for the wood. We must go

up to Mount Calvary if we would secure what is needful for the building of this holy temple of the Lord. To win souls for Christ we need personal cleansing, personal consecration, and a personal enduement of the sacrificial spirit of Jesus. "He that winneth souls is wise." In considering *your* ways, take time to consider God's ways.

THE DESIRE OF ALL NATIONS.
HAGGAI 2. 6-9.

ALL agree that the reference here is to the Coming of the Messiah. But the *birth* of Christ was not heralded by a universal "*shaking*," but rather, we are told that there was universal peace at the first Christmas. So the reference must be to His *Second* Appearing. Note, then—

I. **The Condition of the Nations at His Second Coming.** "I will shake the Heavens, the earth, the sea, and the dry land. And I *will shake all nations*" (vv. 6, 7). Convulsions in nature, and nations being shaken to pieces by internal strife. Our daily newspapers are giving us abundant evidence of this shaking process in operation. "I will overturn, overturn, overturn, *until He come* whose *right it is*" (Ezek. 21. 27). We are not warranted to look for a converted world before He comes, but for these *signs* (see Luke 21. 25-28). And when these things *begin* to come to pass, then look up, for your redemption draweth nigh. "Distress of nations," and "Men's hearts failing them *for fear*" are the warning signals of His near approach.

II. **The Desire of All Nations shall Come.** But do all nations, as nations, desire the coming of the Lord? There is no evidence of this. This word "desire" is of peculiar significance. According to Dr. Young, the word in the Hebrew only occurs in one other place in the Bible (1 Sam. 9. 20), where the sense seems to be, "They desired

the things which a wise and mighty ruler would bring."
"The desirable things of all nations shall come: and I will
fill this house with glory" (v. 7, R.V.). The nations, as
such, do not desire the Coming of the Lord Jesus Christ,
but mutely long for the things which Christ alone can
bring.

1. AS A MEDIATOR. One to stand between the wrongs
of men and the rights of God. His Presence would do more
for peace than a "League of all Nations." He will be the
God-appointed and final Arbiter in all the controversies
of earth.

2. AS A DELIVERER. "There shall come out of Zion THE
DELIVERER" (Rom. 11. 26). All national enemies have
their stronghold in the *hearts* of men. All that is in
the world at enmity with God lies in the human heart.
A Deliverer is needed. When we think of the age-long
blindness of the Jewish nation, of the problem of racial
hatred, of a rapidly growing heathendom, of the growing
army of "seducing spirits," and the comparative impo-
tency of the Church to win the world for Christ. But
when He *Comes*, "All nations shall bow down before Him."

3. AS A PHYSICIAN. He alone can heal *all our diseases*:
all the running sores in our social, industrial, commercial,
and national life. His Presence will be a balm for every
wound. No one shall say, "I am sick."

4. AS A KING. When He came as Redeemer it was in
lowliness and weakness; but when He comes as KING it
will be in kingly fashion—with "great power and glory."
Then shall He judge the poor and save the needy. Then
shall His Presence be like rain upon the mown grass, and
as showers that water the earth. Then in *His days* shall
there be abundance of peace. Then shall the heathen that
dwell in the wilderness bow before Him. Then shall His
enemies lick the dust. Then shall all kings fall down

before Him, and all nations serve Him. Then shall He
redeem from deceit and violence. Then shall be given
unto Him the gold of Sheba, and daily shall He be praised.
Then shall His Name be continued, and all nations shall
call Him blessed. Then shall the whole earth be filled
with His glory. Amen and Amen (Psa. 72). "Even so,
come, Lord Jesus."

THE UNFIT PREPARED.

ZECHARIAH 3. 1-5,

JOSHUA, the high priest, may be regarded as a symbolic
character, representing the degraded priesthood as a whole
at that time. We may regard it as a parable of how
defiled Christians may be restored, and fitted for the
Lord's service.

I. The Cause of His Unfitness.

1. He had FILTHY GARMENTS (v. 3). The *garments*
represent the outward and visible expression of his
character. When the outward life—our acts and deeds—
condemn our profession, then our garments are unclean,
and we become unfit for His holy service. Pure religion,
and undefiled before God, is to *keep himself unspotted*
from the world (Jas. 1. 27).

2. He was like "A BRAND IN THE FIRE" (v. 2). Fire,
like sin, usually has small beginnings. "By *one* man sin
entered into the world." A *brand* is a fit subject for the
fire. A man whose character has become filthy in the light
of God becomes a fit subject for the blackening and consuming power of sin. Like a brand, he is helpless in the
fire.

3. He had an ADVERSARY STANDING BY TO RESIST
(v. 1). Satan, our adversary, is always "standing by,"
ready to resist any efforts that might be made for our
deliverance from uncleanness, and salvation from our

unfitness for the work of our Lord. "Your adversary the Devil" is pleased with your stained garments, and is a standing enemy to the transforming grace of God.

II. The Manner of His Deliverance. "The angel of the Lord stood by" (v. 5). Perhaps the "Angel of the Covenant," the Son of God, to see that Satan was resisted, and that this poor, unclean, and disqualified servant might by the all-sufficient grace of God be cleansed and restored. For here grace reigns.

1. He was FORGIVEN. "I have caused thine iniquity to pass from thee" (v. 4). Forgiveness is our *first* need as sinners and our first need as *backsliders*. Because all sin is against God. Sin is the transgression of His law and of His love. If we lose our *fellowship* with God, we lose our *power* for Him. But we have a God who is *ready to pardon* (Psa. 86. 5).

2. He was CLEANSED. "Take away the filthy garments from him" (v. 4). How inconsistent it would be for any one claiming to have received the forgiveness of God and yet continuing to wear garments that are filthy in the eyes of their fellow-men. "Put off the old man with *his deeds*" (Col. 3. 9). Filthy garments are not to be covered over, but taken away.

3. He was CLOTHED WITH CHANGE OF RAIMENT (v. 4). What a *change*, when we get rid of our soiled and torn garments, and receive that robe of righteousness which Christ alone can bestow. That righteousness which puts us right with God and right for our priestly office in making intercession in His Name for others. Be clothed with humility.

4. He had A FAIR MITRE SET UPON HIS HEAD (v. 5). The mitre was the crown of his priesthood, the symbol of Divine authority. All God's cleansed and clothed ones are crowned with honour. The holy anointing oil was put

upon the mitred head. "Upon man's *flesh shall it not be poured*" (Exod. 30. 32). We should ever remember that the anointing of the Holy Spirit comes upon what God Himself hath given.

III. **The Renewed Promise.** After the cleansing and crowning comes the new purpose. There must now be:

1. A NEW WALK. "Walk in My ways" (v. 7). Hitherto the Lord could say, "My ways are not your ways, neither are your ways My ways." Because there was no *agreement* they could not *walk together*. But now, cleansed in heart and renewed in mind, the only path to be chosen was the "New and living way," as revealed in His Word: the way of faith and willing obedience to the truth. Jesus Christ said: "I am the Way. Follow Me. He that followeth Me shall not walk in darkness" (John 14. 6; 8. 12).

2. NEW MOTIVES. "Thou wilt keep My charge" (v. 7). "Thou shalt be faithful unto Me in the work to which you are called." The new man in Christ Jesus has new motive springs in his soul. His chief desire is to honour his Lord, and to keep true to His charge as revealed in His Word, that God might work in him both to will and to do of *His good pleasure* (Eph. 2. 13). Paul's one motive was: "To me to live is Christ" (Eph. 1. 21). All who are crowned with the mitre of holiness will be able gladly to say: "Not I, but Christ."

THE SUPREMACY OF THE SPIRITUAL.
ZECHARIAH 4. 1-7.

THIS vision of the Candlestick, or Lampstand, teaches us that there is in God's purpose a real and vital relationship between spiritual and visible things. We might look at this vision in connection with—

I. **The Temple of God as a Witness.** The temple

was not yet built, but God saw it already as a perfected thing, as the prophet saw the Golden Candlestick—com-*plete* with its bowls, and lamps, and pipes; with its oil, and the two olive trees standing by as living, unfailing source of supply for the lamps. This is what the temple of God was to be for His people: a witness for Him. But a *lampstand* is not all that was needed. There must be lamps and a plentiful *supply of oil* if light is to shine. Without the oil (emblems of the Holy Spirit) even a *golden* lampstand might become a stumblingblock. So the message of this vision is: "Not by might, nor by power, but by MY SPIRIT, saith the Lord of Hosts" (v. 6). How applicable this truth is to—

II. **The Church of God as a Witness.** The secret of the Church's power lies in the constant flow of the Holy Spirit. This Spirit, like the oil, comes from the living and abiding Sources, the Father and the Son (John 14. 16-18). Let us give heed to Jehovah's warning that this building is not to be reared by mere human might or power, but by His Spirit. In these days there are many substitutes for the power of God's mighty Spirit in doing Christian work. Some trust the power of *money*, some *education*, some *organisation*, some *legislation*, and some the power of *numbers*. None of these are to be despised, but none of them, nor all of them together, can do the work or take the place of the Holy Spirit. None of these can *convict* the world of sin, or righteousness, and of judgment. None of these can *quicken* a dead soul into newness of life and reveal the things of Christ. None of these can *clothe* the message of the Gospel with *power* to win souls for Christ. None of these can be a "Comforter" to the troubled spirit or make intercession for us with unutterable groanings. None of these can breathe the breath of life over a valley of dead bones (Ezek. 37. 9). In this great God honouring work it is the SPIRIT that quickeneth, the flesh profiteth nothing. The secret of the Church's power is the *operation of the Holy Spirit.* What is true of the Church as a whole is true of the *individual* life. "Not by might, nor by power, but by My Spirit, saith the Lord of Hosts." "Ye shall receive power *after* that the *Holy Ghost is come* upon you, and *ye shall be witnesses* unto Me" (Acts 1. 8). "Have ye received the Holy Ghost since ye believed?" (Acts 19. 2).

BEHOLD THE BRANCH.
ZECHARIAH 6. 9-15.

WE believe that there is here—

I. A Symbolic Representation. Joshua is here again brought before us in a symbolic fashion. In chapter 3 we have seen him in filthy garments, then forgiven, cleansed, and adorned with a fair mitre, and so *equipped* for the holy office as high priest. Now he has golden crowns, or a *composite* crown, put upon his head, bestowing on him *kingly honours*; by which he becomes a true type of the Coming Christ, who would be both *Priest and King*, after the order of Melchizedek (Heb. 5. 6).

II. A Prophetic Announcement. "Behold the Man whose name is THE BRANCH." "The Branch" is one of the most significant of Messiah's Names. A branch bears the fruit and *reveals* the character of the tree. Christ as Jehovah's Branch, revealed by His words and deeds the true character of His Father. Jesus said, "I am the Vine, ye are the branches," the fruit-bearing part of the vine. Just as if God should say: "I am the True Vine, and Jesus Christ is *the Branch*, from which My fruit is found." All the blessings that hang on this Branch for our present and future life are the outcome of the love of the Eternal Father. As a Son, Christ is a true and fruitful *Branch* of the Godhead. O the multitudes who have sat under the

shadow of this Branch with great delight! Note what is
said of the Branch as a Person—

1. "HE SHALL GROW UP OUT OF HIS PLACE" (v. 12).
His place was a lowly one: one of humility, sorrow, shame,
rejection, and crucifixion, and burial in a borrowed grave.
But *He grew up*. "Up from the grave *He arose.*" He grew
up, and *up*, till He vanished out of sight and reached the
Throne of the Heavens (Luke 24. 51). His cause shall yet
grow up.

2. "HE SHALL BUILD THE TEMPLE OF THE LORD" (v. 13).
He shall build and see the completion of that great spiritual
temple, "the Church of God," which will be a witness in
the ages to come to the redemptive power of His own
precious Blood (Isa. 53. 11).

3. "HE SHALL BEAR THE GLORY." The glory of the
new temple shall be all *on Himself*. He who bore the
burden of our sins, and of the Cross, shall bear the glory
that was to follow (Heb. 2. 9). The government and the
glory shall be upon His shoulder (Isa. 9. 6).

4. HE "SHALL SIT AND RULE UPON HIS THRONE"
(v. 13). He had His Cross, and He will have *His Throne*.
He was cast out by rulers on earth, but He will yet rule
the nations of the earth. His Kingdom shall be the kingdoms of the world (Rev. 11. 15).

5. "HE SHALL BE A PRIEST UPON HIS THRONE" (v. 13).
What a blessed combination, *King* and *Priest*, an *Enthroned Priest*, a King to govern His people and subdue
His enemies; a Priest crowned to bear His people's needs
before the Throne of His Almighty Father. The King
rules, the Priest intercedes.

6. THE COUNSEL OF PEACE SHALL BE BETWEEN THEM
BOTH. What is that which lies *between* the King and the
Priest? Literally, it may be difficult to define, but in a
spiritual sense, in connection with the character of our

Great High Priest, the meaning is by no means obscure to the spiritually enlightened. Christ, our *High Priest,* offered Himself a Sacrifice for our sins on the Cross. Christ, our Coming King, will yet make His redeemed ones kings and priests to reign on the earth (Rev. 5. 9, 10). The counsel and message of peace and power comes from *between,* or belonging to both the Cross and the Throne.

FORMAL WORSHIP AND POWERLESS PRAYERS.
ZECHARIAH 7. 4-14.

THE Temple at Jerusalem was in process of building, when the question was asked: "Shall I weep and separate myself as I have done these so many years?" (v. 3). Here we have the Lord's answer, which is a charge against them of mere—

I. **Formal Worship.** Formality in worship, or trusting in *the form,* is alas, very prevalent.

1. HYPOCRITICAL FASTING. The Lord asks: "When ye fasted and mourned, did ye at all *fast unto Me?*" (v. 5). When they fasted it was not that they might get into closer fellowship with God, but, like the hypocrites in our Lord's time, that they might appear unto men to fast (Matt. 6. 16-18). It is possible in many things to deny ourselves for the glory of *ourselves* in the eyes of others.

2. SELFISHNESS IN EATING AND DRINKING. "Ye eat and drink *for yourselves*" (v. 6). How little do we think that in our ordinary, every-day "eating and drinking" we should do all to *the glory of God* (1 Cor. 10. 31); thanking Him for such mercies that help to strengthen us for *His work.* Even at the Lord's table we may eat and drink judgment on our own soul by *not discerning* the Lord's body (1 Cor. 11. 29). Our *worthiness* for this is not in our moral goodness, but in our *spiritual discernment.*

3. NEGLECT OF THE WORD OF THE LORD. "Should ye

not hear the words which the Lord hath cried?" (v. 7).
The formalist allows no special value for the *Word* of the
Lord, but is very punctilious about outward acts and
ceremonies. He or she may carry a Bible or Prayer Book
to Church, but they seldom or never seriously read it, or
offer up their own *desires* unto God (1 John 5 15).   Such
have need to pray the prayer of Duncan Mathieson: "Lord,
stamp Eternity on my eyeballs. "

II. **Powerless Prayers.**   There are prayers that are
powerless, because God will not listen to them (v. 13), and
because they come from dishonest and hardened hearts
(v. 12).   Note some of the causes of failure, as recorded
here—

1. THERE WAS A LACK OF MERCY AND COMPASSION.
"Shew mercy and compassion *every man to his brother*"
(v. 9).   Our attitude to our fellowmen has much to do
with the helping or hindering of our prayers.   "First be
reconciled to thy brother, *then* offer thy gifts" (Matt.
5. 24).   We incur God's displeasure if we *from the heart*
forgive not every one his brother (Matt. 18. 35).   He that
loveth God must love his brother also (1 John 4. 21).

2. THEY OPPRESSED THE HELPLESS.   "Oppress not the
widow, the fatherless, nor the poor" (v. 10).   To take
advantage of those because of their helplessness is a
blatant insult to the God who "delighteth in mercy. "
Surely that man's religion is in vain (Jas. 1. 27).

3. THERE WAS EVIL THINKING.   Imagining evil against
another in *your heart* (v. 10).   Thoughts are naked things
before God.   Evil thoughts against your brother will
poison your prayers.   As a man thinketh *in his heart*, so
is he before God.   "The pure in heart shall see God. "

4. THEY REFUSED TO HEARKEN TO THE WORDS which
the Lord hath sent (vv. 12, 13).   To refuse to hear the
voice of His written Word is to close the door of the heart

against Heaven's benediction. "If you will not hear My cry, neither will I hear your cry, saith the Lord of Hosts" (v. 13).

5. THE FINAL RESULT of Unanswered Prayers. A grieved God, scattered hopes, bondage and desolation (v. 14). "Ye ask and receive not because ye ask amiss that ye may consume what you get *upon your own lusts*" (Jas. 4. 3). The remedy for all this is given us in James 4. 8-10.

O JERUSALEM! JERUSALEM!
ZECHARIAH 8. 20-23.

JESUS looked on the city and wept over it, saying: "O Jerusalem, thou that killest the prophets...how often would I have *gathered thy children together*: and ye would not. Behold your house is left unto you desolate. Ye shall not see Me henceforth *till ye shall say*, Blessed is *He that cometh* in the Name of the Lord" (Matt. 23. 37-39). In this prophecy Zechariah gives us the vision of Jerusalem *restored*, the *Presence* of the Lord, and the gathering together of her children.

I. **The Centre of Attraction.** The Holy City (v. 22). Glorious things are spoken of thee, O Jerusalem, the city of the Great King. But the attraction was not the city as such, but the fact that "The Lord Himself had suddenly come to dwell among them" (Mal. 3. 1). What is the chief attraction in our modern religious assemblies? Is it the gorgeous building, the fine music, or the eloquent preacher? The true aim would be: "Sirs, we would see Jesus."

II. **The Gathering of the People.** "Many peoples and strong nations shall come to seek the Lord in Jerusalem" (v. 22, R.V.). What a stirring among the "dry bones" this will be. The Shiloh in Kingly Power has come, and unto Him shall the gathering of the people be

(Gen. **49.** 10). What a holy, Christ-honouring convocation this will be. Sectarianism will have no place in that day. Paul says: "We beseech you, brethren, by the *Coming of our Lord*, and by our *gathering together unto Him*, that ye be not shaken in mind" (2 Thess. **2.** 1).

III. The Purpose of this Gathering. "Let us go speedily *to pray before the Lord*" (v. 21). "They shall come to *seek* the Lord and to *pray*" (v. 22). In those revival days shall ten men (perhaps Gentiles) take hold of a Jew, saying, "We will go with you for *we have heard* that *God is with you*" (v. 23). They heard, they *believed* and *obeyed*. No one will be able, sneeringly, to say on that day, that this Gospel is a failure. Great cities, peoples, and nations flocking to Him, like doves to their windows. In our own days we have a glorious message for *every creature* from the lips of *this same Lord*: "Come unto Me." But with what indifference the tidings is heard. Oh, how much we need the power of the outpoured Spirit, that many may *seek* the Lord and *pray* before Him.

IV. The Blessing to Follow. "He shall *speak peace* unto the nations, and His dominion shall be from sea to sea, even to the ends of the earth" (chap. 9. 10). He shall *speak peace* to the nations, as He spoke peace to the winds and waves on the Sea of Galilee; and His peace-speaking word shall resound to the uttermost parts of the earth. We pray now, "Thy kingdom come." Then His kingdom will have come, and His will being done on earth. Then shall they say: "How great is His *goodness*," and "How great is His *beauty*" (chap. 9. 17). They shall look upon Him whom they have despised and *pierced*, and mourn; but also be constrained to say, "How great is His beauty." The Christ we trust is the embodiment of the Divine fulness. May we so trust Him that the "beauty of the Lord" may be upon us. Walk worthy of your high calling, knowing that the happy day is coming when "Thine eyes shall see the King in His beauty" (Isa. 33. 17).

A HEART-RENDING DISCOVERY.
Zechariah 12. 10-14; 13. 1.

HERE are four great realities in connection with the Second Coming of the Lord.

I. A Precious Opportunity. "I will pour upon the house of David...the Spirit of Grace and of Supplications" (v. 10). This Spirit of *Grace* can only come from the "God of all Grace," and when this Spirit comes He convinces of sin and the need of making supplications unto God, in view of the great revelation that is to follow. Every revival is an evidence of this. We now are living in the days of the poured out Spirit (Acts 2. 16). Days of grace and of personal responsibility. "Behold, now is the accepted time." Days of preparation for the appearing of the Lord.

II. A Great Revelation. "They shall look upon Me whom they have pierced" (v. 10). This will be a heart-breaking sight to the house of David, whose rulers, 1900 years ago, despised and rejected, saying, "We will not have this Man to *reign over us*," and clamoured for His crucifixion. And all these long ages they, as a nation, have been the bitter enemies of Jesus. In that day "this *same Jesus*" (Acts 1. 11) shall appear bearing the marks of His Cross in His hands. And one shall say unto Him: "What are these wounds in Thine hands?" (chap. 13. 6). Ah, these *wounds* are the marks of His identity with the Man who was nailed to a Cross, of whom their fathers cried, "Let Him be crucified." Shall that be the time "when a nation shall be born in a day?" Something like this happens when a sin-smitten soul gets its first

look of Jesus as their sin-bearer. He died for me. My
sins were there at the nailing of Christ to the tree. The
wounds in His hands, even in His *glorified body* (John
20. 20) will remain through all Eternity, as a witness to
the triumphs of His death.

III. **A Real Repentance.** "They shall mourn and be
in bitterness, as one that mourneth for his only son.
Every family shall mourn apart" (vv. 11-13). Their
blindness and unbelief have been great; now they have
discovered their awful guilt in murdering their own
longed-for MESSIAH. What a hallowed time this will be
in Jerusalem, when in every home there will be the
voice of confession, and tears of penitence. While at
the same time a deep well of new-found holy joy
springing up in their hearts. Their long-looked-for
Messiah has come, and brought deliverance (Rom.
11. 26). Like Joseph's brethren, they sold Him, then
saw Him clothed with power and glory, and then
were saved by Him (Acts 5. 31). True repentance needs
no repentance.

IV. **A Great Salvation.** "In that day there shall be
a fountain opened to the house of David...for sin and
uncleanness" (chap. 13. 1). In that day, when "blood
and water" flowed from the pierced side of the crucified
Christ, a fountain was opened for a whole humanity for
sin and uncleanness. "The dying thief rejoiced to
see that fountain in *his day*," and many a living thief
has rejoiced at the same vision. When the Lord
comes and sits upon the throne of His father David,
and when His Word shall go forth from Jerusalem (Isa.
2. 3), then shall there be a fountain opened for the
nation's sin and uncleanness. Meanwhile we rejoice in
the truth that the grace of God, that bringeth salvation to all men, *hath appeared*, teaching us to deny

ungodliness and to look for that *blessed hope*, the *glorious appearing* of the great God, our Saviour Jesus Christ (Titus 2. 11-13).

THE SECOND ADVENT AND SOME OF ITS ACCOMPANIMENTS.

ZECHARIAH 14.

IN this chapter the prophet sees what might be regarded as the final assurance to that prayer taught by our Lord: "Thy Kingdom come, *Thy will be done on earth*" (Matt. 6. 10).

I. The Manner of His Coming.

1. IT WILL BE PERSONAL. "His feet shall stand in that day upon the Mount of Olives, which is before Jerusalem" (v. 4). Some tell us that His *feet* are not to be taken literally. Might they not as well say that He Himself, or the Mount of Olives, are not to be taken literally? It is "the *Lord Himself*" that is to descend from Heaven. It is "this *same Jesus*" that was seen to go up that is "in *like manner*" coming again (1 Thess. 4. 16; Acts 1. 11). It should be remembered that it was while He was making the descent of the *Mount of Olives*, riding on an ass, that the multitude of His disciples began to praise God, saying: "Blessed be the King that cometh in the Name of the Lord. Peace in Heaven and glory in the highest" (Luke 19. 37-38). What a forecast this is of that day when "His feet shall stand on the Mount of Olives" as King of nations.

2. IT WILL BE AS KING OF THE EARTH. "The Lord shall be King over all the earth" (v. 9). In that day there shall be *One Lord*, and His Name One. There shall be no room for any other when He comes; for in *His times* He shall show who is the blessed and ONLY POTENTATE, King of kings, and Lord of lords. To whom be honour and power everlasting. Amen (1 Tim. 6. 15-16). It is

worthy of note that the term Potentate occurs nowhere else
in the Scriptures. In that day the kingdoms of this world
will be compelled to acknowledge no ruler save Jesus
only. His Name shall be *above every name*, and at His
Name every knee shall bow (Isa. 45. 23). The nations
were never in greater need of leadership than they are just
now. But when He comes, who is "the *Wisdom* and the
Power of God," this need will be fully met.

3. IT WILL BE WITH ALL THE HOLY ONES. "The Lord
my God shall come, and all the holy ones with Thee"
(v. 5, R.V.). While Jesus was teaching on the Mount of
Olives, He surely was making reference to this prophecy,
when He said: "The Son of Man shall come in His glory,
and all the holy angels *with Him*. Then shall He sit upon
the throne of His glory" (Matt. 25, 31). Jude also says:
"Behold the Lord cometh with ten thousands of His
saints" (v. 14). It is not customary for kings and princes
on earth to travel alone when fulfilling a public function.
They have a retinue or train of attendants; those who are
in perfect accord with them and their mission. So "the
Lord Jesus shall be revealed from Heaven *with His mighty
angels*" (2 Thess. 1. 7-10), when He shall be glorified
in His saints and *admired in all them* that believe. Glorious
as His ten thousand holy and mighty attendants will be,
yet HE shall still be "the chiefest among ten thousand,
the altogether lovely."

II. Results which Follow His Coming. There
will be—

1. PERENNIAL BLESSING. "In that day living waters
shall go out from Jerusalem" (v. 8). These *living waters*
are symbolic of something that abundantly satisfies;
something ever fresh and abiding. They represent Divine
energy in constant activity on behalf of His people.
"Everything shall live whither this river cometh" (Ezek.

47. 9). Here is something for which civilisation can offer no substitute. Here is a river that cannot be augmented by any earthly tributary. Like the *Gospel* of God, man's wisdom and genius can add nothing to its value. The *living* authoritative Word of the Lord "shall go out from Jerusalem," as streams of blessing from the throne of His glory.

2. UNIVERSAL WORSHIP. "Every one that is left of all the nations shall worship the *King*, the Lord of Hosts" (v. 16). "Who shall not fear Thee, O Lord, and glorify Thy Name; for all nations shall come and worship before Thee, for Thy judgments are *made manifest*" (Rev. 15. 4). Satan tempted the Lord by offering Him the kingdoms of this world if He would fall down and worship him (Matt. 4. 9). But now we see the kingdoms of this world worshipping Him, who submitted to death, defying the Devil and will yet cast him into the abyss (Rev. 20. 10). It is our privilege now to worship the Lord in the beauty of holiness (1 Chron. 16. 29). God is a Spirit, they that worship Him must worship Him in *spirit* and *in truth*. God is not to be mocked.

3. CONSECRATION OF COMMON THINGS. "In that day there shall be upon the bells of the horses, and upon every pot in Jerusalem, *holiness unto the Lord*." Blessed day, when "holiness unto the Lord" shall be stamped upon the bells of the horses and on the pots and pans of the kitchen, and upon our motor cars, city trams, railway trains, and steamboats. When this motto will be read on the gates of our Houses of Commons and places of industry, and on the front door of every Exchange; when every transaction between man and man shall have this holy seal set upon it. Truly these will be "days of Heaven upon earth," when men, because they love the Lord, will love one another, and do all for the honour of His Holy Name. When poor-houses, asylums, law courts, and prisons will be things

of the sorrowful past.   If this is to be written on *bells and pots*, how much more should it be inscribed on the lives of those who have been redeemed by His Blood?   HOLINESS UNTO THE LORD.

A MESSAGE TO MESSENGERS.
MALACHI 2. 1-9.

"AND now, O ye priests, this commandment is *for you*" (v. 1).   A priest was one who ministered before God on behalf of the people.   He is also called "The messenger of the Lord" (v. 7).   We who are priests unto God and ambassadors for Christ, let us note—

I. **The Messenger's Privilege**, as the messenger of God.

1. He was to LAY TO HEART what he *hears*, and to *give glory to His Name* (v. 2).   Our first business as ministers of His Word is to take the truth revealed to *our own hearts*, with the object of giving glory to *His Name*.   We are to speak what *we do know* in our own experience for the honour of His Holy Name.

2. He was a REPRESENTATIVE OF DIVINE TRUTH.   "They shall seek the law at his mouth" (v. 7).   If we are to be worthy of the trust of anxious inquirers, we ourselves must be taught of God, and wear the real garments of the priesthood—humility and godly fear.

II. **The Secret of His Power.**   A powerless ministry is a misrepresentation of this holy order.

1. He is ASSURED OF HIS MESSAGE.   "Ye shall *know* that I have sent this word *unto you*" (v. 4).   He can say: "We speak that we *do know*, and testify that we *have seen.*"   There was no uncertain sound in his testimony.   The waverer receiveth nothing of the Lord (Jas. 1. 6, 7).

2. He is ENJOYING THE GIFT OF LIFE AND PEACE.   "Life and peace, I gave them to him" (v. 5).   It is a joyful

possession. Life in Christ and peace by the Blood of His Cross. The joy of the Lord is your strength.

3. He has "THE LAW OF TRUTH IN HIS MOUTH" (v. 6). When the love of God is in his heart, and the law of grace in his mouth, he is Divinely equipped as a herald of the Gospel of God. *Life, peace, truth,* are an holy trinity in Christian experience.

4. He HAS THE PRESENCE OF GOD. "He walketh *with Me* in peace and equity" (v. 6). Herein lies the secret of all spiritual power. "Lo, I am with you." "Without Me ye can do nothing." For *fruitfulness,* the presence of God in the life is as needful as the presence of the sunshine on the fields.

5. He HAD GOOD SUCCESS. "He did turn many away from iniquity" (v. 6). By their *fruits* ye shall know them. He is *wise* that winneth souls. This is not the wisdom the world gives, but that which cometh by the presence of the Holy Spirit of God.

II. **The Cause of His Failure.** There was failure, even after such high, holy, and happy experiences. God has made no provision for our failure; but, alas, it comes, and always through man's own folly and waywardness. "How are the mighty fallen?"

1. He DEPARTED FROM THE TRUTH. "Ye have departed out of the way" (v. 8). To depart out of *His way* and will is to go outside the sphere of His purpose and blessing. It is easy to depart from His way when our thoughts begin to wander after selfish interests.

2. He CORRUPTED THE COVENANT (v. 8). Made the Word of none effect by false interpretation. We corrupt the Gospel when we make it conditional upon human merit, or that the *grace of God* makes any allowance for continuing in sin (Rom. 6. 1).

III. **The Sad Result of His Failure.** Such is the fall of a backslider who has been used of God.

1. HIS BLESSINGS WERE BLIGHTED. "I will curse your blessings" (v. 2). The gifts and graces divinely bestowed became blighted with God's disapproval, even the seed (Word) which he sows becomes as a rotten thing (v. 3). His life becomes barren and unfruitful, like the branch separated from the vine.

2. HE CAUSETH OTHERS TO STUMBLE. "Ye have caused many to stumble at the law" (v. 8). How many there are who stumble at the Gospel because of failure in professing Christians, especially if they are preachers. *Iniquity* in the Christian life is always a stumbling-block (Ezek. 7. 10). The only remedy for the stumbling-block is to take it out of the way.

3. HE IS DESPISED BY THE PEOPLE. "*Therefore* have I also made you contemptible and base before the people" (v. 9). He preached to others, now he is a castaway. Let us give the more earnest heed to the things which *we have heard*, lest at any time we should slip *away from them* (Heb. 2. 1, *margin*).

————

FULNESS OF BLESSING.
MALACHI 3. 7-17.

MALACHI was the last of the prophets. The times in which he lived, about 400 years before Christ, were typical of any modern community (see vv. 13, 14).

I. **The Condition of Blessing.** There was—

1. THE DIVINE CHALLENGE. "Prove Me now herewith, if I will not open the windows of Heaven and pour you out a blessing, that there shall not be room enough to receive it" (v. 10). What a promise this is, and what a challenge to our faith. "*Prove me.*" "Put Me to the test, and see if I will not do this for you." Don't let the *greatness* of

the blessing make your faith to stagger. Remember that He who hath promised is the Almighty and Unchangeable Lord (v. 6). What He hath promised He is well able to perform.

2. THE CONDITIONS SPECIFIED. "Bring ye all the tithes into the storehouse" (v. 10). The tithe was the tenth of the increase, given for the priests who served in the house of the Lord. It was reckoned as belonging to God. They were to "render to God the things that are God's." But we as Christians are not promised fulness of blessing if we give Him a tenth of our increase, although even this will bring blessing into the soul. We are called upon to give to God that which *belongs to Him.* "*Ye* are not your own, for *ye* are bought with a price" (1 Cor. 6. 20). God is not satisfied when we give Him only part of what is *His own* (Acts 5. 2). If we are to have the "open windows of Heaven" and the "poured out blessing," we must present *ourselves unto God.* This is *our* reasonable service (Rom. 12. 1). "Yield *yourselves* unto God as those that are *alive* from the dead, and your members as *instruments* unto God" (Rom. 6. 13). We can only *prove Him* when we have *fulfilled* His conditions.

II. The Evidences of Being Blessed.

1. "THEY FEARED THE LORD and THOUGHT UPON HIS NAME" (v. 16). Reverential fear is a blessed state of mind, for it leads to a deeper thinking into the preciousness of His Holy Name, that Name which is above every name. O fear the Lord, ye saints of His.

2. "THEY SPAKE OFTEN ONE TO ANOTHER." We are not told what they said, but if they were *thinking* of the wondrous *Name* of the Lord, they were surely speaking of Him. Herein lies the secret and joy of Christian fellowship. They had a common cause.

3. THEY HAD THE PRESENCE OF THE LORD. "The Lord

hearkened and heard" (v. 16). His promise was fulfilled: "Where two or three are gathered together *in My Name*, there am I in the midst of them" (Matt. 18. 20). To the mere onlooker nothing happened. But the Lord was "listening in." *We* have open ears when we hear others speaking of us, and mentioning our name. So the Lord hearkens when we talk of Him. But the Lord is no idle listener. A "book of remembrance" was written, a memorandum was kept. For this thing so precious to Him shall never be forgotten. This thing may be written in that *other book* mentioned in Revelation 20. 12. All spiritual values are associated with His Name.

4. THEY HAD THE LORD'S COMFORTING ASSURANCE. "They shall *be Mine* when I make up My special treasure" (v. 17). "They thought of ME when in the midst of a perverse people, who said, It is vain to serve the Lord" (v. 14). "I will think of them in that day when I gather out all that is worth saving from a wrecked and sinking world." What an encouragement we have here for the prayer and fellowship meeting, for quiet seasons of meditation. The Lord knoweth the thoughts and intents of the heart. His *special* treasure is the Church, redeemed by His own Blood. "They *shall be Mine.*"

TWO GREAT DAYS.
MALACHI 4. 1-3.

IN these verses we think we see a brief prophetic account of two aspects of the Lord's Second Appearing. Both aspects are seen in 2 Thessalonians 1. 7-10.

I. **The Awful Day of Testing.** "Behold the day cometh that shall burn as a furnace" (v. 1, R.V.). This will be the day of the searching power of His consuming presence, when He shall "discern between him that

serveth God and him that serveth Him not" (chap. 3. 18).
A day that when "all the proud and all that do wickedly
shall be stubble. " Stubble in a furnace will stand a poor
chance of escape. In this day it will not be man's *work*
only that shall be tried by fire (1 Cor. 3. 13), but the *man
himself.* "All the *proud.* " "Who shall stand when He
appeareth, for HE is like a *refiner's fire*" (chap. 3. 2).
It is *Himself* that is the "furnace, " in the blazing holiness
of His righteousness. "The Lord Jesus shall be revealed
from Heaven in *flaming fire*, taking vengeance on them that
know not God, and *obey not* the Gospel of the Lord Jesus
Christ: who shall be punished with everlasting destruction
from the presence of the Lord" (2 Thess. 1. 8, 9). How
should this awfully solemn fact effect us in our service for
Him and them? Surely if we realised it, all coldness
and indifference would be melted by pity.

II. **The Joyful Day of Deliverance.** (The Lord's
relationship to His own people.) "But *unto you* that fear
My Name, shall the sun of righteousness arise" (v. 2).
The *sun* also is a "furnace, " but oh, how different its
influence. "But *unto you*" He shall arise "with healing
in His wings. " The *sun* is a brilliant symbol of Christ in
its mystery, majesty, and glorious might; a fit emblem of
the inexhaustible resources of the Son of God, who is the
"Sun of Righteousness. " Then truly "The Son shall *rule*
the day, when, like the sun—

1. CHRIST WILL BE THE CENTRE OF A GREAT SYSTEM.
The sun is the centre of the solar system, bound together
by the law of gravitation. When Christ, as the "Sun of
Righteousness, " shall arise upon the earth, "with the
brightness of His Coming" (2 Thess. 2. 8), He shall be
the centre of the greatest and most glorious system this
world has ever known, bound together by the law of love.
He who is the Centre of all creation will subdue all things
to Himself (1 Phil. 3. 21; 1 Cor. 15. 28). Like the sun—

2. CHRIST WILL BE THE LIGHT OF THE WORLD. Jesus said: "I am the Light of the World," but *now* men "love the darkness rather than the light, because their deeds are evil;" but *then*, when He rules in righteousness, as King, all nations shall come to His light (Isa. 9. 2; 60. 19). All the blessings the sun brings us are emblems of the gifts which Christ will bring to the world in *His Day*: light and life, health and healing, warmth and fruitfulness, beauty and gladness. What a world, perpetually basking in the sunshine of Divine favour. The world for Christ.

AT HIS FEET.
LUKE 7. 37, 38.

1. She **Came** to His feet, ... Faith.
2. She **Stood** at His feet, ... Expectancy.
3. She **Wept** at His feet, ... Contrition.
4. She **Washed** His feet, ... Sympathy.
5. She **Wiped** His feet, ... Submission.
6. She **Kissed** His feet, ... Affection.
7. She **Anointed** His feet, ... Consecration.

JUSTIFICATION.
JOB 25. 4.

1. It is **not** by the deeds of **the Law,** .. Rom. 3. 20
2. It is on the ground of **Christ's** Death
    and Resurrection, ... Rom. 4. 25
3. It is by **His Blood,** ..   ..   .. Rom. 5. 9
4. It is **freely** by His grace, ... Rom. 3. 24
5. It is on the condition of **faith,** .. Rom. 3. 26
6. It is **perfect** in its nature, ... Acts 13. 39
7. It is **God** that justifieth, ... Rom. 8. 33
8. Its result is **Peace with God,** .. Rom. 5. 1

EXPOSITORY OUTLINES.
New Testament.

THE CALL OF GOD.
1 CORINTHIANS 1. 4-9.

ALL true Christian experience has its origin in the call of God: "Ye have not chosen Me, but I have chosen you. " "Whom *He* called, them *He also* justified" (Rom. 8. 30). We shall note some precious things inherent in this call. It is—

I. **The Call of Grace.** "The grace of God which is *given you* by Jesus Christ" (v. 4). This grace by Jesus Christ could never come as a response to human merit. "By grace are ye saved, and that *not of yourselves*, it is the *gift of God*" (Eph. 2. 8). In grace He calls, because that, while "we were yet sinners, Christ died for us. "

II. **A Call to Enrichment.** "In *everything* ye are *enriched* by Him, in all utterance and all knowledge" (v. 5). The new *life in Christ* is enriched with a new value and a new power. There is a deeper knowledge of God, a clear vision of the treasure of His Word, and fuller expression of all these in the life. Truly he is a rich man. Rich in faith, rich toward God.

III. **A Call to Patient Waiting.** "Ye came behind in no gift. Waiting for the Coming of our Lord Jesus Christ. " It is to be feared that many do *come behind* in their gift of looking for the Coming of the Lord. The Christians at Thessalonica had this gift (1 Thess. 1. 9, 10). We should be thankful that this gift is being freely bestowed on God's people in these days.

IV. **A Call to a Blameless Life.** "That ye may be blameless in the Day of our Lord Jesus Christ" (v. 8)

Herein lies the *practical use* of this "Blessed Hope," which if often questioned by the unbelieving. Our lives must be affected by our prospects. "Every man that hath *this hope* in him purifieth himself" (1 John 3. 3). How sayest thou then that there is no good in looking for His Coming?

V. A Call to Fellowship. "Ye were called into the fellowship of His Son Jesus Christ our Lord" (v. 9). Brethren, what a high calling this is! Called into partnership with God's Son in seeking to save the lost and in the building up of His Church, and in the hastening of His Kingdom. In all this we are to be—not *sleeping* partners, but—active "co-workers together with Him." We are called into fellowship with Him, but the "capital" is all His own in this great business. "For in Him dwelleth all the fulness of the Godhead bodily" (Col. 2. 9). And from this fulness have we all received.

VI. A Call by a Faithful God. "God is faithful by whom ye were called" (v. 9). This holy calling does imply serious responsibility. We might well tremble when we think of our own poverty and ignorance and weakness. But then, it was by the God who is ever true to His promise that ye were called. Hear what the apostle says to the merciful Philippians: "My God, so great in His wealth in Christ Jesus, will fully supply every need of yours" (Phil. 4. 19). Only believe!

THE APPEAL OF THE CROSS.
1 CORINTHIANS 1. 18-31.

THE preaching, or message, of the Cross, is treated in these days much in the same way as Christ Himself was treated in the days of His humiliation and sorrow (v. 18). The worldly wise sneered, and official dignity denied Him. By the preaching of Christ crucified the Cross is still making its appeal.

I. To them that are Perishing it is Foolishness
(v. 18). A man must be sinking into the blackness of
final despair who thinks God's method of salvation is
"foolishness." He might as well call it foolishness to
expect light from the sun.

**II. To them that are being Saved it is the Power
of God** (v. 18). To them who are being plucked out of the
fire, like brands from the burning, and being delivered
from the dominion of sin, and translated into the Kingdom
of His dear Son, and being taught by His Holy Spirit and
satisfied with His grace *it is the power of God.*

III. To the Jew it is a Stumblingblock (v. 23). The
poor Jew, blinded by unbelief has been stumbling over the
Cross ever since Christ rose from the dead. The Cross of
Christ lies right across his path. He cannot possibly get
it out of his way. Some of the things spoken of by this
prophet have been literally fulfilled by the life and death
of this Man called Jesus, the Christ (Isa. 53), whom they
crucified. They as a nation will go on stumbling till the
Lord Comes, and they look upon Him whom they have
pierced (Zech. 12. 10).

IV. To the Greek it is Foolishness (v. 23). The
Greeks seek after wisdom, but the message of the Cross,
which is the embodiment of the *wisdom of God*, is to those
worldly-wise ones "foolishness." Surely the "foolishness
of God is wiser than the wisdom of the wisest men" (v. 25).
"The age by its wisdom knew not God" (v. 21). There
are many in our own day, like those Greeks, who are
earnestly seeking after wisdom, and yet deliberately
passing by Him who is the *wisdom of God* (v. 24).

**V. To the Christian, whether Jew or Greek, Christ
and Him Crucified is the power of God and the
wisdom of God** (v. 24). The Gospel of Christ is the
power of God to save to the uttermost of man's need, and

the *wisdom* of God to satisfy to the uttermost man's search for truth. To know God as revealed in His Word is to be made *wise* unto salvation. Our view of Christ in relation to God may be a great thing, but God's view of Christ in relationship to us His people is a much greater thing. It is with HIS reckoning we have specially to do. For by the reckoning of Almighty Grace Christ is made of God unto us—

1. "WISDOM" FOR THE MIND. The quality of being wise belongs more to character than to thought. He has given us capacity to understand spiritual things. He can make us to abound in this wisdom (Eph. 1. 8), so that we might be filled (Col. 1. 9).

2. "RIGHTEOUSNESS" FOR THE HEART. This righteousness comes not by the "works of the law," but by the reckoning of grace. "Abraham *believed* God, and it was counted to him for righteousness." To get right with God means, "Not I, but Christ."

3. "SANCTIFICATION" FOR THE WORK. Set apart, not as a recluse, but as a worker-together with Him. Jesus said: "On their behalf I consecrate Myself, *in order that they* may become perfectly *consecrated in truth*" (John 17. 19, *Weymouth*). We are not saved as a miser saves his money, but as a wise father saves his son, by giving him *fitness* for his life's work.

4. "DELIVERANCE" FOR OUR ASSURANCE. This promise may well put cheer and confidence in our hearts, that He will work deliverance for us, whether as tempted and tried pilgrims, or as warriors for the truth. "Lo, *I am* with you alway."

THE CHRISTIAN REVELATION.
1 CORINTHIANS 2. 9-16.
I. **This Revelation cannot Possibly be the Invention of Men**. The *eye* of man's carnal mind hath never

seen it. The *ear* of man's worldly wisdom hath never heard it. Neither hath it ever entered into the heart of man (apart from the Holy Spirit) the things which God hath prepared for them that *love Him* (v. 9), and since the *beginning of the world* it hath been so (Isa. 64. 4). The world by wisdom knew not God (chap. 1. 21).

II. **It is a Revelation from God.** "But God hath revealed them unto us" (v. 10). God only could reveal the mysteries of His suffering Son. "O the depths of the riches, both of the wisdom and knowledge of God concerning His Son" (Rom. 11. 33). This is the glory of the Gospel message, that it is as true and as gracious as the God who gave it (Gal. 1. 12).

III. **What this Revelation Is.** It is the unveiling of the mystery of Christ and Him crucified (v. 2). The revelation of the fact that He died *for our sins*, and rose again *for our justification*, and that He is coming again for our final deliverance (Heb. 9. 26). It is a revelation of His abounding grace to sinful men, and of His power to save to the very uttermost all that come unto Him.

IV. **How this Revelation is Made Known.** "God hath revealed them unto us *by His Spirit*" (v. 10). It has come from God, and it comes home to the believing heart by the Spirit of God. For "the Spirit searcheth the deep things of God." "The things of God no man knoweth without the Spirit of God" (v. 11). The Holy Spirit is the minister of the things of Christ (1 Cor. 12. 8-11). He is the "Spirit of Truth," and He shall teach you all things bearing on the revealed will of the Father, "for He shall receive of Mine and shall shew it unto you" (John 16. 13). Oh, that all His people were so taught of God. With such a "Teacher, come from God," there is no excuse for spiritual poverty. "Receive ye the Holy Ghost." For ye may know the letter of the word, and yet be strangers to its mighty power.

V. How these Things should be Preached. "My preaching was not with enticing words of *man's wisdom*, but in *demonstration of the Spirit* and *of power*" (v. 4). "Our Gospel came not unto you in *word only*, but also *in power* and in the Holy Ghost" (1 Thess. 1. 5). Without this power, preaching is without authority—"sounding brass." There may be a demonstration of eloquent words and fleshly energy, but without the demonstration of the Spirit it is spiritually powerless (v. 13). "But ye shall *receive power after* that the Holy Ghost is come *upon you*: and ye shall be witnesses unto Me" (Acts 1. 8). Ye ministers of His, "Tarry ye until ye be endued with powers *from on high*" (Luke 24. 49). "For the promise is unto you" (Acts 2. 39).

VI. The Christian's Attitude Towards this Divine Revelation. "I am determined not to know anything among you, save Jesus Christ *and Him crucified*" (v. 2). In Corinth there were many contentions, as there are in the world everywhere to-day. But Paul knew that the one thing needed by all was the power of the Gospel of Christ. The worldly, in their wisdom, would call this narrow-minded; but it is the wisdom of God to offer the *Divine remedy* for all the world's woes. "I am *determined*," he declared. "This one thing I do." Would God that this determination was the settled motive in the hearts of all who serve in the preaching of God's Word. The whole counsel of God radiates from the "Christ and Him crucified." "I count all things but loss for the excellency of the *knowledge of Christ Jesus*, my Lord" (Phil. 3. 8).

OUR LIFE'S WORK TESTED.
1 CORINTHIANS 3. 10-20.

PAUL, as a master builder, is here dealing with some fundamental facts concerning the Christian's life and work.

I. A Foundation has been Laid. "Other foundation *can no man lay* than that is laid, which is *Jesus Christ*" (v. 11). A foundation was needed, *first,* by God Himself, in which to build the structure of His redeemed Church; *second,* by man, on which to build his hopes for this life and the life to come. This foundation has been *well and truly* laid by the hand of infinite wisdom. Laid as deep as the grave, and as stable as the Eternal Throne. "Upon this Rock (Christ) I will build My Church, and the gates of Hell shall not prevail against it" (Matt. 16. 18). "For the foundation of God standeth sure" (2 Tim. 2. 19). Since God the Father has purposed to build His Church and His Kingdom on that Rock, which is Christ, let us have *the faith of God,* and build *our all* on Him.

II. A Superstructure is Being Raised. "If any man *build upon* this foundation, gold, silver, precious stones," etc. (v. 2). Here are two different classes of builders—

1. THE WISE BUILDER. Who builds "gold, silver, and precious stones." He puts in this foundation that which is consistent with its precious character (Rev. 21. 19). He is careful about *his doctrine,* that the things he teaches in God's Name are in harmony with His Word. He is careful also about *his manner of life.* In 2 Peter 1. 5-7 there is laid down before us a whole load of suitable material for a wise builder.

2. THE FOOLISH BUILDER. He uses "wood, hay, and stubble, or timber, hay and straw." The foolish builder is wise in his own conceit. He thinks that as long as you *believe* in the foundation it matters little what you build upon it, and so false teaching becomes easy, and the vain philosophies of the proud in heart become attractive. He is careless and indifferent in *practice, his* faith in Christ has brought no change in his life and outlook. He still

believes in building with "wood, hay, and stubble." These may be useful in some ways, but they are "*after the tradition of men and not after Christ*" (Col. 2. 8).

III. A Testing Time is Coming.   "That day in which the fire shall try *every man's work* of *what sort it is*" (v. 13).   The foundation has been already *tried* (Isa. 28. 16).   But the work done that has been associated with His Name will be tried with the fire of God's searching judgment.   "Behold the day cometh that shall burn as an oven, when the *proud* and all that do *iniquity* shall be as stubble" (Mal. 4. 1).   If the *proud* and the workers of *iniquity* are reckoned as stubble, so also are the *works* of the proud self-seeking Christians.   This fiery test is not to reveal whether we are Christians or not, but whether *our works* as Christians are worthy of Christ or not.   Will *He* own them, or will He burn then?   That depends on their own intrinsic character, whether they are gold, or wood, silver or hay, precious stones or stubble.   What *they are* will determine their destiny.

IV. The Results.

1. SOME REWARDED.   "If any man's work—or building which he has created—stands the test, he will be rewarded" (v. 14).   He is not rewarded because he is a Christian. Salvation is not a reward for good works.   It is the *gift* of God.   The reward comes for the good works done in His Name, that are *well pleasing* in His sight; works that are consistent with the character of the Foundation.   True and good, precious in His eyes, and that bear the stamp of eternal value.

2. SOME NOT REWARDED.   "If any man's work shall be burned, *he shall suffer loss*, but he himself shall be saved, yet so as by fire" (v. 15).   If his work is burned up it is because it is as wood, hay, and stubble, fit fuel for the fire. He may have a saved *soul*, but he has a lost *life*.   Such

will be the poorer through all the coming ages, as the result of his present ignorance and folly. The wages of this sin is also death. Death to the prospect of being rewarded for *faithful* service at the Coming of the Lord (1 Peter 5. 4), who shall try every man's work of what sort it is. For we must all of us appear before Christ's judgment, set in our true characters, *in order* that each may then receive *an award for his actions in this life,* in accordance with what he has done, whether it *be good or worthless* (2 Cor. 5. 10). "Let no man deceive *himself*" (v. 18), for we are assured that God will not be mocked. He cannot mistake the hollow, heartless, worth-less hay and stubble service for the faith, love and works of the consecrated life. Let every man take heed how he buildeth *thereupon* (v. 10).

THINGS WE OUGHT TO KNOW.
1 CORINTHIANS 6.

AT this time the Corinthian Church was unstable in doctrine and factious in fellowship. Some things are specially emphasised by the prefix: "Do you not know" or "Know ye not." See what some of these things are. KNOW YE NOT that—

I. **The Saints shall Judge the World** (v. 2). Daniel, in his vision, saw the Ancient of Days come, and the time that the saints possessed the kingdom (Dan. 7. 22), Jesus said: "Ye which have followed Me in the times of regeneration, when the Son of Man shall be enthroned, *ye also* shall sit upon thrones judging" (Matt. 19. 28). They lived and reigned *with Christ* a thousand years (Rev. 20. 4). It is a small matter for His saints to be judged of men now. Their day is coming.

II. **Your Bodies are the Members of Christ** (v. 15). "The body is for the Lord, and the Lord for the body"

(v. 13). Know ye not that these bodies of yours belong
to Christ as really as your souls? The Lord is for your
spirit, He also is for *your body*. Your body is a visible
working member of Christ. The temptations of the Devil
often come by way of the body. Keep it in subjection,
lest by any means it might lead to uselessness (1 Cor.
9. 27).

III. **Your Body is the Temple of the Holy Ghost**
(v. 19) In Solomon's Temple the glory of the Lord
rested on the mercy seat, right in the centre of the Holy
of holies, making the Temple a true witness to His
Presence and power. The Church of God is also His
temple. "*Ye* are the temple of the living God; as God hath
said, I will *dwell in them*, and walk in them; and I will
be their God, and they shall be My people" (2 Cor. 6. 16).
"Ye also are *builded together* for a habitation of God,
through the Spirit" (Eph. 2. 21, 22). We are all one in
Christ, as a corporate body, it is the temple of God. But
the body of each individual believer becomes a temple of
the Holy Ghost. This is a more humbling, searching, and
inspiring thought than that God dwells in His Church.
Your body is the temple of the Holy Spirit Right in
the centre of this temple, in the Holy of holies, the *heart*,
the Holy Spirit broods and works, bringing comfort and
guidance in life, and power for testimony. God *in the
midst*.

IV. **Ye are Not Your Own for Ye are Bought with a
Price** (vv. 19, 20). Is this freedom or bondage? It is
both. It means the freedom of the sons of God, the
liberty of the Spirit; and the bondage of a conquered love.
Independence is an impossibility. To be independent
we must be without a country, without a body, and without a God. "Ye are bought with a price. " A price which
only God Himself could pay: the precious Blood of His
own dear Son (1 Peter 1. 18, 19). Christ is much more

than an *Example* for us, He is our *Ransom.* Having been
bought by His Blood, ye *belong to Him*; therefore, "ye
are not your own, " and should "glorify God in your body
and in your spirit, *which are God's*" (v. 20). The love of
Christ ought to constrain us, that we who live by His
redeeming grace should not henceforth live unto ourselves, but unto Him who died for us and rose again
(2 Cor. 3. 14, 15), that we might show forth the praises
of Him who hath called us out of darkness into His marvellous light (1 Peter 2. 9).

THE MINISTRY.
1 CORINTHIANS 9. 7-27.

THE apostle is here vindicating both his ministry and his
method, and there are suggested some qualifications for
a successful ministry.

I. He had a Personal Experience of Jesus Christ.
"Have I not *seen* Jesus Christ our Lord?" (v. 1). He had
both seen Him and heard Him, and knew the transforming
power of His revelation. He could truthfully say: "I
know Him whom I have believed. " Should not this be the
initial experience of every messenger of the Gospel? How
can we say, "We speak that we do know, " if we have no
personal experience of His saving power?

II. He had Faith in God for the Supply of his Need.
Although he asked nothing from those to whom he ministered the Word, but showed them that if he sowed spiritual
things it was no great thing if he should reap their carnal
things (v. 11), he reminded them that it was an ordination
of the Lord, "that they which preach the Gospel should
live of the Gospel (v. 14). The Gospel of Christ is without
charge, and he would put no price on it for his own advantage (v. 18). He could say: "My God will supply all your

need" (Phil. 4. 19). It is a sorry service that can be bribed with money.

III. **He has Enthusiasm for the Gospel.** "Necessity is laid upon me; yea, woe is unto me if I preach not the Gospel" (v. 16). This is not that kind of enthusiasm that can be worked up for a special occasion; not a convulsive effort that may be produced by a torrent of words. It is the result of the holy fire from the altar of the Cross blazing in the heart, where the "wood, hay, and stubble" of all self-seeking has been burned up, and where the Holy Spirit has taken possession of the life, and focused the energies of the soul in Christ and Him crucified. "To me to live is Christ."

IV. **He has Humility of Spirit.** "I have made myself the *slave of all*, that I might gain the more" (v. 19). He was ready to take the lowest place that he might, if possible reach the lowest down. Like his Master, he took the towel of humility and girded himself, that he might wash the feet of others (John 13. 4, 5). "He that humbleth himself shall be exalted." "The proud He knoweth afar off." "If any man have not the Spirit of Christ he is none of His" (Rom. 8. 9).

V. **He has the Power of Adaptation in Method.** "To the Jews I become as a Jew, that I might gain the Jews. To them under the law, as under the law, that I might *win them* that are under the law" (vv. 20, 21). He declares further: "That I am made all things to all, that I might by all means save some. And *this I do for the Gospel's sake*" (vv. 22, 23). In all this we may be assured Paul never condescended to pander to that which was evil, or encourage customs and practices which were dishonouring to the Name of Jesus. He simply and lovingly stooped down far enough to get a hold of them, that he might lift up into God's salvation. No weakling in the faith should attempt this. It takes a strong man to swim against this tide.

VI. **He is Self-denying that he might Keep Physically Fit.** "I keep my body in subjection, lest I myself should be rejected" (v. 27). The body is a sacred instrument for the work of God. In eating and drinking, in work or in physical exercise, let us remember that the body is for the Lord, and the Lord for the body (1 Cor. 6. 13). "Ye are not your own," therefore take care of the Lord's property.

GOD'S PROVISION FOR HIS PILGRIM PEOPLE.
1 CORINTHIANS 10. 1-4.

PAUL assures us here twice over (vv. 6. 11) that these things happened unto them as types, or examples unto us, upon whom the ends of the ages are come. We, like them, are pilgrims and strangers on the earth, enjoying great spiritual mercies. They had the "shadows," we have the realities.

I. **The Moving Cloud.** "All our fathers were under the cloud" (v. 1). The cloud of shelter by day, and of fire by night as their protection and guide (Exod. 13. 21). The cloud was the symbol and evidence of the Divine Presence, in itself a mystery. When it moved they moved. It seemed to move easily, but nothing on earth *outside* could move it. What a suggestive emblem of the revealed *Word of God*! They all were *under it*, and God was *in it*, and all were baptised into the one name (Moses), their leader and law-giver (v. 2). They were infallibly led by the God-created cloud, just as we can be by His unerring Word. To move *without* the cloud was to go in their own name, wisdom, and strength, which would mean for them confusion and failure. This is what it means for us when we choose our way, and act without His authority.

It was because they *believed* and *followed* the cloud that they
were able to go into the midst of the sea upon dry ground
(Exod. 14. 22).   It is because we have believed and acted
on the "Word of the Lord" that we have passed from death
into life, from the place of bondage into the liberty of
the land of the promises.   Keep on believing.   Keep your
eye on the God-inspired cloud.

II. The Daily Manna. "They did all eat the same
spiritual meat" (v. 3).   "He gave them bread from
Heaven to eat" (John 6. 31).   Those who follow the Word
of God will surely be fed by the "Bread of God."   Jesus
said: "I am the Living Bread which came down from
Heaven" (John 6. 48-51).   The manna, then, is typical
of Jesus Christ, who came down from Heaven as "the
Bread of Life."   The manna was like Christ in that—

1. IT WAS THE GIFT OF GOD.   Of course all bread is
God's gift, whether it comes out of the earth or out of
the Heavens; but the wilderness could do nothing by way
of producing it.   So Christ was God's gift to a starving
world (John 3. 16).   God knew what the hungry heart of
man needed when He gave His Son as "the Bread of Life."

2. IT WAS SUITED FOR ALL.   All alike found it what it
pretended to be: something to satisfy the craving of
hunger.   What Christ has to give is just what all the sons
of men need, that which exactly suits them, the forgiveness of sins and grace to help in every time of need.
Satisfied with His abundance.

3. IT WAS OFFERED TO ALL.   From the youngest to the
oldest, without money, without price.   The rich and the
poor alike needed it.   In this offer of Heaven's bread, God
is no respecter of persons, for all have sinned.   So Christ
as the "Living Bread" from Heaven is offered, in God's
grace, to *any man* who will eat this bread (John 6. 51),
promising that he that eateth shall *live for ever*.

4. IT WAS PERSONALLY USED. "They did all *eat* the same spiritual meat. " It was not enough to gather and boast of how much they had gotten. To be personally profited there must be a personal appropriation. We may possibly gather much knowledge about Christ, and yet receive little strength and satisfaction from it, if the truth is not assimilated in our own spiritual life. "He that eateth Me shall live by Me" (John 6. 47).

III. **The Rock that Followed Them.** "They drank of that Spiritual Rock that followed them, and that Rock was Christ" (v. 4).

1. LIKE CHRIST, THIS ROCK WAS REVEALED BY GOD. It may only have taken God a few moments to show Moses this rock in Horeb, but it took Him over thirty years to show the Rock, Christ; for all the years of His earthly life was an unveiling of His character as the Chosen One. "This is My beloved Son, in whom I am well pleased. "

2. LIKE CHRIST, THIS ROCK WAS DIVINELY POSSESSED. 'Behold I will *stand* before thee there *upon the rock* in Horeb" (Exod. 17. 6). At Christ's baptism the Holy Spirit rested upon Him. There was to be no mistaking Him as the God-appointed medium of blessing to His trusting people. "God was *in Christ* seeking to reconcile a wandering world to Himself" (2 Cor. 5. 19).

3. LIKE CHRIST, THIS ROCK WAS RICH IN UNREALISED BLESSING. The Israelites might say, "How can any good come out of this rock?" as they said of Christ, "Can any good come out of Nazareth?" or, "How can this Man save us?" but it pleased God that in Him should all fulness dwell (Col. 1. 19). But they could say later on: "Of His fulness have all we received" (John 1. 16).

4. LIKE CHRIST, THIS ROCK MUST BE SMITTEN. "Thou shalt smite the rock, and there shall come water out of it, that the people may drink" (Exod. 17. 6). The rock was

not smitten for itself, but for the salvation of the people.
He was wounded for our transgressions, the rod of God's
judgment fell upon Him, and by His stripes we are healed
(Isa. 53).

5. LIKE CHRIST, THE SMITTEN ROCK POURED FORTH
ITS HIDDEN TREASURES.   "He clave the rock, and gave
them drink as out of the great depths" (Psa. 78. 15).   O
wonder of wonders, that from His *smitten* Son there should
come forth streams of redeeming mercies, out of the *great
depths* of God's eternal purpose.   In that day in which
Christ was pierced, there was opened a fountain of cleansing
for a sinful world.   "Ho, every one *that thirsteth*, come
ye to the waters" (Isa. 55. 1).

6. LIKE CHRIST, THIS SPIRITUAL ROCK FOLLOWED
THEM.   They drank of that Spiritual Rock that followed
them: and that Rock was Christ" (v. 4).   This water
from the Rock was to them an *abiding* blessing.   It followed them.   Something to satisfy all the way.   Jesus
said · "The water that I shall give him shall be *in* him a
well, springing up into *everlasting life*" (John 4. 14).   And,
"Lo, I am with you, and will never leave you nor forsake
you. "   He is our Rock, the Rock of our eternal salvation
and eternal supply.

OVERTHROWN BY SIN.
1 CORINTHIANS 10. 5-15.

THEY went up out of Egypt a mixed multitude (Num: 11. 4),
but not a man of them saw Caleb and Joshua enter into
the promised possession (Num. 26. 65)   What a warning
we have here against *secret sin*, which leads to backsliding
and to final overthrow

I. **Who were They that Fell in the Wilderness**?
They had been—

1. SAVED OUT OF EGYPT.   They passed through the sea,

and knew something of the God of Deliverance. They had identified themselves with the ransomed host.

2. BAPTISED into the Name of the God-appointed leader, acknowledging his authority, and professedly his followers.

3. IN FULL COMMUNION. They did all eat of the same bread and drank from the same Rock (vv. 3, 4). What privileges were theirs, but how hollow their profession.

II. **Their Failure.** It was great, and brought fatal results. "They were *overthrown* in the wilderness." There fell on one day twenty-three thousand (v. 8). The character of their failure as backsliders may be seen in that they—

1. DISPLEASED GOD. With many of them God was not well pleased (v. 5). God's displeasure may not be apparent for a time, as He is slow to anger, but if not repented of will certainly ripen into judgment.

2. MISSING THE MARK. The mark was the Land of Promise, but they missed it because of their unbelief (Jude 3). They failed because they lost their faith in God.

3. PREMATURE DEATH. Every one of them died, we might say, before their time. God was willing to bring them into the "good land," but *evil* slays the wicked (Psa. 34. 21). Those who wander in heart away from God scarcely realise how they are cutting short their lives.

III. **The Causes of Failure.** They are many, but all have their root in heart-departure from the Living God, by ceasing to honour and obey His Word. Their sins are the sins of many in our own day, who have turned aside in heart from following the Lord.

1. THEY LUSTED AFTER FORBIDDEN THINGS (v. 6).
VOL. X. 9

The pleasures of the old unregenerate life are longed for, the bread of God has become stale (Num. 11. 4), God Himself has become unreal.

2. THEY WORSHIPPED OTHER GODS (v. 7). When any other object is loved and honoured more than the Lord our God, then we are idolaters, whether it be our business, our pleasures, our children, or ourselves. "He that loveth any one or anything more than Me," saith Christ, "is not worthy of Me" (Matt. 10. 37, 38).

3. THEY INDULGED IN SOCIAL IMPURITY (v. 8). This secret, soul-withering sin is without a covering in the eyes of God. "Be sure your sin will find you out."

4. THEY MURMURED AT THE PROVIDENCE OF GOD (v. 10). They murmured against Moses, against Aaron, against God's method of dealing with them, and became discontented even with the manna from Heaven (Num. 14. 2). When a professing Christian begins to murmur against God's servants, and to criticise and find fault with God's Word and message, be sure that in heart they are estranged from God, if they ever truly knew Him.

IV. **The Present Application.** These things are all examples unto us (vv. 6-11). All sins, secret or open, have still the same effect in separating the soul from fellowship with God, and overthrowing the testimony of the life as a witness to the power of Christ. Discontent with the provision and promises of God is the blighted fruit of a doubting heart. Brethren, let us labour therefore to enter into that "rest of faith," lest any man fall after the same example of unbelief (Heb. 4. 11). "Thou *standest by faith*; be not high-minded, but fear" (Rom. 11. 20). "The end of all things is at hand: be ye therefore sober, and watch unto prayer" (1 Peter 4. 7).

THE LORD'S SUPPER.

1 CORINTHIANS 11. 23-29.

THIS ordinance is the heirloom of the Christian Church. The emblems are of a most simple and homely character— "Bread and Wine." Yet the significance of them in the hands of Christ embody the profoundest facts in the Christian faith. The bread, *"My Body;"* the wine, *"My Blood."* Symbols of His character and mission.

I. **His Incarnation.** "He *took bread* and said, This is My Body" (v. 23). A *body* hast Thou prepared me. He took on Him not the nature of angels, but the *"likeness* of sinful flesh" (Rom. 8. 3). He took the body prepared for Him by the Father, that He might have somewhat to offer as a visible sacrifice for the sin of the world. The taking of the bread as a symbol of His body was a voluntary act, for He *made Himself* of no reputation when He took the form of a servant (Phil. 2. 7).

II. **His Devotion.** "He gave thanks" (v. 24). He took the bread, emblem of His body, and gave thanks to God for it. Think of it! Giving thanks to God for a body that was to be bruised and broken on a Cross: thanks to the Father for the privilege of dying for a guilty and thankless humanity! In this simple, common act, see the whole-hearted devotion of our Lord to the awful work the Father had given Him to do. "Not My will, but Thine be done."

III. **His Suffering.** After giving thanks *He brake it.* Every word and act seems full of meaning. He did not ask Judas to break it. He Himself broke it. He *gave Himself* a sacrifice for our sins. He could say: "No man taketh My life from Me: I lay it down of Myself." *He* broke the bread, of which He said, "This is My Body" (John 10. 18). It was because He *loved* us that He gave Himself for us an offering unto God (Eph. 5. 2). His life was a life of thanksgiving; His death was a voluntary offering. "Father, I will. "

IV. **His Substitution.**   "This is My Body which is *broken for you. "*   Not broken by accident.   He was wounded for *our* transgressions, bruised for *our* iniquities, the chastisement of *our* peace was upon Him.   He was "broken for you" (Isa. 53. 5).   The wine of His precious blood was poured out for our redemption (1 Peter 1. 19). We are apt to speak lightly and think little of these words uttered at His last meal on earth.   *"My body,* broken for " you.   What would be the thoughts in His mind when uttering them?   He already saw the Cross, and perhaps already felt the pangs of Gethsemane in His soul.   But love constrained Him.   When we sit at the Lord's table and handle the bread and cup, do we realise this as we should: "My Body broken *for you, "* "My Blood shed *for you?"*

V. **His Invitation.**   "Take, eat. " "Do this in remembrance of Me. "   After atonement has been made by His suffering and death, there comes (symbolically) the invitation to partake of the benefits purchased.   "Take, eat, " appropriate to yourselves what is here set before you. This is the message of the Gospel.   "Do this *in remembrance of Me. "*   There is no virtue in the mere *eating* and *drinking.*   The soul of the ordinance is in *remembering Him.*   The elements are but the memorials of what He hath done for us in giving His body and His Blood a Ransom for our souls.

VI. **His Purpose in It.**   "As often as ye eat this bread and drink this cup, *ye do shew forth the Lord's death. "* There is no symbolic ordinance left us to *show forth* His Incarnation, or His Transfiguration, or His Ascension, but there is for His *Crucifixion.*   Why is that *His death* is to be so prominently and persistently kept before our minds?   Because all our salvation has come out of it, and all the hopes of the ungodly are in it. "God forbid that I should glory, save in the Cross of Jesus Christ our Lord" (Gal. 6. 14). Preach Christ and *Him crucified*.

VII. **His Prospect**. "Ye do shew forth the Lord's death *till He come*" (v. 26). When He comes again, according to His promise, the Church will have no need of this memorial of Him. We have little need for an absent friend's photograph when He Himself has come to us. The present dispensation is an interval between His Cross and His Throne. While we may sit at His table with sorrowful, yet peaceful, hearts; while we think of His sorrow and shame on our behalf, we can look hopefully up, knowing that He is coming again to receive us unto Himself (John 14. 1-3). When we think of the Lord's table we must recognise that it is not the table of any particular Church or sect. It is *the Lord*'s, and all have the right to it who are able to *discern* the Lord's body in the emblems. Our worthiness or unworthiness to sit at His table lie, not in our good education, not in our moral character, or religious profession, but in our *spiritual discernment* (v. 29).

THE CHURCH AS THE BODY OF CHRIST.
1 CORINTHIANS 12. 12-31.

THE human body is a perfect metaphor, or image, of the Church of Jesus Christ, as it is a living organism with many members, controlled by one spirit

I. **The Church is One Body.** A body with two heads would be a monstrosity. So would a head with two bodies. "Ye are the body of Christ" (v. 27). "Ye, being many, are one body in Christ" (Rom. 12. 5). We have Churches many, but Christ has only one.

II. **The Members are all United by One Spirit**. "By *one Spirit* are *we all* baptised into one Body" (v. 13).

We may be admitted into a local Church on a *profession*
of faith, but to be united to the Spiritual Body of Christ
we need the regenerating power of the Holy Ghost. "It is
the Spirit that quickeneth, the flesh profiteth nothing"
(John 6. 63). The Lord knoweth them that are His.

III. **The Body of Christ includes Every Member.**
"Whether they be Jew or Gentile, bond or free" (v. 13).
Whether they be black or white, brown or yellow, rich or
poor, young or old, learned or ignorant, living or dead:
all who in every age have been made to drink of the one
soul-nourishing Spirit (v. 13), all are His. All who have
been brought nigh by the Blood of Christ (Eph. 2. 13).
Is the Church a failure? It may be. But the Church
which is the Body of Christ is no failure, for when He
comes to gather up His precious treasure, He will have a
body that will be a glorious witness to the triumph of His
sufferings.

IV. **Each Member has its Own Function.** "God
hath set the members every one of them, in the body as it
hath *pleased Him*" (v. 18). The foot is not expected to
do the work of the hand, nor the eye to do what the ear
is made for. There are diversities of gifts (see vv. 28-31),
but one Spirit and one purpose. Be not discouraged if
your gift is not so prominent and helpful as some others.
The eye doth not covet the function of the ear, nor the ear
that of the eye. Let us prayerfully seek to find out what
that gift is which God hath been pleased to bestow. If
you *are* a member of Christ's Body, there is something
you *can do* for Him. A paralyzed member is a betrayal
of His character.

V. **All the Members are Interdependent.** "The eye
cannot say unto the hand, I have no need of thee," etc.
(v. 21). Each member of the body needs the help of the
others. We ought to praise God for the gifts of other

members, when the work of the Lord is being helped on.
What does it matter which member has the special gift,
so long as the will of the Head is being done through the
body.

VI. **There is no Division in the Body in His Sight**
(vv. 25-27). "Ye are all one in Christ Jesus" (Gal. 3. 28).
"The same Lord over all is rich unto all that call upon
Him" (Rom. 10. 12). "There is *one* body, and *one* Spirit,
even as ye are called in *one* hope" (Eph. 4. 4). Things
that divide the members of His Body, in the eyes of men,
are things devised by the pride and prejudice of men.
As Christians, let us "Endeavour to keep the *unity of the
Spirit* in the bond of peace" (Eph. 4. 3).

VII. **All the Members of the Body are in Mutual
Sympathy.** So the members of Christ should have the
same care one for another. "If one member suffer, all
the members suffer 'with it: if one be honoured, all the
members rejoice with it" (vv. 25, 26). There is no place
for envy or jealousy here. In the Lord's service such
unclean spirits must be cast out. For "though I speak
with the tongue of an angel and have not love, I am
become as sounding brass" (chap. 13. 1). "Love seeketh
not her own." Follow after love and desire spiritual
gifts (chap. 14. 1).

THE SIGNIFICANCE OF CHRIST'S
RESURRECTION.
1 CORINTHIANS 15 12-23.

HERE the apostle reasons on this great truth from two
different standpoints—

1. The NEGATIVE. "If Christ be *not* risen"—then
what?

2. The POSITIVE. "But now *is Christ risen,*"—then
what? As if one should say: "If the sun should not rise

again, then what would happen?" But now the sun is risen and becomes self-evident.

I. If Christ be Not Risen.

1. THEN CHRIST'S OWN TFSTIMONY WAS UNTRUE. He had given His promise: "I will rise again." "Destroy this temple (body) and in three days I will raise it up" (John 2. 19). If He failed here, how could He be "the Resurrection and the Life?" (John 11. 25).

2. THEN HIS DISCIPLES WERE COMPLETELY DECEIVED. For this was the keynote of their joyful testimony. "They taught the people, and preached through Jesus the resurrection from the dead" (Acts 4. 2). When their Lord was crucified, the disciples were of all men the most miserable, hiding in shame from their countrymen. But suddenly they became the most joyful and courageous of mortals. What had happened? They had seen their Lord risen from the tomb.

3. THEN THE CHRISTIAN CHURCH IS A GIGANTIC FRAUD. It is a majestic structure, without any foundation. If there was no empty grave in Joseph's garden on the third day, then this is the emptiest thing on earth. It is built on the supposition that Christ rose from the dead. If He did not rise from the grave, then how are we to account for its strength and perpetuity all these long ages?

4. THEN CHRISTIAN EXPERIENCE IS A GRAND DELUSION. Our assurance of forgiveness, our joy in being justified in the light of God, our peace of heart and mind, our answered prayers, our sweet fellowship with God, our bright hopes for the world to come, are all imaginary; and all the millions in every age who have had these experiences have been fatally betrayed.

5. THEN WE WHO BELIEVE IN IMMORTALITY HAVE BEEN LIVING IN A FOOL'S PARADISE. Instead of "departing to be with Christ," those who have died in this faith have

perished like the beast. The joys, hopes, and visions of the dying Christian have all been delusive. Their expectation of seeing Jesus and meeting the loved ones gone before have been but a treacherous empty fancy. Their whole life has been a mere hallucination.

6. THEN WE ARE OF ALL MEN THE MOST MISERABLE. For we, of all men, have stood on the highest pinnacle of expectation, having the brightest outlook and the most confident hopes of any other man. It means for us to be cast down from the high tower of our personal blessedness into the abyss of darkness and despair. If Christ be not risen then the Christian life is but a ghastly mirage, for there will be no resurrection of the dead (v. 12), our *preaching* has been in vain, and our *faith* is also vain (v. 14). We have been *false witnesses*, and we are yet *in our sins*, and all who have died in the faith *are perished* (v. 18).

II. **But Now is Christ Risen** (v. 20). What a joyful ring there is in this shout. It is like the blast of the trumpet of victory. "Now is Christ risen," and the foundations of Hell have been shaken. The sun has arisen in His strength and scattered the darkness, and brought health and beauty with His healing beams. "Now is Christ risen."

1. THEN OUR PREACHING IS NOT IN VAIN. The great commission still stands good and true: "All power is given unto Me in Heaven and in earth. Go ye *therefore*" (Matt. 28. 18-20). "Lo, I (the Risen One) am with you alway." He will not fail you, be not discouraged. The Gospel of the Risen Christ is still the *power of God* unto salvation to every believer.

2. THEN OUR FAITH IS NOT VAIN. We are not trusting a dead Saviour, but Him who is "the Resurrection and the Life" (John 11. 25). It is no vain thing to trust in the Living Lord, who had the power to lay down His life

and to *take it again.* He who conquered death and the
grave can easily restore our sickly faith and raise our
dying efforts from the tomb of uselessness.

3. THEN WE ARE NOT NOW IN OUR SINS (v. 17). He
died for our sins, "but He rose again for our justification."
His death was the paying of the price. His resurrection
was the evidence that God had accepted the price paid for
our redemption. Now we who believe are accepted in
Him, being raised together with Him in the purpose of God.

4. THEN THOSE WHO HAVE FALLEN ASLEEP IN CHRIST
ARE NOT PERISHED (v. 18). They are with their Lord,
who was the *firstfruits* from the dead (v. 23). "For if
we believe that Jesus died and *rose* again, *even so* them also
which sleep in Jesus will God bring *with Him*" when He
comes to be glorified in His saints (1 Thess. 4. 14, 15)
"Knowing that He which raised up the Lord Jesus shall
raise up us also by Jesus" (2 Cor. 4. 14).

5. THEN WE ARE NOT OF ALL MEN THE MOST MISERABLE
(v. 19). Christians should be the happiest people on the
face of the earth. They have the best of all friends in
Jesus, the sweetest of all promises in God's Word, the
greatest of all treasures in the fulness of Divine Grace.
They hold the highest of all earth's positions in being the
servants of the Lord, crowned with honour and glory.
They enjoy the brightest of all prospects in the Coming
Kingdom. They shall *reign with Him* a thousand years
(Rev. 20. 6).

THE FINAL VICTORY.

1 CORINTHIANS 15. 51-58.

"THANKS be to God, who giveth us the victory through
our Lord Jesus Christ" (v. 56).

I. **Victory over Sin.** "The sting of death is sin."
"O death, *where is thy sting?*" (vv. 55, 56). Death is as

common as birth, as impartial as the law of gravitation,
and as uncertain as a thief. To the Christian death is
stingless, for the *sting* of sin was buried in the Crucified
Christ, who bore our sins in His own body to the tree.
The strength of sin is the *Law*, but His obedience-unto the
death on our behalf met the just demands of the righteousness of God. "Sin shall not have dominion over you; for
ye are not under the law, but under grace" (Rom. 6. 14).
The Law was given by Moses, but grace and truth came by
Jesus Christ (John 1. 17). Thanks be to God, who
giveth us the victory *over sin*.

II. **Victory over Mortality.** "For this corruptible
must put on incorruption, and this mortal (body) must
put on immortality" (v. 53). These *bodies* of ours are to
share the victory of our Saviour's resurrection when He
comes again. Then "in a moment, in the twinkling of an
eye, the dead shall be raised incorruptible, and we (those
who are still alive) shall be changed" (v. 52). "We that
are in this tabernacle do groan, being burdened (with the
infirmities of the body): not that we are ourselves to be
unclothed but clothed upon, that *mortality* might be
swallowed up of life" (2 Cor. 5. 4). He is longing for that
"house which is from Heaven," the new abode of the
Spirit. "It is sown a natural body, it is raised a spiritual
body" (v. 44). Our resurrection bodies may differ in
lustre, according to the lives we have lived. "For one
star differeth from another star in glory. *So also* is the
resurrection of the dead" (vv. 41, 42). "Thanks be to
God who giveth us *this* victory through our Lord Jesus
Christ."

III. **Victory over Death.** "O death, where is thy
sting?" He hath swallowed up death (Isa. 25. 8). Christ
Himself took part of the same flesh and blood that through
death He might destroy him that had the power of death,
that is, the Devil, and *deliver them* who through *fear of*

death were in their lifetime subject to bondage (Heb. 2.
14, 15). Death has always been a winged monster to the
human race, where Christ and His resurrection is unknown.
For Jesus Christ hath abolished death, and hath brought
life and immortality to light through the Gospel (2
Tim. 1. 10). Thanks be to God who giveth us *this* victory
through our Lord Jesus Christ.

IV. **Victory over the Grave.** "O grave, where is thy
victory?" The hour is coming in the which all that are
in the graves shall hear His voice and come forth (John
5. 28). "The LORD HIMSELF shall descend from Heaven
with a shout, with the voice of the archangel and the trump
of God, and the dead *in Christ* shall rise *first*" (1 Thess.
4. 16). Those who are the members of His Body shall be
the first to share in the triumph of their Lord over the
bondage and corruption of the grave. This is the *first*
resurrection. "Blessed and holy is he that hath part in
the first resurrection, the terrors of the second death and
the second grave will have no power over them" (Rev.
20. 5, 6). "Therefore, beloved brethren, be ye stedfast,
unmoveable, always abounding in the work of the Lord,
forasmuch as ye know that your labour is not in vain in
the Lord" (v. 58). Thanks be to God who giveth us *this*
victory through our Lord Jesus Christ.

THE TRIUMPHANT LIFE.

2 CORINTHIANS 2. 14-17.

"THANKS be unto God, who always causeth us to triumph
in Christ" (v. 14). The life that has always been led on
in triumph should indeed be a *thankful* one. There are so
many seeming failures in one's experience. What are the
secrets of a victorious life? In those few verses as above,
we note some of them.

I. **A Life in Christ.** "God causeth us to triumph *in Christ.*" There is no possibility of living the victorious life, in God's sight, out of Christ. To be *in* Christ is to be at one with Him, and so entirely yielded to His will that His will will be done in us. As the apostle put it, "I am crucified with Christ: nevertheless I live, yet not I, but Christ liveth in me" (Gal. 2. 20). "We know that we *dwell in Him*, because He hath given us of His Spirit" (1 John 4. 13).

II. **A Life that Reveals Something of the Wisdom of God.** "He maketh manifest the savour of His knowledge by us" (v. 14). The guiding principle in the Christian life is the truth revealed in His Word (2 Cor. 4. 2). Those led by the Spirit of God will surely be witnesses to something higher and nobler than the wisdom of this world, which is foolishness with God.

III. **A Life that has a Sweet Savour of Christ unto God.** "For we are unto God a *sweet savour of Christ*" (v. 15). "Christ gave Himself for us an offering to God for a sweet smelling savour" (Eph. 5. 2). Those who have been partakers of that offering are to be partakers also of the same sweet savour *unto God*. He could say: "This is My beloved Son, in whom I am well pleased," for He knew that all His interests committed to His Son would be safe and successful. Let us so seek to please God.

IV. **A Life that Affects both Saved and Unsaved.** "A savour of Christ in them that are saved and in them that perish" (v. 15). The influence of one Christian's life can be made a confirmation to another who loves the same Lord. The "savour of Christ," like the fragrance of the rose, can be easily detected by those who are saved, but to those who are perishing it smells condemnation, so they don't like it (v. 16).

V. **A Life True to the Word of God.** "We are not as

many which corrupt the Word of God" (v. 17). Those who walk in craftiness are sure to handle the Word of God deceitfully (chap. 4. 2). If the heart is not true to God, the life will not be true to His Word. It is easy to corrupt God's message by mingling it with Christ-dishonouring philosophies and the traditions of men. There can be no spiritual victory for those who have gone out of *the way* (Col. 2. 8).

VI. **A Life Lived in the Presence of God.** "In the sight of God speak we in Christ" (v. 17). Abiding in Christ and practising the presence of God in the daily life is the evidence of vanquishing power. This is the victory that overcometh the world, our faith. Faith in Him who is greater than all that can be against us. "If ye abide in Me, and *My words* abide in you, ye shall ask what ye will, and it shall be done unto you" (John 15. 7). Not that we are sufficient of ourselves to think anything as of ourselves; but our sufficiency is of God. "Thanks be to God who giveth us the victory through our Lord Jesus Christ."

THE GOD OF THIS AGE.
2 CORINTHIANS 4. 1-7.

"THE god of this age hath blinded the thoughts of the unbelieving, that the light of the *Gospel of the glory of Christ*, who is the image of God, should not dawn upon them" (R.V., *margin*). This Scripture is burdened with neglected but tremendous realities. There are mighty spiritual forces that war against the higher interests of the souls of men. "For we wrestle not against flesh and blood, but against *principalities*, against *powers*, against the *rulers* of the darkness of this world, against spiritual wickedness" (Eph. 6. 12). All under the leadership of "the god of this age."

I. **His Personality.** This god is no mere phantom,

but a great and mighty spiritual individuality. So great that even "Michael the archangel" did not dare to use abusive terms when contending with him (Jude 9). It was no ordinary wicked spirit that could dare to tempt the Lord Jesus Christ with the kingdoms of this world (Matt. 4. 8, 9). Even the Lord did not sneer at his folly and ridicule his presumption. He simply said: "Get thee hence, Satan." This is not language suitable to some unseen evil *influence*, but to the "prince of devils."

II. **His Position.** He is "the god of *this age*." This age is the dispensation of the ministry of the Holy Spirit; it is also the "hour and the power of darkness" (Luke 22. 53). In John's Gospel Satan is called "the prince of this world" three times; also "the *prince* of the *power of the air*, the spirit that now worketh in the children of disobedience" (Eph. 2. 2). It was doubtless under his influence that the rulers of this world killed the Prince of Life, for he "deceiveth the whole world" (Rev. 12. 9). The *god* of this age is not worshipped and obeyed as an ugly, cruel-faced devil, but as an "angel of light," for Satan has so transformed himself (2 Cor. 11. 14). He is the great arch-deceiver in these latter days, when knowledge has increased and multitudes run too and fro upon the earth.

III. **His Purpose.** It is to blind the thoughts that the light of *the Gospel of the glory of Christ* should not dawn upon them (v. 4). The Gospel of the *coming glory of Christ*, when He shall *put down* all authority and power, and take unto Himself His right to reign, must strike terror into the heart of Satan; for then he will be spoiled of his goods; then "that great dragon, that old serpent called the Devil and Satan, will be cast out" (Rev. 12. 9). Why in this age is Satan so anxious to hinder, if possible, the dawning of the light of the truth about His Coming again in power and great glory? Is it because this revelation brings fresh inspiration and a more joyful confidence into the hearts of Christ's servants in these last and testing days?   But this diabolical purpose is being largely thwarted now, in that multitudes of God's people are rejoicing in the light of the Gospel of that glory of the kingdom of our Lord Jesus Christ, which is surely drawing nigh.

IV. His Manner. How does he manage to blind the thoughts of men to the light of the Gospel of the glory of the coming Christ? See how he dealt with our Lord when tempting Him. Was he not trying to blind the thoughts of Christ to the Father's time and method of giving Him the dominion of this world when he "showed Him all the kingdoms of the world, and the glory of them," and offered them to Him for an act of obeisance? Does he not still show men the honours and pleasures of earth that he might blind their thoughts to the greater and more enduring things of the Kingdom of God and of His Christ? By putting a special lustre on material things it is not difficult for the great deceiver to blind the eyes of men to the things that are eternal. Even when the seed of God's Word has been sown in the heart, it is easy for this wicked one to catch it away, by blinding the understanding with confused interests (Matt. 13. 19). We are not ignorant of his devices. Let us watch and be sober.

V. His Subjects are those which *believe not* (v. 4). Those whose hearts are closed to the "light of the know-ledge of God in the face of Jesus Christ" (v. 6), and fit subjects and willing dupes to Satan's delusions. They cannot enter into the light and liberty of the sons of God because of unbelief. They may have a growing desire for the *fictitious*, the *theatrical*, and the *sentimental*, but the things that belong to their eternal peace are still hid from their eyes, and those counterfeits of the god of this age become increasingly attractive. If he can only hide the

Gospel of Jesus Christ from their eyes he knows that his purpose will be successful—they will *be lost* (v. 3). For this is the condemnation that *light is come* into the world, and men love darkness rather than the light. He that believeth not is condemned already (John 3. 18, 19).

VI. **His Overcomers** are those into whose hearts "the light of the knowledge of the glory of God hath shined" (v. 6). The light of God's truth alone, as revealed in the face of Jesus, can deliver from the power of *darkness*, which is the domain of Satan's operations. Here spiritual death reigns; but Christ, by His death, has delivered us from this death and from him that had the *power of death*—the Devil (Heb. 2. 14). Christ our Redeemer and Conqueror now holds the keys of Hell and of death (Rev. 1. 18). He that is born of God keepeth himself, and that wicked one toucheth him not (1 John 5. 18). Jesus said to Peter, "Simon, behold Satan hath desired to have you, but I have prayed for you that your faith fail not" (Luke 22. 32). Listen to this joyful shout of final and eternal victory that will ring from the Heavens: "Now is come *salvation* and strength *and the kingdom* of our God, and the power of His Christ; for the accuser of our brethren is cast down! They overcame him by the Blood of the Lamb" (Rev. 12. 10, 11). "Thanks be unto God who giveth us the victory."

THE IDEAL LIFE.
2 CORINTHIANS 4. 7-11.

GOD is being pleased to manifest Himself. In creation God is manifesting His wisdom and almightiness in the works of His hands. "The heavens declare the glory of God, and the earth His handiwork." In Jesus Christ God is manifesting His love in merciful plenitude for our salvation. In the lives of the redeemed He desires to

manifest His saving and satisfying grace for a witness
and encouragement to the unbelieving; for the *life of
Jesus* is to be *made manifest* in *our mortal flesh* (vv. 10, 11).

The life of Jesus is *the ideal life*, and the life of the Christian is to be, in measure, a spiritual reproduction.
Many lives of Christ have been *written*, but the most
effective and God-honouring is the *living* one. "The *life*
of Jesus made manifest in our body.". Let us think of it.
The life of the Lord Jesus was—

I. A Life from God. He was born from above (Luke
1. 35). He could say: "I am from above: I came down
from Heaven." He was God manifest in the flesh (1 Tim.
3. 16). If then, the life of Jesus is to be manifest in our
mortal flesh, we must be born of God, born from above.
"Except a man be born again, he cannot *see* the Kingdom
of God." How then can he live the life of Jesus if he has
not received the Jesus' life? Christ must live in us if
His life is to be manifested by us (Gal. 2. 20).

II. A Life Entirely Yielded to God. It was a life
fully surrendered to the Divine will. At His baptism he
gave Himself up to fulfil the righteousness of God. He
said: "The Son can do *nothing of Himself*, but what He
seeth the Father do" (John 5. 19). He also spake the
words of the Father (John 14. 10). "My doctrine," he
declared, "is not Mine, but His that sent Me" (John
7. 16). The keynote of His life was: "Not My will, but
Thine be done." What an example for all who desire to
live the life of Jesus in their mortal bodies. Entire
surrender to God's Word and will and work was needful
for Him. How can it be less needful for us in seeking
to live His life and to do His work? "Yield *yourselves*
unto God as those that are alive from the dead" (Rom. 6. 13).

III. A Life Empowered by the Spirit of God. John
bare record, saying: "I saw the Spirit descending from

Heaven like a dove, and it *abode upon Him.*" God *anointed* Jesus of Nazareth with *the Holy Ghost* and with power (Acts 10. 38). Being made in the likeness of sinful flesh, He made Himself dependent on the power of the Holy Spirit given Him by the Father (see Isa. 11. 2, 3), and when He began His public ministry He testified that "the Spirit of the Lord is upon Me, because He hath anointed Me to preach the Gospel" (Luke 4. 18). He knew that *all His disciples* needed this spiritual enduement from on high if they were to be true witnesses for Him. So He told them to tarry at Jerusalem *until* they were endued. How can we expect to live this life of Jesus without this gift? There is no substitute on earth for spiritual power. There is no excuse for being without it. For the promise is to you and to all that are afar off (Acts 2. 29).

IV. **A Life of Unwavering Faith in God.** His face was steadfastly set to do the will of His Father at any cost. Because of this attitude and His devotion, He must needs suffer. The holiness of His character brought suffering, because He could not be understood by sinful and wicked men. He suffered through His faithfulness in testifying against the world's evil works (John 7. 7). He was not of the world, therefore the world hated Him (John 15. 9). He suffered because of His intense love for blind, deluded sinners, as seen in His tears over guilty Jerusalem. Yet withal, His faith in the Father had no tremor of doubt. "If any man will live godly he must suffer." How ready we are to shrink from seeking to live "the life of Jesus" in our mortal bodies, because of the testing conditions that are sure to follow. This is when a steadfast faith is needed. But who is sufficient for these things? Our sufficiency is of God (2 Cor. 3. 5). "For it is God Himself who worketh in you both *to will* and *to do* of His good pleasure" (Phil. 2. 13).

V. A Life of Concentrated Activity. His first recorded utterance was: "Wist ye not that I *must* be about My *Father's business?*" The *Father's* business was *His life's business.* Never was there any one more diligent in business than Jesus. "Lo, I come, in the volume of the Book it is written of Me. *I delight to do Thy will,* O My God" (Psa. 40. 7). In our Lord's ministry there was no dissipation of interest or of energy. Everything was subordinate to the known will of His Father. If this feature of the character of Jesus is to be manifest in our present life, then we also must be willing to make ourselves of no reputation, and take the form of *a servant,* by putting on *His yoke,* that we might learn of Him meekness and lowliness of heart; and so in fellowship with Him in service, manifest in our bodies the devotion of Jesus Christ. "This one thing I do."

VI. A Life Crowned with Victory. It was one prolonged battle, with one prolonged victory. His words were all victories of wisdom. His miracles were all victories over human weaknesses. His dying was His victory over the world's sin, in the breaking down of the great barrier that stood in the way of man's approach to God. His resurrection was His victory over mortality, death, and the grave. He knew no defeat. May we who are called upon to manifest "the life of Jesus" in our mortal flesh, expect to have victory all along our pilgrim life? Has God made provision for victory or defeat? Was the apostle fearful because of the infirmities of the flesh when he said: "Thanks be to God, who *always causeth* us to *triumph in Christ*" (2 Cor. 2. 14). Again, "Thanks be to God who giveth us the victory *through our Lord Jesus Christ*" (1 Cor. 15. 54). If Jesus Christ has conquered in us, then in all these things we are more than conquerors (Rom. 8. 37). We have this treasure in *earthen vessels,* that the excellence of the power may be of God (v. 7). "Bear about . . . the *dying* of the Lord Jesus, that the life of Jesus may be manifest in the body" (v. 10). "Not I, but Christ. "

THE GREAT CHANGE.
2 CORINTHIANS 5. 14-21.

THE experiences of a Christian may not all be Christian experience. Experiences may be as varied as Christians themselves. But there are some radical and fundamental experiences that lie at the root of every real Christian life. Here are some of them. We shall note—

I. **The Change Needed.** "If One died for all, *then were all dead*" (v. 14). "Death passed upon all men, for *that all have sinned*" (Rom. 5. 12). "The wages of sin is death. " Sin separates from God, and to be separated from God is spiritual *death*. A change is needed, not in God, but in the condition of the soul that is already lost to Him because of sin.

II. **The Change Wrought.** "If any man be *in Christ, he is a new creation*" (v. 17). To be *in* Christ is to be trusting Him so entirely that God is pleased in grace to reckon the righteousness of His Son as *for us*. In this new *creation* old things have passed away. No man can create himself. We are *His workmanship*. "Created in Christ Jesus unto good works" (Eph. 2. 10). The change is so great that "all things become new, " both in us and around us, because the *heart* is renewed and the *eyes* are enlightened.

III. **The Divine Method in Accomplishing this Change.** "God was *in Christ* reconciling the world to Himself" (v. 19). Yes, in Jesus of Nazareth this lowly Man of Sorrows, GOD was seeking to reconcile a world at enmity with Himself. *In* Christ we meet with this seeking and forgiving God, finding salvation and newness of life, being justified freely by *His* grace, *through* the redemption that is *in* Christ Jesus (Rom. 3. 24). "By grace are ye saved through faith." "It is of *faith* that it might be *by grace*" (Rom. 4. 16).

IV. The Evidence of this Change. "He died for all that *they which live* should not henceforth live *unto themselves*, but *unto Him* who died for them" (v. 15). The evidence that we have of being redeemed and transformed is a changed attitude towards ourselves and our Lord. It is not "I" now, but "Christ." He gave *Himself* that He might redeem us. Now henceforth it must be *ourselves* for Him. This new purpose in life is surely what is expected from a new creature. Let the time past suffice for the love of self, the will of the flesh, and the pride of place. The grace of God that saved us now teacheth us to deny worldly lust and to live soberly, righteously, and godly in this present world (Titus 2. 12). For God hath called us unto holiness (1 Thess. 1. 7).

V. The Responsibilities Connected with this Change. "Now then we are ambassadors for Christ" (v. 20). We are Christ's representatives in the world, both as to His *character* and His *purpose*. In Christ's stead we are to beseech men to be reconciled to God. Having been reconciled to God by Jesus Christ, there is committed unto us "the *ministry of reconciliation*" (v. 18). Thank God, it is not the ministry of hopeless damnation. God is not waiting to be reconciled to men, but to reconcile men to Himself. As ambassadors, we are not left to our own resources. We are workers *together with Him* (chap. 6. 1). Out of His fulness are we all to receive. Let us labour and pray that souls may be won for Christ and His Kingdom

A CALL TO SEPARATION.

2 CORINTHIANS 6. 14-18; 7. 1.

THE Christian is not of the world, but has been sent into it as a new creature, to be a witness for Jesus Christ (John 17. 18). The danger is to compromise with the evil customs and false doctrines with which he is surrounded.

I. Why is Separation Needed? Because the two great currents of influence in the world are diametrically opposed to each other. "The Spirit of Truth and the spirit of error." The purpose of the Lord Jesus Christ and "the god of this age" are vastly different.

1. "WHAT FELLOWSHIP hath righteousness with unrighteousness?" How can the righteousness of God and the unrighteousness of Godless men abide in fellowship?

2. "WHAT COMMUNION hath light with darkness?" Darkness, it is said, is the natural condition of the universe. Light is its conqueror. "Ye were sometime darkness, but *now are ye light* in the Lord." Walk as children of light. Have no fellowship with the unfruitful works of darkness (Eph. 5. 6-11).

3. "WHAT CONCORD hath Christ with Belial?" What harmony can exist between the Holy Christ and pure vileness and worthlessness? (Deut. 13. 13).

4. "WHAT PART hath he that believeth with an infidel?" The part of the believer is the knowledge of God and the joy of His salvation. What is the part of the infidel?

5. "WHAT AGREEMENT hath the temple of God with idols? "Ye are the temple of God, and the Spirit of God dwelleth in you" (1 Cor. 3. 16). How could the *Spirit of God* agree to that which would dethrone God? Separation is absolutely needed.

II. The Call to Separation. "Come out from among

them, and be ye separate, saith the Lord, and touch not
the unclean" (v. 17). God at the first *"divided* the light
from the darkness" (Gen. 1. 4), and ever since man has
been trying to blend them. The carnal and the spiritual,
the works of the flesh, with the works of the Spirit. In
our minds and hearts, in our thoughts and affections, there
is to be an exodus from the dominion of world influences,
and a complete surrender of ourselves to the call of God.
"Set your affections on things above, *not on things on the
earth,* for ye are risen with Christ, and your life is hid
with Christ *in God"* (Eph. 3. 1-3). They are reckoned
enemies of the Cross who are devoted to earthly things
(Phil. 3. 18, 19). "Ye cannot serve God and mammon."
Therefore come out and be separated for God and for His
Christ.

III. The Promises Made to the Separated.

1. "I WILL RECEIVE YOU" (v. 17). You are not going
out into cold isolation. When you separate yourself *for*
God, you are but going closer into His arms, and nearer
to His heart. The man of the world may look upon you
with wondering pity, because *he* has no experience of
fellowship with God or of victory by His constraining
Spirit.

2. "I WILL BE A FATHER UNTO YOU" (v. 18). Our God
knows how very much we shall need Him when we are
separated *for* Him. So He *promises,* and will act the true
Fatherly part toward His devoted children. They can
joyfully say: "Behold, *what manner of love* the Father
hath bestowed upon us" (1 John 3. 1). Fear not, He will
not fail thee.

Having, therefore, *these promises,* dearly beloved, let
us cleanse ourselves from all filthiness of the flesh and
spirit, perfecting holiness in the fear of the Lord (chap.
7. 1). Father, I will.

OUR WARFARE.

2 CORINTHIANS 10. 3-7.

THE idea of warfare here is very emphatic. It is a bloodless struggle for the higher life. Being deserters from the camp of Satan, we must expect conflict, but greater is He that is for us.

I. **Our Enemy.** Our enemy consists of allied forces. There is—

1. THE FLESH, OR CARNAL MIND. "Though we walk in the flesh (body) we do not war after the flesh" (v. 3). "The flesh lusteth against the Spirit, and the Spirit against the flesh." The carnal mind is a sworn enemy to the things of the Spirit. It is a rebel against the law of God (Rom. 8. 7). The *worldly* mind is essentially opposed to the mind of the Spirit. To be carnally minded is death.

2. IMAGINATIONS. "Casting down imaginations" (v. 5). Those high-flying renegade thoughts that would carry us to the palace called vanity, and that seeks to put the crown of pride, upon our self-satisfaction. Such vain imaginings are dangerous to the soul's highest good (Psa. 2. 1).

3. EVERY THING THAT EXALTETH ITSELF AGAINST THE KNOWLEDGE OF GOD (v. 5). Every thought and feeling and act that springs up from a doubting heart against the word, the will, and the wisdom of God is vile presumption. Everything that is moral in the "old man" seeks to exalt *itself*. Beware of pride.

II. **Our Weapons.** The weapons of our warfare—

1. ARE NOT CARNAL (v. 4). They don't belong to the "old nature." They are not man-made. Not a product of human ingenuity. Spiritual enemies cannot be overcome by material weapons. We cannot overcome evil with evil. "Railing for railing" and such like are of the flesh and not of God.

2. THEY ARE MIGHTY THROUGH GOD. They are mighty because God's hand grips them, and that hand is almighty. These are His weapons for bringing down the "strongholds" of unbelief, sin, and Satan, and breaking the wings of our vain and lofty imaginations, and *everything* that would exalt itself "against the knowledge of God." This unbending and never-failing weapon is the "Word of God" in the hand of the Holy Spirit, for the sword of the Spirit is the Word of God (Eph. 6. 17). With this weapon of His Truth, we are also, through faith, to be more than conquerors. "For the Word of God is quick and *powerful*, sharper than any two-edged sword, and is a discerner of the *thoughts* and *intents* of the heart" (Heb. 4. 12). Like the sword of Goliath, "There is none like it. Give it me."

III. Our Victory

1. IS SURE. "The *pulling down* of strongholds" (v. 4). The first stronghold that has to be pulled down is our own self-will. This is the citadel of the carnal man. Here we have victory by surrendering to the Prince of Life. When our wills have been conquered by the subduing power of His mighty love, then we become partakers of the Divine nature, and are brought into league with Christ Himself, and so become, by His grace, victors over sin and the strongholds of Satan. "Be strong in the Lord, and in the *power of His might*" (Eph. 6. 10).

2. IT IS TO BE COMPLETE. "Bringing into captivity *every thought* to the *obedience of Christ*" (v. 5). When a fort has been captured, then all that are in it are taken prisoners. *Thoughts* are fugitive things, and have to be watched and restrained, "for as a man *thinketh*, so is he." Thoughts constitute character. Pure thinking leads to noble action. They are the subtle weapons of life's warfare. How important then it is that our *thoughts* should be brought *into captivity* to the will of Jesus Christ.

Thoughts require mastering. Who can guide, sanctify, and use them as Christ can? Under His control they become weapons of triumph. Thoughts are difficult things to get hold of, but when captured by Christ, He will hold them for thoughts are captured when they are *captivated*. Like Rebekah, they say, "I will go with this Man" (Gen. 24. 58). We can bring out thoughts into the captivity of obedience of Christ by keeping steadfastly *"looking unto Jesus,"* who is the *Author* and *Finisher* of our faith, the *Subduer* of our wills, the *Winner* of our affections, the *Captor* of our thoughts, and the *Giver* of every good and perfect gift. "What think ye of Christ?"

POWER IN WEAKNESS.
2 CORINTHIANS 12. 1-10.

THE personal experiences of the apostle, as recorded in those verses, are deep with significance for all who are persistently staggering after his example.

I. **A New Revelation.** "He was caught up, and heard unspeakable words" (v. 4). This revelation was for himself alone, therefore it was unutterable to others. We can only know its character by its fruits, for by their fruits ye shall know them; and the fruits as seen here are worthy of the God of all grace. Special revelations are given to many of God's faithful servants, when their minds and thoughts are *caught up* by the Holy Spirit, as on wings of faith and hope, into the highest Heavens (Ezek. 11. 24; Acts 8. 39), where they see and hear things which the language of mortals cannot fully express. They are precious seasons of the consciousness of God's presence, and the reality and power of eternal things.

II. **A New Trial.** "There was given to me a thorn in the flesh, the messenger of Satan, to buffet me, lest I should be exalted above measure" (v. 7). New trials usually come after new visions. God knows that *pride* goeth before a fall, so He permitted Satan to drive this *stake* of affliction into his body. What it really was it is difficult to say. To the Galatians he wrote: "Ye know that through the *infirmity of the flesh* I preached unto you the Gospel" (Gal. 4. 13). He was still more anxious to *preach the Gospel* than glory in his special *revelation*. It is better, in His eyes, that we should be witnessing for Christ than revelling in our new discoveries, but know that these are not contradictory, but complementary.

III. **A New Promise**. "My *grace* is sufficient for thee: *for My strength is made perfect in weakness*" (v. 9). The power of this weakness is abundantly evident in 1 Corinthians 2. 3-5. This is not the weakness of ignorance or of unbelief, but that of conscious *self-inefficiency* and entire dependence on the offered grace of God. If God's strength is to be made perfect in *weakness*, surely here is an opportunity for all of us. But it is much easier for some to be self-confident than self-emptied. To be full of self-confidence is to be empty of the power of God. God will not give His glory to another for self-display. Humble thyself, and He will exalt thee.

IV. **A New Source of Gladness**. "Most gladly therefore will I rather *glory in infirmities*, that the power of Christ may rest upon me" (v. 9). *Glorying* in our infirmities is something nobler than merely submitting to them. But no one can glory in afflictions because they are afflictions; but if by faith we can see them to be the Divinely appointed means whereby we are made more effective witnesses to the power of Christ, then we may gladly glory in them. It is common for Christian workers to find gladness in their *gifts*, but not so common to find gladness in their *infirmities*. Rejoice in the Lord alway: He doeth all things well.

V. A New Resolution. *"Therefore* I take pleasure in infirmities, in reproaches, in necessities, in distresses for *Christ's sake*: for when I am weak, then am I strong" (v. 10). He took pleasure in every trial and hardship that made him feel more keenly the measure of his *weakness*, knowing that this only made more room in his life for the grace and power of God. We glory in tribulation, knowing that tribulation *worketh* patience, experience, hope (Rom. 5. 3). "No chastening for the present *seemeth* to be *joyous*, but grievous, nevertheless *afterward* it yieldeth peaceable fruit unto *them that are exercised thereby*" (Heb. 12. 11). Let this *afterward* strengthen our faith for the present.

THE GOSPEL OF CHRIST.
GALATIANS 1. 3-9.

THE *Gospel* of Christ is simply the good news concerning Christ. The Law was given by Moses, but grace and truth, that is, the *favour* and *exact expression* of God, came by Jesus Christ (John 1. 17, 18).

I. What is Offered to Men in this Gospel?

1. FORGIVENESS. "He gave *Himself* for our sins" (v. 4). Here we have God's best, in contact with man's worst. The Holiest One in Heaven, with the foulest thing on earth. What must sin be in the eyes of God, when it took the life and death, and all the wealth of the character of His own Son to put it away? Now in Him we have redemption through His Blood, and the *forgiveness of sins* (Eph. 1. 7).

2. DELIVERANCE. "That He might deliver us from this *present evil age*" (v. 4). Although forgiven and justified, we are still here in the midst of all the evils of this present age, and need to be delivered and continually kept from their enthralment. "He is able to keep you from falling."

3. GRACE AND PEACE (v. 3). Grace sufficient to meet your every need, and the peace of God to keep your hearts and minds through Christ Jesus (Phil. **4. 7**). Bless God for such a full salvation.

II. How are these Blessings to be Received? How can I make sure that they are mine? "Him that *called you into the grace* of Christ" (v. 6). The Gospel brings God's call to the soul to enter into the full enjoyment of that grace abounding which is in Christ Jesus. There is no other way but by the *obedience of faith*. You believe the message, you obey the call, and the grace of God does all the rest (1 John 3. 5). "He is faithful that hath promised."

III. How Can this Gospel be Perverted? "There be some who would pervert the Gospel of Christ" (v. 7). The Gospel in itself cannot be perverted: it is always and everywhere the same. But it can be so *misrepresented* that the minds and thoughts of men may get a very distorted view of its real character. The Judaizer taught that they must be circumcised to receive the full benefits of the Gospel of Christ. We Gentiles are not concerned about being circumcised; but there are many who think that they ought to be *compromised*, that God will save them because of their moral character and good works. This is a perverted view of the Gospel of Christ. Anything we can do, or be, will never add any value to the saving *grace of God* in Jesus Christ. "While we *were yet* sinners, Christ died for us" (Rom. 5. 8). Therefore it is *by faith* that it might be *by grace* (Rom. 4. 16). "The *gift* of God is eternal life, *through* Jesus Christ our Lord."

IV. There is No Other Way. "Though we, or an angel from Heaven, preach any other Gospel, let him be accursed" (vv. 8, 9). Neither the wisdom of the ages, nor all time, nor eternity, will ever produce another

Gospel whereby sinful men—without the grace of God in Jesus Christ His Son—can be saved. "There is *none other Name* under Heaven given among men, whereby ye can be saved" (Acts 4. 12). Jesus said: "I am the Way, the Truth, and the Life; *no man* cometh unto the Father *but by* ME." "He that believeth *on the Son* hath everlasting life, and he that believeth *not the Son* shall not see life, but the wrath of God *abideth* on him" (John 3. 36). Believest *thou* this?

"THE LIFE I NOW LIVE."
GALATIANS 2. 16-21.

THIS was certainly not the life he used to live, when he was "breathing out threatenings and slaughter against the disciples of the Lord" (Acts 9. 1), but it is a brief spiritual autobiography of the life he now lived. It is—

I. **A Life Justified Without the Deeds of the Law**. "By the works of the law shall no flesh be justified" (v. 16). If we have offended in *one* point, we have broken the law. The law *cannot forgive* sin, but by the law is the knowledge of sin (Rom. 3. 20). To be justified in God's sight is to be free from *guilt*. So free from punishment.

II. **A Life Imparted Through Faith in Jesus Christ**. "We have *believed* in Jesus Christ that we might be *justified by faith* in Christ" (v. 16). Thus by faith in Christ the righteousness of God is imputed to the believer. The law is but our schoolmaster to *bring us to Christ*, that we might be justified *by faith* (Gal. 3. 24). "Abraham *believed* God, and it was counted unto him *for* righteousness" (Rom. 4. 3). This is the Divine law of grace. "Therefore being justified by faith, we have peace with God."

III. **A Life Lived Unto God**. "I am dead to the law that I might live unto God" (v. 19). Being now delivered from the terrors of the law, and the ensnaring power of sin ; saved out of the self-life into the happy freedom wherewith Christ hath made His believing ones free, his one absorbing purpose is to love, honour, and obey Him who hath redeemed by the Blood of His Son and brought into sweet communion with Himself.

IV. A Life Crucified with Christ. "I am crucified with Christ" (v. 20). The *old man*, with all his fleshly passions and lusts is crucified with Christ, that the body of sin might be destroyed (Rom. 6. 6). In the Cross of Christ he sees the whole body of his sinful nature nailed to the tree, and in this he gloried. "God forbid that I should glory, save in the Cross of our Lord Jesus Christ, by whom the world is crucified unto me, and *I unto the world*" (chap. 6. 14). Crucifixion is a painful remedy, but it is effectual.

V. A Life Indwelt by Christ. It is now, "Not I, but Christ liveth in Me. " He has now become, as it were, a new personality. A new will, a new purpose, and a new power now rules and reigns. Where Christ dwells is always a centre of attraction, like the home in Bethany. To be strengthened with might by His Spirit in the *inner man* is as Christ dwelling in the heart. This comes by faith (Eph. 3. 16, 17). Christ's indwelling is manifested by the Holy Spirit's presence and power. "Herein know we that we dwell in Him, and *He in us*, because He hath given us of His Spirit" (John 4. 13).

VI. A Life Continued by Faith in the Son of God. "The life I now live in the flesh, I live by faith in the Son of God" (v. 20). This life begun by faith in Christ, is to be perpetuated by a *continuous* act of faith in Christ. By grace are we saved *through* faith, all the way long. Ours is a *life* of faith in the Son of God. We live by faith, not by sight. Continue in the faith, and be not moved away from this doctrine. He that endureth to the end in this steadfast attitude of unfailing trust will be saved with a full salvation. "Without faith it is impossible to please Him" (Heb. 11. 6).

LAW—GRACE—FAITH.
Galatians 3. 6-14.

These three, but the greatest of these is "grace." The law shows us our need. Grace reveals God's provision to meet that need. Faith is the personal application of that provision to meet that need.

I. By the Law there is Condemnation.

1. It Demands a Perfect Obedience. "Cursed is every one that continueth *not in all things* written in the law *to do them*" (v. 10). "He that offendeth in *one point* is guilty of all." You cannot break *one* link without breaking the whole chain.

2. It Cannot Justify a Transgression. "No man is justified by the law in the sight of God" (v. 11). It is easy for us to justify ourselves in *our own* eyes, but then it is *with God* we have to do. This was the delusion of the Pharisees (Luke 16. 15).

3. To be Trusting the Works of the Law is to be Under the Curse (v. 10). That is a withering sentence against those who are hoping to earn eternal life by their trying to obey the just demands of the law. "Whatsoever things the law saith, it saith to them that *are under the law*, that every mouth may be stopped" (Rom. 3. 19). The law would shut us up, that we might look to Christ.

II. By Grace there is Salvation. "Grace came by Jesus Christ" (John 1. 17).

1. "Christ hath Redeemed us from the Curse of the Law" (v. 13). Jesus Christ hath bought us with His

VOL. X. 11

own Blood.   We now belong to Him and are not under the
law.   So we are freed from its curse.   One is your Master
now, even Christ.

2. BY "BEING MADE A CURSE FOR US. "   "He was made
under the law, that He might redeem them that *were under
the law*" (Gal. 4. 4, 5).   He became under the law, that
He might come into contact with those who were under the
curse.   He could not be made a curse for us by becoming
disobedient to the law.   He said: "I am not come to
destroy the law, but *to fulfil*" (Matt. 5. 17).   He willingly
took the place and curse of those under the law, and bore
their penalty when He was hanged on a tree (v. 13).   He
died for us, the Just for the unjust, that He might bring
us to God.

3. CHRIST REDEEMED us "that we Might Receive the
Promise of the Spirit" (v. 14).   It is a great blessing for
us to be delivered from the curse and dominion of the law.
It is also a great honour to Christ that we should be
possessed by His Spirit and made witnesses for Him.   Is
not this the ultimate purpose of our redemption?   Saved
to serve.   He hath redeemed us that *we might receive* the
promise of the Spirit.   The Holy Spirit is promised to
every believer in Jesus, and a *promise* is for faith.   "Have
ye received the Holy Ghost since ye believed?" (Acts 19. 2).

III. **By Faith there is Justification.**   "The just shall
live by faith" (v. 11).   Abraham was justified by faith
because he believed the promise (v. 6).   This was 430
years before the law was given.   The *promise* of eternal
life, given us in Christ, which the Scripture foresaw before
Abraham (v. 8) is an infinitely greater revelation of God
than the law given by Moses.   The law offers no promise,
but is a command with a penalty for disobedience.   Having
no promise, then it cannot be by faith.   The Gospel is a
glorious God-honouring *promise*, therefore the appeal is

to *faith*. "All that *believe* are justified from all things." "He that heareth *my Word*, and believeth in Him that sent Me, hath everlasting life, and *shall not come* into condemnation" (John 5. 24). As the Gospel is offered in promise, then salvation *cannot* be by works. Where is boasting then? It is excluded. By what law? Of works? Nay, but by the law of faith (Rom. 3. 27).

THE PURPOSE OF THE INCARNATION.
GALATIANS 4. 4-7.

I. The Time. "When the *fulness* of the time was come" (v. 4). There is no *premature* action in the Divine Providence. He does not pluck unripe fruit. The time was ripe for the coming of the long promised Seed (Gen. 3. 15). The Mosaic age had come to its close. "Now once in the *end of the age* He appeared to put away sin" (Heb. 9. 26). The psychological moment had arrived, prophetically and politically, for the Coming of Him who was to bring to the sons of men the new age of saving grace.

II. **The Person.** "God sent forth *His Son*" (v. 4). The pre-existence of the Son is clearly implied. "In the beginning was the Word" (John 1. 1). "He is *before all things*" (Col. 1. 17). "He only could speak of the glory which He had with the Father *before the world was*" (John 17. 5). "It was by His Son God *made* the world" (Heb. 1. 2). Now by His Son He seeks to save it. What a "good-bye" among the angels when He left His Father's Home to take the form of sinful flesh, and become "God manifest in the flesh." It is humiliating to think that there are teachers so blind and so presumptuous as to say that this Christ was a product of the age. "God loved the world, and sent His only begotten Son" (John 3. 16).

III. The Manner. *"Made of a woman"* (v. 4). With regard to His physical nature, He was born of a woman; but He was never called the Son of Mary. He was not the Son of Joseph. But He called Himself *"The Son of Man,"* the Son of humanity, as if the blood of the whole race was in His veins. He was the Child of all ages and of all nations. "Unto *us* a child is born; unto us a *Son is given."* As a child in *human* form He was *born*; but as a *Son* in the likeness of His Father He was *given* (Isa. 9. 6). *"Made under the law."* No angel ever knew what it was to be under the law, yet He who was higher than the angels, humbled Himself to become a debtor to do the whole law, and to be obedient unto death, even the death of the Cross. Neither the law, nor any of His accusers, nor the prince of this world, could find anything against Him (John 14. 30). Worthy is the Lamb!

IV. The Purpose. When the clock of time struck the appointed hour, God sent forth His Son.

1. TO REDEEM "them that were *under the law*" (v. 5). All were under the *law*, and all were under the *curse* (chap. 3. 10), and the only way of escape from the curse was by a Divinely ordained redemption: for no man could "redeem his brother." He gave *Himself* as the Surety for an insolvent humanity.

2. "THAT WE MIGHT RECEIVE THE ADOPTION OF SONS" (v. 5). This sonship is based on redemption. There are those who teach that Christ came to reveal the Fatherhood of God and the brotherhood of man. These facts are implied in the teaching of Christ, but NEVER is it stated that He came and suffered and died to make this known. "He came to seek and to save the lost." He came to *redeem us*, that we might *receive* the adoption of sons. All men are God's creatures, but only those who have been reconciled to God by the death of His Son can have

the true spirit of sonship (v. 6). Sonship implies family *likeness.* "All one in Christ."

3. "IF A SON, THEN AN HEIR OF GOD." "An *heir* of God *through Christ*" (v. 7). "If children, then heirs of God, and *joint-heirs* with Christ" (Rom. 8. 16). All who are in Christ are heirs with Him of that inheritance of "honour and glory" which is now His, being exalted to the right hand of God. This is an inheritance incorruptible, undefiled, and reserved in Heaven for you (1 Peter 1. 3, 4). "All are yours, for *ye are Christs,* and Christ is God's" (1 Cor. 3. 23). "What think ye of Christ?"

SOWING AND REAPING.
GALATIANS 6. 7-9.

IN chapter 5, verses 17-25, there is a description of the *works* of the flesh and the *fruit* of the Spirit. The contrast is between rottenness and perfect soundness, between the basest and the best. The works of the flesh are separate individual acts. The fruit—not fruits—of the Spirit are all of one, but manifold in its expression. This fruit is the outcome of the energy of the indwelling Spirit, and "against such there is no law," because they are above and beyond the law. Now he speaks about *sowing* to the flesh and sowing to the Spirit. Here we have—

I. **An Unalterable Law.** "*Whatsoever* a man soweth *that* shall he also reap" (v. 7).

1. THE SEED. The harvest will not be according to how much we *know,* but how much we *sow.* There may be a large stock of seed in the barn of the mind, but unless planted in suitable soil there shall be no profit in the time of harvest. The seeds of thought are sown in words and deeds. The "Word of God" is the incorruptible seed (1 Peter 1. 23). That always brings forth fruit "after its kind."

2. THE SOIL. There are two classes of soil: the *flesh*
and the *Spirit*. To sow to the flesh is to sow rotten seed,
in a poisonous soil. Nothing can come from it but corruption. We sow to the flesh when we sow to our carnal
self-pleasing, worldly lives. There is nothing in this for
the honour of God, so it will rot like a lifeless carcass.
To sow to the Spirit is to sow to the revealed will of God,
that which is pleasing unto Him. Then the fruit of the
Spirit will appear.

II. **A Solemn Reminder.** "Be not deceived, God is
not mocked" (v. 7). No one can ever gather "grapes from
thorns," or "figs from thistles," or the fruit of the Spirit
from the works of the flesh. The flesh is bad, and cannot
bring forth good fruit in the sight of God. The Spirit is
good, and cannot bring forth evil fruit (Matt. 7. 17, 18).
By their fruits ye shall know them.

1. BE NOT DECEIVED. It is easy to deceive ourselves
by false expectations, by trusting to *appearances*, by
being guided by our *feelings*, instead of God's Word.
We deceive ourselves when we think it matters not what
we sow, if only we mean well. Would that be wholesome
advice for a farmer? Most certainly the *self-life* will never
produce the fruit of the Spirit.

2. GOD IS NOT MOCKED. He is not going to be silenced
and put to shame by men's indifference and unbelief, in
regard to this great eternal law, that spiritual things can
never be produced by carnal things. The unrenewed man
cannot bring forth the fruits of the new creation. The
flesh and the Spirit are as different as death and life. The
Christless man sows to the fleshly life, and reaps corruption. The Christian sows to the Eternal Spirit and reaps
life everlasting (v. 8).

III. **A Word of Encouragement.** "Be not weary in
well-doing: for *in due season* we shall reap if we faint not"

(v. 9). We have much need of this cheerful word in these conflicting days. The *season* for us to reap the final harvest from all our spiritual sowing is not yet *due*; but the firstfruits are being gathered, when the personal character is being made rich with the graces of the Holy Spirit. Some weary themselves looking for the fruits of *their* labours, and get discouraged because they seem so scanty and poor. Let such seek more earnestly that the *fruit of the Spirit* may be manifested *in* their own lives, and God will look after the fruit of their labours (John 15.5)

CHRISTIAN EXPERIENCES.
EPHESIANS 1. 3-14.

THIS is a marvellous and comprehensive statement of Divine *grace* and of the believers' progressive discovery of its riches. "Blessed with all spiritual blessings in the heavenlies in Christ" (v. 3). The apostle's view is from the Divine standpoint. "Chosen in Him *before* the foundation of the world" (v. 4), then following step by step down to the day that "ye heard the Gospel of your salvation" (v. 13). It might help us to reverse this order, and take the truths as they appeal to Christian *experience.*

I. "Ye Heard the Word of Truth, the Gospel of your Salvation" (v. 13). What a Gospel this is. Good news of Christ's redeeming love, that has its origin away back in the eternal purpose of the Eternal God. To hear it is to behold the open door into the fulness of blessing in the favour of a reconciled God.

II. "Ye Trusted after that ye Heard the Word of Truth" (v. 13). It is not enough to hear, there must needs be the committal of the heart's affections and confidence. This *trust* is the personal *appropriation* of the offer God has made in Jesus Christ. "Ye are all the children of God *by faith in Jesus Christ*" (Gal. 3. 26).

III. Ye were Sealed with the Holy Spirit of Promise
"After that ye believed" (v. 13).   The Holy Spirit *of
Promise* has been given as an earnest in our hearts of all
that God hath laid up in store for His children (2 Cor.
1. 22).   "Ye are sealed until the day of final and perfect
redemption" (Eph. 4. 30).   Ye are claimed by Him and
stamped with His signature.

IV. Ye have Redemption through His Blood (v. 7).
Ye were not sealed that ye might be redeemed, but because
ye *have been* redeemed.   He gave Himself for us that He
might redeem us from all iniquity (Tit. 2. 14).   He was
the "Lamb slain from before the foundation of the world. "
Redemption is an older thought than *creation*, and will be
the theme of the final song (Rev. 5. 9).

V. Ye have the Forgiveness of Sins, and that
"According to the riches of His grace" (v. 7).   *Bought*
by the precious Blood of Christ, and *forgiven* according to
the infinite riches of almighty grace.   Oh, how marvellous
is His lovingkindness to us, who deserved nothing but His
righteous condemnation.   He hath loved our souls
out of the pit, and called us sons of God (1 John 3. 1).

VI. Ye are Accepted in the Beloved (v. 6).   Yes,
already accepted in Him in all our ignorance, weakness,
failure, and conscious helplessness, through faith in
Christ.   God is pleased to wrap the trusting soul within
the folds of the riches of His grace in Christ Jesus that
we might be to the praise of His glory (v. 6).   How
gladly and fully did the Father accept the Son when He
raised Him from the dead.   That is the measure of your
acceptance in Him.

VII. Ye have Obtained an Inheritance.   "In Him
also we have obtained an inheritance" (v. 11).   Not only
accepted in the Beloved, but a partner in His inheritance.

"If children, then heirs: *heirs of God* and joint-heirs with Christ; for if we suffer with Him, we may be *glorified together*" (Rom. 8. 17). This will be the inheritance of the saints in light (Col. 1. 12). "Heirs of God?" What can this mean? Jesus Christ is God's only begotten Son and Heir. The Church is the Bride of Christ. All saved by His grace and possessed by His Spirit are one with Him. The redeemed Bride shall share the glory and honour of the Bridegroom in that day when the "Marriage of the Lamb" is come.

VIII. **Ye were Predestinated unto the Adoption of Children** (v. 5). Having been forgiven, accepted, and honoured as heirs, we make this great discovery that all these experiences were according to the predetermining purpose and good pleasure of His will (v. 5). "Whom He did foreknow, He also did predestinate to be conformed to the image of His Son" (Rom. 8. 29, 30). We in our simplicity, may have thought that when we first trusted in Christ we were adding some fresh lustre to the glory of Christ, but now we see that we were only fulfilling the promise of the Father to the Son, that He would give Him an inheritance from among the nations of the earth. Jesus said: "All that the Father giveth Me shall come to Me" (John 6. 37).

IX. **Ye were Chosen in Him before the Foundation of the World** (v. 4). The origin of the Church, as the body of Christ, may date as far back as, "In the beginning was the Word" (John 1. 1). Pentecost was the visible manifestation of this eternal purpose (2 Thess. 2. 13). There was nothing haphazard about the covenant God made with His Son to give Him a people for the eternal honour of His Name. Christ did not die in chance that some might believe in Him and be saved. He knew that the Father had given Him power over all flesh, that He should give eternal life to as many as the Father had

given Him (John 17. 2).   So our Lord could say: "This
is the Father's will which hath sent Me: that of all which
He hath given Me, I shall *lose nothing*" (John 6. 39).
What a halo of glory is here seen on the brow of the Church
of God; that it was a completed thing in the Divine
purpose a thousand ages before the incarnation of His
beloved Son.   The Christ who loved the Church before it
was born, and gave Himself for it, will, one day present
it to Himself a "glorious Church, not having spot, or
wrinkle, *or any such thing*" (Eph. 5. 27).   Then shall He
see of the travail of *His soul* and shall be satisfied.   "Now
unto Him that is able to keep you from falling, and to
present you faultless before the *presence of His glory* with
exceeding joy.   To the only wise God our Saviour, be glory,
and majesty, dominion and power for ever and ever"
(Jude 24, 25).

A COMPREHENSIVE PRAYER.
Ephesians 1. 15. 21.

The spirit in which this great prayer was offered was that
of *thanksgiving* and abounding faith.   Prayer and thanksgiving are twin sisters (v. 16).

I. **To Whom it was Offered.**   The *manner* in which
men approach God is often a revelation of their spiritual
character.   This prayer was offered—

1. To "the God of our Lord Jesus Christ" (v. 17).
He is doubtless thinking of the manifestation of His own
character in the person of *His Son*.   He is praying to the
God of infinite love and super-abounding grace.

2. To "the Father of Glory."   The Father of
all the glory that belongs to His eternal Son, in whose
face this glory was seen (John 1. 14).   Christ's personality was the Shekinah of God, unveiled before the
eyes of men.

II. The Petitions. They are in sweet harmony with such a gracious God.

1. That He may "give unto you the SPIRIT OF WISDOM, and REVELATION, in the KNOWLEDGE OF HIM." This would mean a precious inheritance to any possessor. Wisdom to discern spiritual things. Fresh revelations and a growing knowledge of the glorious character of *Him* who is the Wisdom and the Power of God. All such gifts are for the magnifying of Jesus Christ in our hearts and lives.

2. THAT THE EYES OF YOUR HEART MAY BE ENLIGHTENED (v. 18). There may be things Spiritual and Divine which we can see with our *hearts*, that we cannot comprehend with our minds. The affections of the heart may lay hold on what the intellect is inclined to doubt, as when doubting Thomas said, "My Lord and my God" (see 2 Cor. 4. 4-6).

III. The Expected Results. That ye may know—

1. WHAT IS THE HOPE OF HIS CALLING. Not what is the hope of *your* calling. But what is the hope of *His* calling. The greatness and grandeur of that hope into which the grace of God hath called us, how few can realise. "Walk worthy of God who hath *called you* unto *His Kingdom and glory*" (1 Thess. 2. 12). Our calling as *we* view it, and our calling as God views it, may be vastly different things. The apostle had the Divine outlook when he said: "I press toward the mark for the prize of the *high calling of God in Christ Jesus*: for our citizenship is in Heaven, from whence also we look for the Saviour, the Lord Jesus Christ, who shall fashion our bodies *like unto His glorious body.*"

2. WHAT IS THE RICHES OF THE GLORY OF HIS INHERITANCE IN THE SAINTS? We often think of our inheritance *in Christ*, but here it is the riches of Christ's inheritance

in *the saints* (v. 18). All are His saints—or separated
ones—who have been born from above, possessed by His
Spirit and yielded to His will. They are Christ's peculiar
treasure. The Lord's portion is His people; and in the
coming ages the glorified Church will be an everlasting
witness to the riches of the glory of Christ's saving grace.

3. WHAT IS THE EXCEEDING GREATNESS OF HIS POWER
TO USWARD? We believe that God is Almighty. We see
His power in the creative work of His hands. But what
is the greatness of His power in operation *toward us*, who
are now His needy children? It is the same mighty power
that wrought in Christ when He raised Him from the dead
and set Him in the heavenlies, far above *every form of
power* and *every name that is named* in this world, and also
in that which is to come (vv. 20, 21). This is the power
at the disposal of the Church of God to-day; for it is given
to Christ to be Head *over all* to the Church (v. 22). "All
power is given unto Me. Go ye, therefore." "Ye are
complete in Him" (Col. 2. 10).

————

THE BELIEVER'S PAST, PRESENT, AND FUTURE.

EPHESIANS 2. 1-13.

I. Their Past. This constitutes a dark and dismal
review. They were—

1. WITHOUT LIFE. "Ye were *dead* in trespasses and
sins." Spiritually dead to God, and buried in graves of
their making—"trespasses and sins." No response to all
the overtures of Divine mercy in Christ Jesus. "To be
carnally minded is death."

2. WITHOUT STRENGTH. "Ye walked according to the
course of this world" (v. 2). Carried away by the current
of the world's influences, and, like a dead fish in the
stream, without any power of resistance.

3. WITHOUT CHRIST. "At that time ye were without Christ" (v. 12). All thàt Christ *now* stands for in our personal experience and future hopes, at that time had no existence in our lives. Here see the poverty and desolation of unregenerate souls. Destitute, afflicted, tormented.

4. WITHOUT PROMISE. Strangers from the covenants of promise (v. 12). It is said that there are thirty thousand promises in God's Book, but not one for the man whose mind is at enmity with God. There are "exceeding great and precious promises," but the worldly, carnal, Christless soul sees no value in them.

5. WITHOUT HOPE. "Having no hope" (v. 12). Being without a promise, they are without hope. This is God's judgment of their case: but it is not theirs. Jesus Christ said: *"No man* cometh unto the Father *but by me"* (John 14. 6). But at that time we were "without Christ," and so could not come to the Father in His own appointed way. "He that believeth not is condemned *already.*" Without hope.

6. WITHOUT GOD IN THE WORLD. Without God, in a world teeming with evidences of His wisdom and power. In the world, loved by God, where God's own Son lived, loved, and died to save sinners (John 3. 16). Yes, such were some of us, "but ye are washed."

II. Their Present. But NOW *in Christ Jesus.* What a change!

1. YE ARE QUICKENED (v. 1). The Holy Spirit of God hath breathed into you the breath of a new life. Your eyes have been opened to see the mysteries and realities of eternal things. The darkness is past and the true Light now shineth. The clouded promises now appears like stars of the first magnitude. Christ has become an overshadowing reality.

2. YE ARE MADE NIGH. "Now made nigh by the

Blood of Christ" (v. 13). Christ has been trusted, and He who died, the Just for the unjust, has brought us to God (1 Peter 3. 18). The sins that separated have been put away. We have now the fellowship of the reconciled.

3. YE ARE RAISED together with Christ (v. 6). In the purpose of God we were one with Him in the Cross. Now we share His resurrection life and power. "He died for our sins, but He rose again for our justification."

4. YE ARE SEATED together with Him in the heavenlies (v. 6). His last word on earth was, "It is finished," then He ascended to the Father's right hand and sat down. Our blessed privilege now is to *rest* with Him in the work accomplished for us.

5. YE ARE HIS WORKMANSHIP. It is all His doing. Through faith we are saved *by grace*, that not of ourselves, it is the gift of God" (v. 8). "For it is God which worketh in you both *to will* and *to do* of His good pleasure" (Phil.2.13).

III. **Their Future.** "That in the *ages to come* He might shew the exceeding riches of His grace in His kindness toward us through Christ Jesus" (v. 7). In this present age we have seen much of God's kindness toward us through Christ Jesus in His saving, keeping, satisfying fulness. But in the age to come we shall be witnesses of the glory that was to follow. When the Lord Himself shall appear, and when all His redeemed shall be caught up together to meet Him and to be glorified together with Him as "heirs of God," we shall then have entered into our glorious inheritance (Rom. 8. 17-19, Luke 22. 28-30).

THE CHURCH AS A NEW MAN.
EPHESIANS 2. 14-22.

IN by-gone ages the Church's character "was not made known unto the sons of men" (chap. 3. 5). It was "a mystery hid in God" (chap. 3. 9). In all ages God had His Holy ones; but the Church *as a new man*, a new created Body of Christ, through which the manifold wisdom of God was to be make known (chap. 3. 10) had not yet been revealed. This is the theme before us now.

I. **The Divine Plan**. This was to *make in Himself* of twain (Jew and Gentile) one new man, one new *Body*, so making peace (v. 15). This new Body was to be—

1. COMPOSED OF JEW AND GENTILE. These terms represent the whole human race. He that is *not* a Jew is a Gentile, whatever be the colour of his skin or the language he may speak. The Church is to be composed of "called out" ones from every nation and people under the heavens.

2. RECONCILED ONE TO ANOTHER. No more strangers and foreigners, but *fellow-citizens* and of the *household of God* (v. 19). "All one in Christ Jesus." In being brought to God, each member is to be brought into sympathy and fellowship with one another. They all belong to the "household of faith" (Gal. 6. 10).

3. RECONCILED TO GOD. "That He might reconcile *both* unto God *in one body*" (v. 16). Before God there is now neither Jew nor Gentile, but *one* body, made nigh by the Blood of Christ (v. 13). All are saved by grace. This "new man" is "accepted in the Beloved" for the Head of this new creation is Christ Himself.

II. **The Divine Preparation**. Before this gracious purpose of God could be accomplished a great work had to be done, a work that God only could do. There was—

1. A WALL OF PARTITION TO BE BROKEN DOWN. "He hath broken down the middle wall of partition" (v. 14). In the temple worship the Gentile court was cut off from the inner court by a separating wall or partition. But in this new creation in Christ all such prejudice, sectarianism, and every dividing thing is to be *broken down*. But

men are still building partition walls in their priestly pride, religious bigotry, and pagan superstitions; but, thank God, that *in Christ* all are done away, "broken down."

2. ENMITY TO BE SLAIN. "He hath reconciled both unto God *by the Cross*, having slain the enmity *thereby*" (v. 16). The Cross of Christ is God's mighty weapon for breaking down barriers between individuals and nations, between human hearts and a Holy God. The greatest of all partition walls is the *enmity* of the carnal mind (Rom. 8. 7). This enmity cannot be cured, it must be *slain*; and the humbling and melting vision of Christ crucified for our own sins can slay it.

3. BOTH MUST BE POSSESSED BY THE SAME SPIRIT. "Through Him we both have access by one Spirit unto the Father" (v. 18). This union between Jew and Gentile is not a mere expediency for a temporary end. It is a vital and eternal work of God's grace. *One Spirit* animates the whole body. "For by *one Spirit* are we all baptised into one body, whether we be Jew or Gentile, bond or free; and have all been made to drink *into one Spirit*" (1 Cor. 12. 13). Christ is the Fountain Head of this Spirit-life that flows through every member of the body. "If any man thirst, let him come unto Me and drink" (John 7. 37).

III. **The Divine Purpose** is to have this "new man" *as a fixed abode of God through the Spirit* (v. 22, Weymouth trans.). Does that mean that in the coming age the Church will be the fixed abode of the Holy Spirit for the manifestation of the glory of Christ? "He shall abide with you for ever."

1. ALL BUILT ON THE ONE FOUNDATION. Built upon the foundation of the apostles and prophets, Jesus Christ *Himself* being the chief corner stone (v. 20). The prophets as well as the apostles built upon the truth revealed,

whether by the Holy Spirit or by Christ Himself (Heb. 1. 1, 2). In both instances Jesus Christ Himself was the chief corner stone, binding the whole spiritual fabric as one to Himself. The strength and stability of the structure depends on the presence and *position* of the "Chief Corner Stone" (Matt. 21. 42).

2. ALL FITLY FRAMED TOGETHER. "In HIM all the building is fitly framed together, *groweth* unto an *holy temple* in the Lord" (v. 21). In Christ every separate believer is depending on Him as the foundation of all their hopes, but they are also individually to be "*fitly framed together*" with their local fellow-believers. There is to be "no schism in the body." Stones which do *not fit with each other* make an untrustworthy or uncomely structure. Christians have often ruined their testimony by being out of harmony with their brethren. The Church is a *growing* concern, "growing unto an holy temple in the Lord."

3. ALL UNITING TO MAKE A FIXED ABODE FOR GOD THROUGH THE SPIRIT (v. 22). When this holy temple in the Lord will be ready as a fixed abode for Him to whom it belongs, no tongue of angel or pen of scribe can tell. But the day will come when the last addition will be made, and when the top stone will be put on, with "shoutings of Grace, Grace, unto it" (Zech. 4. 7). Truly every stone in the building is a monument of the grace of God through Christ Jesus. Thus this "new man," full-grown and glorified, will become the temple of the Lord, and a witness to the triumph of Christ's sacrifice in the kingdom that is to come. Well may we pray: "THY KINGDOM COME."

BELIEVERS' POSSIBILITIES.
EPHESIANS 3. 14-21.

"FOR *this cause* I bow my knees." This was no mere formal prayer. Paul deeply realised the immense impor-

tance of the petitions he was about to offer. He knew
that as Christians these experiences were needed.

I. **What these Blessings Were**. He prayed that they
may have—

1. SPIRITUAL POWER. "Strengthened with might by
His Spirit in the inner man" (v. 16). The *might* of the
Holy Spirit in the *inner* man is the supreme need of every
Christian in our own day. Herein lies the secret of our
real influence for God. This power He is ready to give to
the faint (Isa. 4. 29-31).

2. THE INDWELLING PRESENCE. "That Christ may
dwell in your hearts by faith" (v. 17). There can be no
spiritual power where Christ is not honoured. If *by faith*
Christ dwells in us, then the Spirit will take the things
that are Christ's and show them through us. This *indwelling* is assured by an unfailing faith in Him.

3. STABILITY OF CHARACTER. "Ye being *rooted* and
grounded in love" (v. 17). The downward growth of the
roots of our being are to be in the rich, fruitful soil of God's
love, and the upward growth of the building of character
is to be *based* also in love. "Rooted and *built up* in Him,
and established in the faith" (Col. 2. 7).

4. ENLARGED COMPREHENSION. "That ye may be *able
to comprehend* with all saints…and to know the love of
Christ which passeth knowledge" (v. 19). It will take
the comprehension of "all saints" in every age to find out
the breadth, length, depth, and height of that love of
Christ which in itself passeth knowledge. It is a great
discovery to find out the immeasurable magnitude of that
love wherewith Christ hath loved us. And who shall
separate us from that love? (Rom. 8. 35).

5. COMPLETE AND ABIDING SATISFACTION. "That ye
might be filled with all the fulness of God" (v. 19). Filled
out of this fathomless fulness of God. "That ye might be

complete in accordance with God's own standard of completeness (Weymouth). Already "from His fulness have all we received, and grace upon grace" (John 1. 16). But, Lord, increase our faith, that we may rise to the *Divine standard* of fulness.

II. **The Unfailing Source.** "Now unto Him that is able to do *exceeding abundantly above all we ask or think*" (v. 20). These were great requests, but the apostle knew that he was coming to a great and gracious God. He knew and believed what we so easily forget, that "He that spared not His own Son, but delivered *Him up for us all*, how shall He not *with Him* also freely give us *all things*" (Rom. 8. 32). If this princely truth reigned over our prayers, how different many of them would be. God has given us His Son, this is the proof and pledge that He will withhold no good thing from those that love Him and ask Him. But the measure of our receiving is "according to the *power that worketh in us*" (v. 20). "According to your *faith.*" This power worked mightily in the apostle, and mighty things were done (see Heb. 11).

III. **The Measure of God's Giving.** "According to the *riches of His glory*" (v. 16). We think that we know something of "the riches of *His grace*" (Eph. 1. 7), but what can we know of the "riches of *His glory*?" In dealing with His pleading servants, it is the larger measure of His eternal glory that He uses, according to the wealth of His risen and glorified position. If in His poverty He could so bless and enrich needy souls, how much more now, since He has entered into the inheritance of His Father's glory. "All power is given unto Me in Heaven and on earth." Believest thou this? "Ask, and ye shall receive." "He giveth liberally and upbraideth not."

CHARACTER AND CONDUCT.
EPHESIANS 4. 17-32.

As those who have learned of Christ (v. 20), the apostle
exhorts the Ephesian brethren that their manner of walk
must be different from "other Gentiles," who walk in the
"vanity of their mind," with the *understanding darkened*
and *"alienated from the life of God,"* because of *ignorance* and
blindness of heart (vv. 17-19). What a sad picture this
is of the unrenewed man. "Such were some of us, but ye
are washed." The difference grace makes must be apparent
in character and conduct. To this Christ-honouring end
he calls upon them and us to—

I. **Put Off the Old Man** (v. 22). This old man is just
the same age as yourself. You cannot put him off like an
old coat, nor can you put him off with promises. It is the
natural carnal mind, whose motto was "Me first"—the
self-seeking, self-praising, self-satisfying spirit. It is
the old, corrupt heart, that loved the things that dis-
honoured the Christ. Shake him off as you would a
poisonous viper! Let him be crucified (Rom. 6. 6).

II. **Put on the New Man.** This new man is after the
image of God in righteousness and true wholeness (v. 24).
This new man is the "second man, the Lord from Heaven."
"Put ye on the Lord Jesus Christ, and make no provision
for the old man" (Rom. 13. 14). To put on Christ is to
put on His Spirit and the yoke of His will. When He has
His rightful place in the heart and life there is no room
for any other. "Jesus must reign."

III. **Put Away all Unreality.** Every deceptive and
untruthful thing (v. 25). Does it seem strange to be
warning those who have been made anew after the likeness
of Christ, of lying, anger, and stealing? We all know that
the *thoughts* of the heart, as well as the words of the tongue,

often betray. In their most incipient stage these things are to be hated and disowned.

IV. Give No Place to the Devil (v. 27). The Devil is always in search of a *place* in our lives. He knows that if he can but get his poison into the blood, that the whole man will be affected. Paul forgave others, "lest Satan should get an advantage of us" (2 Cor. 2. 10, 11). The hasty temper and the unforgiving mood gives Satan a great advantage. "Resist the Devil and he will flee from you."

V. Let your communications be free from corruption, and Good for Edifying (v. 29). When conversation degenerates into mere gossip, or a display of repartee, there is little thought of obeying this injunction of making it a *"ministry of grace to the hearers."* Many a God-given opportunity has been utterly lost by the frivolous mood displayed at times by God's servants in the presence of quiet, thoughtful, anxious souls (Col. 4, 6).

VI. Grieve not the Holy Spirit. This is an awful possibility on the part of a Christian worker. He may be grieved by *ignoring His presence*, by *unholy talk* and *temper* which falsifies His character, by *resisting His teaching*, by *depending on our own wisdom* and strength. A grieved Spirit means the loss of the enjoyment of God's love, the loss of communion which is by the Holy Spirit, the loss of power for service (Isa. 63. 10). Grieve Him not, for by the Holy Spirit are *ye sealed* and secured unto the day of Christ's final redemption (v. 30).

VII. Be Kind and Tender-hearted. "Forgiving one another, *even as God for Christ's sake hath forgiven you*" (v. 32). Be kind, tender-hearted, forgiving one another for *Christ's sake*: *even as* God for Christ's sake hath forgiven you. This measure is "until seventy times seven" (Matt. 18. 22).

BE FILLED WITH THE SPIRIT.

EPHESIANS 5. 16-18.

To "redeem the time" (v. 16) and to "understand what the will of the Lord is" (v. 17), we must be "filled with the Spirit." God does not now thunder from a mount or send prophets with *new* messages. The last of the prophets was His Son from Heaven, and His last great gift for this age is the Holy Spirit, who reveals the will of God and inspires with power to do it.

I. A Striking Contrast. "Be not drunk with wine, but be filled with the Holy Spirit." A contrast between being drunk and Spirit-filled. Between man's most debasing vice and God's holiest and highest virtue. Between that which genders mockery and self-deception and that which gives Divine illumination. Between that which gives license to lust and shame and that which gives liberty and power in God's service. The one means waste and loss of self-control, the other means new gifts and self-renewal. The one leads to vain imaginations and regretful deeds, the other guides into truth and makes strong to do the will of God. "Wine is a *mocker*." The Holy Spirit is the great *Teacher* come from God to take the place of the Lord Jesus Christ.

II. A Needful Exhortation. "Be filled with the Spirit." This implies—

1. THAT THE HOLY SPIRIT HAS BEEN GIVEN, and that as surely as God gave His Son, Pentecost is a witness to that (Acts 2. 1-4). Just as there is an ample provision in the Sacrifice of Christ to meet all our needs as sinners in the sight of God, so there is sufficiency in the Holy Spirit to meet our need as sons and servants of God in the presence of men.

2. EVERY BELIEVER HAS BEEN INFLUENCED BY THE SPIRIT. It was He who first convinced of sin (John 16. 8).

It was He who gave the first quickening touch to our spiritually dead souls (Eph. 2. 1), and since we first trusted in Christ has been in many ways helping, guiding into truth, and revealing the things of Christ to our lagging hearts. "If any man have not the Spirit of Christ, he is none of His. " But there is something more than this—

3. EVERY BELIEVER SHOULD BE FILLED WITH THE SPIRIT. When the Spirit was first poured out, He rested upon *each of them*, and they were *all filled* with the Holy Ghost (Acts 2. 3, 4). Again, after prayer, we read that *all assembled together* were filled with the Holy Ghost (Acts 4. 31). While Peter yet spake, the Holy Ghost fell on *all them which heard the word* (Acts 10. 44). It is perfectly clear that the apostles, at the beginning of their ministry, were taught by the providence of God that *every believer* in the risen Lord was to be, or might be, filled with the Spirit. Paul's first question to the Ephesian disciples was: "Did ye receive the Holy Spirit when ye believed?" (Acts 19. 2). There are many young disciples to-day that could give the same answer they gave: "We have not so much as heard whether there be any Holy Ghost to be received. " "By grace are ye *saved*, " but by the Holy Spirit are ye to be *filled*. This filling is for you. Seek it.

III. **A Powerful Inducement** to seek this filling is presented to us in the peaceful, faithful, and fruitful lives of those who were filled with the Spirit in Bible and in modern times. We can only note some of the more prominent characteristics.

1. A DEEP SENSE OF PERSONAL UNWORTHINESS. The more of the Spirit the less of self. "Not I, but Christ. " They know that apart from Him—nothing.

2. A HUNGER FOR THE WORD OF GOD. When the Spirit has full control within, and reveals afresh the things of

Christ, there is a growing love and reverence for the living Book.

3. A QUICKENED REALISATION OF THE PRESENCE OF GOD. There are wonderful sights and sounds in nature, which cannot be seen nor heard without some special instrumentality. There are more wonderful things in the spiritual sphere, that the natural eye or ear hath never seen or heard, but God hath revealed them unto us by His Spirit (1 Cor. 2. 9, 10). We know *Him.*

4. A DESIRE FOR, AND A DELIGHT IN, PRAYER. Prayer now means having fellowship with God in our need. There is no misgivings as to God's Personal interest in His trusting child. His prayers are mingled with notes of thanksgiving and heart-felt praise.

5. A YEARNING FOR THE SALVATION OF OTHERS. Paul wept over those who were the enemies of the Cross of Christ (Phil. 3. 18). Spiritual things have become so vital and precious that compassion and pity have been intensified for those who are out of the way. The love of Christ constraineth.

6. A MORE REAL CONFLICT WITH SPIRITUAL ENEMIES. Hitherto we were but onlookers and students of spiritual forces, but now we are right in the arena of battle, "wrestling against principalities, against powers, against the rulers, of darkness and wickedness in high places" (Eph. 6. 12), and know the power of the Sword of the Spirit, which is *the Word of God.*

7. A MORE CHRIST-LIKE ATTITUDE IN THE FACE OF OPPOSITION. When misunderstood and misrepresented (Acts 2. 13), not giving railing for railing, but contrariwise, praying for them that despitefully use you, as Christ and Stephen prayed: "Father, forgive them." To be filled with the Spirit is to be filled with the knowledge of His will and a desire to please Him.

IV. **What Doth Hinder?** There is no hindrance on the Divine side. He says: "Be filled with the Spirit." Then, if we are not, the hindrance must be in us. Is it *ignorance* of its possibility and need? Is it *unbelief* in its reality? It may be *indifference* as to its vital importance, or it may be love of the world and sheer *self-satisfaction*. Whatever it is, we are responsible for *not* being filled with the Spirit. Then, for the sake of Jesus Christ, and your own eternal honour, "Be filled with the Spirit." "If ye, being evil, *know how* to give good gifts unto your children: *how much more* shall your heavenly Father *give the Holy Spirit* to them that *ask Him*" (Luke 11. 13). "If thou knewest the *gift of God* thou wouldst have *asked of Him*" (John 4. 10).

CHRIST AND THE CHURCH.
EPHESIANS 5. 21-33.

THE union brought about by a truly Christian marriage is here used by the apostle as a metaphor of that spiritual union between Christ and His Church. Let us examine—

I. The Relationship of Christ to the Church.

1. It is that of A LOVER. "Christ loved the Church" (v. 25). When did this love begin? He loved it before it was born, as the promised gift of the Father. His love is an abiding benediction, a love that passeth knowledge (chap. 3. 19).

2. It is that of A REDEEMER. "He gave *Himself* for it" (v. 25). Like a true lover, He gives *Himself* first. He has bought the Church for Himself by the ransom of His own precious Blood (Eph. 1. 7). "Ye are not your own."

3. It is that of A HUSBAND. "The husband is head of the wife, even as Christ is the Head of the Church" (v. 23). The *Head* is the seat of *authority*. With the Head also

rests the *responsibility* of supplying the needs of the wife—the Church. Why, then, for the work of the Head, do we constantly appeal to the wife for the means to carry on? If we are doing the Lord's work we ought to do it in the Lord's way, by trusting Him who is "able to supply all our need" (Phil. 4. 19).

4. It is that of A SANCTIFIER. "That He might sanctify and cleanse her with the washing by His Word" (v. 26). He sanctifies, or *separates*, her for Himself. He found her in rags and wretchedness, but He looked on her in love and spread His skirts of mercy over her. He washed and clothed her with broidered work. He anointed her and decked her with ornaments and jewels, and made her perfect with the comeliness He put upon her (Ezek. 16. 5-14). It is all *His* doing. Praise His Name.

5. It is that of A SATISFIER. "He nourisheth and cherisheth it" (v. 29). No mother was ever more careful over her child than the Lord is over His Church. He nourisheth her with the milk of His Word, and fondles her in the arms of His love (John 17. 14, 15). He satisfies with good things by His comforting Spirit (John 16. 13, 14).

6. It is that of A BRIDEGROOM. He longs to "present it to Himself a glorious Church, not having spot or wrinkle, or *any such thing*" (v. 27). A Bride without blemish in *His eyes*. Seeing that this is His ultimate purpose concerning all His own, should we not expect Him to work out that which is pleasing to Him now in each individual life? Let us ever remember that we are always in the hands of Him who is able to *keep* us from falling, and to *present* us faultless before the *presence of His glory* with exceeding joy (Jude 24, 25). That will be the happy day of the "Marriage of the Lamb."

II. The Relationship of the Church to Christ. It is that of—

1. SAVED ONES. "He is the Saviour of the body" (v. 23). It can never be forgotten that the Church is as a brand plucked out of the fire.

2. MEMBERS OF HIS BODY, of His flesh, and of His bones (v. 30). So close is the relationship that "they two shall be one flesh" (v. 31) The *members* of the body are the operators on behalf of the Head (Rom. 12. 5).

3. SUBMISSION. "Therefore the Church is *subject* unto *Christ*" (v. 24). The members of the body that is *not subject* to the control of the Head is either *separated* or *paralyzed*.

4. REVERENCE. "The wife see that she reverence her husband" (v. 33). We reverence our Lord when we believe His Word, love His will, and adore His Holy Name. This is the happy slavery of love. "Thou art worthy, O Lord, to receive honour."

THE WARRIOR'S ENEMY.
EPHESIANS 6. 11, 12.

(FOR Notes on "The Whole Armour of God," see Vol. IX., page 179.) Here we shall briefly look at "Your Adversary the Devil." The Christian's great enemy is "not flesh and blood" (v. 12). Not even human nature, as such, but a real spiritual and powerful personality. "Called the Devil and Satan" (Rev. 12. 9).

I. **His Character.** There is but one Devil, or Satan, but there are many "demons." "The Devil and *his* angels." He has had long experience in sinning. "The Devil sinneth from the beginning." He is great. Called "the Son of the Morning" (Isa. 14. 12). He is also called a "lion" for strength, a "dragon" for fierceness, the "old serpent" for subtilty. Even our Lord called him "the *prince* of this world." When he led the revolt in Heaven

it was the great Archangel Michael who fought against
him (Rev. 12. 7).   This is the passage we have to deal
with: Who is the *"accuser of the brethren"* (Rev. 12. 10).

II. **His Sphere.**   When cast down from Heaven, he
seems to have pitched his camp in the aerial regions near
this world, and became "the prince of the power of the
air," and the god of this age (2 Cor. 4. 4), and "the spirit
that now worketh in the Children of disobedience" (Eph.
2. 2).   Although his stronghold is spiritual wickedness
in high places, he is found "going to and fro in the earth,
and walking *up* and *down* in it" (Job 2. 2).

III. **His Resources.**   These are difficult to define.
But when we take our "stand against the wiles of the
Devil" (v. 11) we are in conflict with the despotisms, the
empires, the forces that control and govern this dark
world—the *spiritual hosts of evil* arrayed against us in the
heavenly warfare (Weymouth).   But, thank God "greater
is He that is *for us.*"

IV. **His Methods.**   We are not to be "ignorant of his
devices," lest he should get an advantage of us (2 Cor.
2. 11).   His devices are varied—

1. He tries "WILES" (v. 11).   Something *attractive,* but
deceptive and ensnaring.   This was his method with
Christ in His great *temptation.*

2. He tries "FIERY DARTS" (v. 16).   Poisoned tipped
arrows, that strike as suddenly as an unclean *thought* or a
dishonest and evil imagination.   If you do not *love* such,
but hate them, you need not worry over them.   *Disown
them.*

3. He tries the PROLONGED STRUGGLE, or "wrestling."
"We *wrestle* against the *rulers* of darkness, against spiritual
wickedness" (v. 12).   The conflict may be severe, but
resist the Devil and he will flee from you.

V. **His Subjects** are not those who are warring against

him, but those who are his willing, because *blinded*, slaves (Eph. 2. 2; 2 Cor. 4. 4). They live in his "kingdom of darkness, " being captured by his powers, his signs, and *lying wonders* (2 Thess. 2. 9). They are in bondage to a great delusion. This is the condition into which sin and unbelief had brought us, and where all unsaved ones now are. May the love of Christ constrain us to seek their deliverance.

VI. **His Victors.** Our Lord Jesus Christ, the *stronger* One, has come into the Devil's dominion, and has overcome him, and spoiled him of his goods (Luke 11. 21, 22). By His life and death, and triumphant resurrection, He has spoiled *principalities* and *powers*. He shook them off, and boldly displayed them as His conquests, when by His Cross He triumphed over them (Col. 2. 15). The Son of God was manifested that He might *destroy the works of the Devil*, even him that had the power of death (Heb. 2. 14). Now we who believe in Him have been delivered from the power and dominion of Satan, and *translated* into the *Kingdom* of God's dear Son (Col. 1. 13). We know that we have passed *from death into life* (John 5. 24), and that the darkness is passed, and the *true light* now shineth (John 2. 8). "Thanks be to God, who hath given us *the victory*" (Rev. 12. 11).

THE SELF-HUMBLED BUT GOD-EXALTED CHRIST.
PHILIPPIANS 2. 5-11.

I. **His Humiliation.** The pre-incarnate position and glory of the Lord Jesus Christ is frequently referred to in the Scriptures. "He was in the form of God, and thought it not d'shonouring to claim equality with God" (v. 6). "In the beginning was the word...and the *Word was God*" (John 1. 1). He is before all things (Col. 1. 17). It was

He who "laid the foundations of the earth, and the heavens are the works of His hands" (Heb. 1. 10). This is He who was "the Lamb slain before the foundation of the world" (Rev. 13. 8). This is He who—

1. MADE HIMSELF OF NO REPUTATION (v. 7). Think of the reputation *He had* in the Heavens, before the world was, and how much He stripped Himself off when He appeared amongst men to be despised and rejected. "A man of sorrows, acquainted with grief."

2. TOOK UPON HIM THE FORM OF A SERVANT. He who was the Creator of the ends of the earth, whom angels delighted to serve and adore, who *was in the form of God*, takes the form of *a servant*, that He might bring blessing to a rebel world (Luke 22. 27).

3. WAS MADE IN THE LIKENESS OF MEN. He Himself took part of the same flesh and blood, for it behoved Him to be made *like unto His brethren* (Heb. 2. 14-17). "The Son of Man came not to be served, but to *serve*, and to *give*" (Matt. 20. 28). He who was the "express image of the invisible God" takes upon Him the likeness of a sinful humanity.

4. BECAME OBEDIENT UNTO DEATH (v. 8). OBEDIENT! but not to the clamoring of a proud, sin-blinded race, but to the *will of His Father*. "I delight to do Thy will, O my God" (John 6. 38). Nothing on earth or in Hell could turn Him aside from His great and gracious purpose. "He set His face like a flint."

5. Became obedient EVEN UNTO THE DEATH OF THE CROSS (v. 8). From our natural standpoint it is simply appalling to think of the Eternal and Beloved Son of God submitting to be nailed to a Cross by those whom He lovingly sought to save. The utter unworthiness and guilt of men could never make itself more hideous before the eye of Heaven. But yet the infinite grace of God is

hereby revealed. He was *giving "Himself* a ransom for us all." The Just One was willingly suffering for the unjust, that He might *bring us to God* (Gal. 3. 13).

II. His Exaltation. *"Wherefore* God hath *highly exalted Him"* (v. 9). Because of His voluntary humility and suffering, in the fulfilling of His Father's purpose, He hath highly exalted Him as the *Son of Man,* as the Eternal *Son of God.* He could not be exalted above His pre-natal position, "as One with the Father" (John 14. 9). There was given unto Him—

1. A PRE-EMINENT NAME. "A Name which is *above every name"* (v. 9). The *Name* which is for ever above every name is "JEHOVAH." Now the *Man,* Christ Jesus, who became a "Man of Sorrows," has been lifted up above every name that is named. He who was crowned with the thorns of shame for us is now crowned with glory and honour (Heb. 2. 9) as our Representative.

2. UNIVERSAL AUTHORITY. At the Name of Jesus every being in Heaven and on earth, and in the under world shall yet bow (v. 10) "All power is given unto Him in Heaven and on earth" (Matt. 28. 18). He who now bears the eternal stigma of the Cross upon His hands and feet, will "subdue all things unto Himself," not only in this world, but also in that which is to come (Eph. 1. 20, 21).

3. UNIVERSAL WORSHIP. "Every tongue confess that Jesus Christ is *Lord* to the glory of God the Father" (v. 11). It was God the Father who sent His Son to seek and save the lost, and He shall be honoured and satisfied when a whole redeemed world shall confess *Jesus as Lord.* For He shall be Lord both of the dead and the living (Rom. 14. 9). Now we see Jesus, who *tasted death* for every man, crowned with glory and honour. "Thine is the kingdom, and the power, and the glory for ever. Amen." "He that humbleth *himself* shall be exalted."

HOLY ASPIRATIONS.

PHILIPPIANS 3. 7-14.

WHEN Paul met the Lord on his way to Damascus (Acts 9) his whole being was revolutionised. His eyes being opened, he discovered that in Him he had found a limitless store of spiritual wealth, for which he counted everything else as worthless (v. 7). We have here some of the experiences which his holy ambition aimed at. May our own hearts also be stirred up to seek them.

I. **That I may Win Christ** (v. 8). Christ had already won him (Acts 9). But the apostle realised that although he was now in the land of promise, there was still much land to be possessed. He evidently wished to find Him as a *daily* prize. He was determined not to know anything among them but Jesus Christ (1 Cor. 2. 2).

II. **That I might Know Him** (v. 10). There are, of course, many degrees in knowledge. All Christians know *Him* whom to know is life eternal. But the Christ some saintly men and women know is a much greater Christ than many have ever experienced. It is the same Jesus, but they have a much deeper and more intimate knowledge of His character and capabilities. It will take all eternity to know Him as He really is. We are to "grow in grace," but also *"in the knowledge of Him."*

III. **That I may be Found in Him** (v. 9). It is an abiding victory for all those whose faith and works are found *in Him.* If He abides in us we shall be found in Him (John 15. 4), and at last, when the time of our departure is at hand, it will be a joy to us, an honour to Christ, and glory to God, when HE finds us enveloped in the worthiness of His own Son. To be found *in Him* will be to find us blameless and complete (Rom. 8. 1).

IV. **That I Might Know the Power of His Resurrection** (v. 10). There is no doubt as to the *fact* of Christ's resurrection. He had seen Him, and had such exultant faith in Him, that he longed for the *power* that raised Jesus from the dead, that the risen life of Jesus might be manifested in his mortal flesh (2 Cor. 4. 10). If we have been crucified with Christ, then are we raised *together with Him*. The power of His resurrection is the power of His life-giving Spirit. The vitality of the Gospel has its source in *His* resurrection.

V. **That I may Know the Fellowship of His Suffer-ings** (v. 10). With the sufferings of Christ as our atoning *Substitute*, we can have no fellowship. He was alone, and will be for ever alone in that, but in suffering because of His holy, God-honouring devotion to His Father's will, He hath left us an example, that we should follow His steps; for "if any man will *live Godly* he must suffer" (2 Tim. 3. 12). We cannot know the fellowship of *His* sufferings unless we are possessed by the same Spirit and faithfully serving in the same cause. This fellowship demands a *consecrated life*, a life willing to be "made con-formable unto His death."

VI. **That I Might Attain unto the Resurrection from Among the Dead** (v. 11). At the coming of our Lord the *dead in Christ* shall rise first (1 Cor. 15. 20). This is called "the *first* resurrection." "Blessed and holy is he that hath part in the first resurrection, for they shall be priests of God and *of Christ*, and shall reign *with Him* a thousand years" (Rev. 20. 5, 6). Doubtless this is the truth the apostle refers to here in being raised *from among* the dead. (The rest of the dead lived not till the Millennial reign had closed.) He desired to attain a place of honour and service in the coming Kingdom of his Lord; and cer-tainly he will, for he "fought the fight and finished the course," he kept the faith and expected the crown (2 Tim. 4. 7). "Seek those things which are above."

VII. **That I may Apprehend that for which also I am Apprehended** (v. 12). It was Jesus Christ who suddenly apprehended him, while on a persecuting expedition (Acts 9). He still yearns to know and to carry out to completion the whole purpose of His Lord in saving him. Many there are who are satisfied just because they are saved from the penalty of sin. They have no concern as to *the work* the Lord has saved them to do. Saul was very practical and reasonable, for as soon as he was converted he said: "Lord, what *wilt Thou* have *me to do,*" and he made it his life's business to do that will. "To me to live is Christ" is the faithful Christian's motto.

VIII. **That I might Gain the Prize of the High Calling of God in Christ Jesus** (v. 14). The higher the calling the greater is the reward. To be *"called of God,"* and that *"in Christ Jesus,"* is the greatest honour Heaven can bestow upon a sinful man. What can the prize of this heavenly calling be? It must be perfectly consistent with the glory of the calling. That surely means a *perfected character*, not only in the world to come, but here and now, as the reward of true-hearted obedience (1 Peter 5. 10). "Let us therefore as many as be perfect, *be thus minded*" (v. 15). For they shall know who *follow on* to know the Lord (Hosea 6. 3).

THE BELIEVER'S POSITION, EXPECTATION, AND PREPARATION.

PHILIPPIANS 3. 20, 21; 4. 5, 6.

I. **Their Position.** Their "citizenship is in Heaven" (v. 20). They have been *born from above*, and have their home in the City of God So they have "no continuing city" here, but they look for that city whose "Builder and Maker is God" (Heb. 11. 10). They know that in their

Father's house there are many rooms, and that a place is prepared for them there (John 14. 1, 2). Knowing that they are citizens of a *better country*, they love not the world nor the things of this world, but are loyal to Him who rules in the "Heavenly Jerusalem."

II. **Their Expectation** The expectations of the *believer* are as great as the promises of God.

1. They expect that CHRIST WILL COME AGAIN. "They eagerly *look for* the Saviour, the Lord Jesus Christ" (v. 20). They believe that He will appear the *second time* without a sin-offering unto a perfected salvation (Heb. 9. 28). They are obedient to His Word in *waiting* for the Coming of the Lord Jesus Christ (1 Cor. 1. 7; 1 Thess. 1. 10). Happy are they who hold this "Blessed Hope."

2. They expect A TRANSFIGURED BODY. "Who shall change our mortal body, that it may be fashioned *like unto His glorious body*" (v. 21). The Lord Jesus showed His disciples a pattern of this new body, when on the mount He was transfigured before them (Luke 9. 29). So when Christ, who is our life, shall appear, then shall we appear with Him *in glory* (Col. 3. 4). We are sons of God now, but "it doth *not yet* appear what we shall be, but we know that when He shall appear we shall be *like Him*" (1 John 3. 2). For this corruptible body must be changed for the incorruptible (1 Cor. 15. 53). Then shall "death be swallowed up in victory." "Believe ye that I am able to do this?"

III. **Their Preparation.** The watchword of the early Christians seem to have been, "The Lord is at hand" (chap 4 5). In view of His appearing, they were exhorted to—

1. BE CAREFUL FOR NOTHING (v. 6). Let no harassing care trouble your mind with regard to the seemingly conflicting experiences of this life or the signs of the times.

He who is Coming again would have us to cast all our care
upon Him, because *He careth for us* (1 Peter 5. 7). He who
bore our sins is the same Lord who carries our sorrows.
Roll thy burden on the Lord, and He shall sustain thee
(Psa. 55. 22). "Be careful for nothing."

2. BE PRAYERFUL IN EVERY THING. "In *every thing*
by prayer let your requests be made known unto God"
(chap. 4. 6). Nothing that troubles us is too trifling to
bring to God. Those who have learned this holy practice
know what it is to "pray without ceasing." The blessedness of it is unspeakable. In these closing days of this age,
with the end of present conditions at hand, "Be ye therefore sober and *watch unto prayer*" (1 Peter 4. 7).

3. BE THANKFUL FOR ANYTHING. "In *every thing...
with thanksgiving*" (chap. 4. 6). For "all things work
together for good to them that *love* God." "This is the
will of God in Christ Jesus *concerning you*," that ye should
in every thing give thanks (1 Thess. 5. 18). It is easy to
thank God when we receive the things we desire and that
please us; but when disappointment comes, when our
plans are thwarted or friends betray us, it may be easy to
forget this: but it is *then* that we need the faith that God
doeth *all things well*, that we may still say, "Thanks be
to God."

THE POWER OF THE GLORIFIED CHRIST.
COLOSSIANS 1. 9-14.

IN this prayer the apostle shows his great faith in the all-
sufficiency of his Lord, when he pleaded for the "brethren
in Christ," that they might be blessed *"according to* his
glorious power," or rather, His power in glory. Let us
remember that we have the same Lord who is rich unto all
that call upon Him.

I. What the Lord has Done for Us.

1. He has REDEEMED US. "We have redemption through His Blood" (v. 14). He "gave *Himself* for us that He might redeem us" (Titus 2. 14). Our redemption *price* is *incorruptible* (1 Peter 1. 18), and so possesses eternal value.

2. He has FORGIVEN US. "Even the forgiveness of sins" (v. 14). Yes, God, for *Christ's sake,* hath done this (Eph. 4. 32), and, for *His sake,* He is ready and willing to do for them all that His forgiven ones really need.

3. He has RESCUED US. "Delivered us from the power of darkness" (v. 13). Rescued from the grip of sin, from the fear of death, the terrors of darkness, and the dominion and delusions of the Devil.

4. He has SETTLED US. "Translated into the Kingdom of His dear Son" (v. 13). We who were strangers and foreigners have, by the grace of God, been taken and settled in a new kingdom, under a new King, and in entirely different conditions. "Passed from death into life."

II. **What the Lord is Able to Do for Us**. He is able—

1. To "FILL WITH THE KNOWLEDGE OF HIS WILL" (v. 9). With regard to God's character and purposes, there is no place for mere speculation. *His will* for us is clearly revealed in His Word, and the Holy Spirit is ready to teach, giving "wisdom and spiritual understanding." If any man lack wisdom, let him ask of God. who giveth liberally.

2. To make us "WALK WORTHY OF THE LORD" (v. 10). There are many references in the Word concerning the Christian's *"walk,"* that is the outward and visible expression of their every-day life before men should be *pleasing to God.* "Walk worthy of Him who hath called you" (1 Tim. 2. 12). Walk worthy of your vocation (Eph. 4. 1). Walk in newness of life (Rom. 6. 4). **Walk** as the wise (Eph. 5. 15). Enoch had this testimony that

he pleased God (Heb. 11. 5). To walk and not faint is a crowning blessing (Isa. 40. 31).

3. To make us "FRUITFUL IN EVERY GOOD WORK" (v. 10). What a victory this would mean to many a discouraged worker. This is possible, for it is God-honouring. "Herein is My Father glorified, that ye bear much fruit" (John 15. 8). A barren ministry is dishonouring to God, and is a betrayal of the worker's weakness. Where the Holy Spirit controls the "fruit of the Spirit" will be manifest (Gal. 5. 22, 23). The Holy Spirit is fruitful in all His work. Abide in Christ, and let His Word abide in you, and your fruit will remain (John 15. 16).

4. To "STRENGTHEN WITH ALL MIGHT." All the might of our glorified Lord awaits His needy, believing people. The *strength* referred to here is that they might be *"patient* and *longsuffering with joyfulness"* (v. 11). It needs strong faith to be patient and joyful in the midst of prolonged suffering. Many of God's saints in the past have "out of weakness been made strong" (Heb. 11. 34).

5. To make us MEET FOR THE INHERITANCE OF THE SAINTS IN LIGHT (v. 12). Paul did not believe that the saints were buried in the darkness of the grave, or lost in the abyss of "eternal oblivion." He knew that they had entered into the fuller *light* of the Presence of His glory, and had found their inheritance in the fellowship of their Redeemer. He longs to be a *partaker* with them of the "glory that is to follow." This is not the morbid desire of a faint heart, but the longing of a truly loving heart. "Absent from the body, present with the Lord."

THE PRE-EMINENCE OF CHRIST.
COLOSSIANS 1. 15-19.

JESUS CHRIST, as God's Beloved Son, and as the Redeemer of men, has been so honoured by the Father that *in all* things, in all spheres, in all times, and in all Eternity He should have the PRE-EMINENCE. He has the pre-eminence:

I. In Power "For by Him were all things created." All things in Heaven and on earth, visible and invisible (v. 16). It pleased God that "by" Him, *"through"* Him, *"in"* Him, and *"for"* Him, were all things brought into existence, and *without* Him was not anything made that was made (John 1. 3). By Him also He made the universe (Heb. 1. 2). Think of it. This is the *same Christ* by whom, through whom, in whom, and for whom, God is now seeking to save sinners for the glory of His Name.

II. In Birth. "He is the *Firstborn* of every creation" (v. 15). He could say: "I am the *First*: the Beginning and the End" (Rev. 21. 6). He is also the "Firstborn from among the dead" (v. 18). This has been called His "second birth." Christ the firstfruits, *afterwards* they that are Christ's at His Coming (1 Cor. 15. 23). The first-born usually becomes the *heir*. God hath "appointed Him heir of all things" (Heb. 1. 2). And now by His marvellous grace, we who believe in Him are made "heirs together with Him."

III. In Likeness. "He is the *image* of the invisible God" (v. 15). Angels are *holy*, many of His people in every age have been *Godly*, but Christ alone in His essential character was the *express image of His Person* (Heb. 1 3). He could say: "He that hath seen Me hath seen the Father" (John 14. 9); also: "I and My Father are One." If the Gospels were read in the light of this glory from the "face of Jesus," surely they would have a deeper meaning, a more humbling, yet more inspiring influence on our hearts and lives. Here we see grace pre-eminent

IV. In Authority. "By Him all things *are held to-gether*" (v. 17). The law of gravitation as an ordinance of God has a mighty balancing effect in holding material things *together*. But this law has no influence over heavenly things. The things invisible, the theories, dominions, principalities, and spiritual powers (v. 16). Christ upholdeth *all things* by the *Word of His power* (Heb. 1. 3). His wisdom and His will are in constant activity over all the works of His hands. His will is done in Heaven, and the time is coming when it will be done on earth. The *enmity* of man's *free will* is meanwhile a perennial obstacle. But all power has been given Him in Heaven and on earth, and He will yet *subdue all* unto Himself. The Lord shall *reign*.

V. In the Church. "He is *the Head* of the Body, the Church" (v. 18). Here His pre-eminence is generally acknowledged, but does He get His true place as such in the practical life? It is the *Head* of the body, and not the *hands*, that does the thinking and the planning. In *His Word* we have His mind, and will concerning us clearly revealed. The secret of the Church's authority and power lies in obedience to His Word, both in doctrine and in polity. What is displeasing to the Head must be dishonouring to the body. The head takes all the responsibilities of the body, therefore we should cast *all our care* on Him, both for men and resources. He supplies all the needs of His Body.

VI. In Riches. He is pre-eminently rich, "for it hath pleased the Father that *in Him should all fulness dwell*" (v. 19). This is a Divine act of grace, that God should *be pleased* that in Jesus Christ the world's *Redeemer*, *all fulness* should dwell, that all who are *in Him* by faith may be in touch with all the fulness of God. "He who was rich, for our sakes became poor: that we through His grace may become rich." "And of His fulness have all we received" (John 1. 16). All the blessing we have received has come *out of His fulness.* Our cup may be full, but the oceans of *His fulness* still remains (Eph. 1. 3). His *Name* shall be called "WONDERFUL" (Isa. 9. 6).

COMPLETE IN CHRIST.
COLOSSIANS 2. 9-15.

I. **Where this Completeness is Found.** "Ye are *complete in Him.*" In *Him* in whom *"dwelleth all the fulness of the Godhead* in human form" (v. 9). This fulness is *abiding* in Him for ever, that all His loved and loving ones may be filled up and eternally perfected. He is made of God unto us wisdom and righteousness, and sanctification, and deliverance (1 Cor. 1. 30). This is part of His fulness, which we have "all received with grace upon grace" (John 1. 16). In Christ we dwell in God's storehouse of infinite grace, and with Him who is "the *Head* of all principality and power." In Him there is *fulness* to satisfy and *power* to protect, to guide, and to keep, to strengthen, to deliver, and to make the life abundantly fruitful. "Ye are *complete* in Him."

II. **How this Completeness is Attained.** Simply by being *in* Christ. But what is implied by this experience? The statements which follow in verses 11-15 explain.

1. BY BEING FORGIVEN. "Having forgiven you all trespasses" (v. 13). Forgiveness is our first necessity, and God's forgiveness is complete. *All trespasses.* It is against God that we have sinned, and the reconciliation must begin by His act of grace in *not imputing* their trespasses unto them (2 Cor. 5. 19)

2. BY HAVING THE BOND THAT WAS WRITTEN AGAINST US CANCELLED. Blotting out the handwriting that was against us, and contrary to us, and took it out of the way,

nailing it to His Cross. The law was a bond against us, saying: "*Do this* and live, disobey this and die." But this bond as the condition of life, Christ hath for us blotted it out by *nailing it* to His Cross—making it a part of His Cross (v. 14). Now ye are not under the law, but in the kingdom of His grace. For He hath abolished in His flesh "even the law of commandments," and by His Cross He hath slain the enmity (Eph. 2. 15, 16).

3. BY BEING BURIED WITH HIM. "Buried with Him in baptism" (v. 12). This is no mere symbol or figure of speech, but a deep and real spiritual experience. Through faith we are baptised *into the death* of Jesus Christ (Rom. 6. 3). Now the "old man" is to be thrown off and left in the grave (1 Peter 3. 21). Paul refers to this when he says, "I am crucified with Christ." The Cross should be to us the death of the self life.

4. BY BEING RAISED WITH HIM. "Ye are risen with Him through God-given faith" (v. 12). Having been identified with His death, we have been *quickened together* with Him (v. 13) into the new resurrection life. Having been planted together in the *likeness* of His death, we shall be also in the *likeness* of His resurrection (Rom. 6. 5). The Christian life, then, is a life *hid with Christ* in God; a life whose birth is "from above;" a life that is the life eternal, for He hath *begotten us again* unto a living hope, by the resurrection of Jesus Christ (1 Peter 1. 3). Then what doth the Lord now require of us? Surely it is this: "Yield yourselves unto God as those that are *alive* from the dead" (Rom. 6. 13). The life we now live in the flesh has been given us through Jesus, then surrender it to Him in thankful service.

5. BY HAVING OUR ENEMIES CONQUERED BY HIM. "He hath spoiled principalities and powers, triumphing over them" (v. 15). All power is given unto Him, and

He is able, and hath made His faithful followers more than conquerors through His own unfailing and inseparable love (Rom. 8. 37-39). "All the hostile princes and rulers He shook off from Himself, and boldly displayed them *as His conquests*, when *by the Cross* He triumphed over them." In Christ. "Greater is *He* that is for us, than *all* that can be against us." "Ye are complete in Him." "Thanks be to God who *giveth us the victory*, through our Lord Jesus Christ."

THE HIDDEN LIFE.
COLOSSIANS 3. 1-4.

THE essence of Christianity is not a "creed," not a "system of doctrine," not a particular mode of worship, but a *life*, and that life *Christlike*. It is—

I. **A Life from the Dead.** "Ye *were* dead" (v. 3) "Dead in trespasses and sin." Dead to God, in that there was no faith in Him, no response to His love, no felt need of His mercy; as insensible to spiritual and heavenly things as the dead in their graves are to the things of earth.

II. **A Resurrected Life.** "Risen with Christ" (v. 1). The carnal man, as a corn of wheat, has fallen into the ground and died, and the new life, quickened by the Spirit of God, hath appeared (John 12. 24). "For that which thou sowest is not quickened *except it die.*" The dead leaves of the *old life* fall off in the springtime of the new. If we have been buried with Christ in His death, we are risen with Him in newness of life. This life in Christ is eternal, for He who is *our life* dieth no more. We have passed from death into "the life everlasting."

III. **A Life Supported by Heavenly Things.** "Seek those things which are above. Set your *affections* on things above, not on things on the earth" (vv. 1, 2). This

life which is *from above* can only be fed and nourished with
the things that belong to the heavenlies.   Material things
can never satisfy a quickened spirit.   They that are *after
the Spirit* must mind the things of the Spirit (Rom. 8. 5).
The spiritual life is often choked with the riches of this
world.   Seek ye first the things of God, and all other
things will be added (Matt. 6. 33); and by so doing ye
shall lay up for yourselves treasures in Heaven.   "If
any man love the world, the love of the Father is not in
him (1 John 2. 15).

IV. A Substitutional Life.   "Christ, *who is our life*"
(v. 4).   If His death was a substitute for us, so also is His
resurrection and life.   "I live, yet *not I, but Christ* liveth
in me."   "We are in Him that is true, even *in His Son*
Jesus Christ.   This is the true God and eternal life (1
John 5. 20).   Truly we "live, and move, and *have our
being in God.*"   He was judged for us on the Cross.   Now
we are justified *by His life* (Rom. 5. 10).   "Because *I live*,
saith the Lord, *ye shall live also*" (John 14. 19).

V. A Secure Life.   "Your life is *hid with Christ in
God*" (v. 3).   In grace God was in Christ reconciling
sinners unto Himself.   In glory, Christ is in God representing His ransomed people.   By faith, "Ye are in Christ
as the fruit of His victory, the special treasure which He
found in the field of the world (Matt. 13. 44).   "Hid with
Christ in God," ye are as safe as Christ Himself.   As Noah
was shut up in the ark by God, so has His Church as His
Body been shut up and sheltered in the ark of His anointed.
"I give unto them eternal life, they shall never perish,
neither shall any power be able to pluck them out of My
hand" (John 10. 28).

VI A Life Yet to be Manifested.   "When Christ who
is our life *shall appear, then* shall ye also *appear with Him
in glory*" (v. 4).   "It doth *not yet* appear what we shall be."

"Here we suffer grief and pain," because of the world's sins and sorrows, and because of our own weakness and shortcomings. But when He shall appear we shall be like Him, seeing Him as He is (1 John 3. 2). For "He shall change our mortal body, and fashion it like unto His glorious body" (Phil. 3. 21). "What we now suffer, count as nothing in comparison with the glory which is soon to be manifested in us" (Rom. 8. 18). Christ came and died that we might have life. He rose and ascended that we might have it in abundance (John 10. 10). "Fear not, little flock."

CHRISTIAN CHARACTER.
COLOSSIANS 3. 8-24.

THE believers at Colosse are here reminded that as Christians there are some things they must *put off* as inconsistent; some things they must *put on* as absolutely needful; some things *to do* as a proof of their faith; and *how* they should be done as an evidence of true-hearted devotion.

I. **Some Things to Put Off.** Put off—

1. "THE OLD MAN with his deeds" (v. 9). The old carnal mind which is corrupt, and which lives under the spell of deceitful lusts (Eph. 4. 22). Throw him off.

2. "ANGER, UNHOLY PASSION, ill-will, evil-speaking, personal abuse: put off all these" (v. 8). Why should Christians need to be told to put off things that are more like the Devil than their Redeemer? These are sins that do beset some (Heb. 12).

II. **Some Things to Put On.** Put on—

1. "THE NEW MAN, which is after the image of God" (v. 10). To put on the new man is to give the Lord Jesus Christ—the Second Man, the Lord from Heaven—His true

place in the life.   Act as if He is mantling you with His presence.

2. "TENDER-HEARTEDNESS, kindness, lowliness of mind, longsuffering" (v. 12).   Note that these are the features of the Divine image, as seen in the face of Jesus (This is the fruit of the Spirit).   "And above all, we are to put on love" (v. 14).   "God is love, and he that dwelleth in love dwelleth in God and God in him" (1 John 4. 12-16).   May the love of Christ constrain us to be more like Him.

III. Some Things to Let In.

1. THE PEACE OF GOD.   "Let the peace of God rule in your hearts" (v. 15).   What a blissful kingdom our hearts would be if the peace of God ruled therein (Rom. 14. 17).   "Thou wilt keep him in perfect peace whose mind is stayed on Thee" (Isa. 26. 3).   We can let this peace rule in our hearts by a trustful submission to the will of Him who is able to say, "Peace, be still."

2. THE WORD OF GOD.   "Let the Word of God dwell in you richly" (v. 16).   "That Word, which is quick and powerful, and a discerner of the thoughts and intents of the heart" (Heb. 4. 12).   "Search the Scriptures, for they are they which testify of Me."   It is Himself that our souls need if our character is to be enriched and our testimony made fruitful.

IV. Some Things to Let Out.   What we have by faith taken in, should in service be let out.   "Freely ye have received, freely give."   We are to—

1. SERVE LOYALLY.   "Whatsoever ye do in *word or deed*, do all in the *Name of the Lord Jesus*" (v. 17).   How different life would be if our ordinary duties were done for "Christ's sake.   "In His Name" would take the sting of shame out of many a lowly deed.   "One is your Master, even Christ."

2. SERVE HEARTILY.   "Whatsoever ye do, do it *heartily*

as unto the Lord" (v. 23), "not with eye-service, as men-pleasers." Heartless service must be a solemn mockery in His eyes. Formal lip-service is rank hypocrisy.

3. SERVE THANKFULLY. "Do all in the Name of the Lord Jesus, *giving thanks* to God the Father by Him" (v. 17). We should give thanks always for all things (Eph. 5. 20). The Lord hath done great things for us, and is still doing them on our behalf, therefore "His praise should be *continually* in our mouths" (Psa. 34. 1). In giving and in taking away, His Name is still to be blessed (Job 1. 21).

V. **Some Things for which we Look Up.** "Ye serve the Lord Christ, and from the Lord ye shall receive the reward of the inheritance" (v. 24). Every good thing done is to be rewarded (Eph. 6. 8). The inheritance as a harvest will be according to our works. He shall render to every man according to his deeds (Rom. 2. 6). But to *see* Him, and be made *like Him*, and to *dwell with Him*, this is the reward of grace alone.

THE MODEL CHURCH.
1 THESSALONIANS 1. 6-10.

THE beauty of this Church did not consist of a gorgeous material building, but of a people who are said to be "*In God* the Father and *in the Lord Jesus Christ*" (v. 1). And that they were *ensamples* to all believers (v. 7). Note their character.

I. They were **Saved from Wrath.** "They were delivered from the wrath to come" (v 10) It should never be forgotten that there is "wrath to come" (Rev. 6. 17) Wrath against all ungodliness. Blessed are they whom "God hath appointed to obtain salvation by our Lord Jesus Christ" (1 Thess. 5 9). Christ our Refuge. "Flee from the wrath to come."

II. They were **Converted to God**. "They *turned to God* from idols" (v. 9). Christ is the propitiation for the sin of the world, but that fact in itself does not save the world; there must needs be a personal *turning to God* from sin and unbelief. The idols of the unconverted are numerous and varied. To *turn to God* is to forsake everything that would divide our affections or hinder our whole-hearted trust.

III. They were **Receivers of the Word of God**. 'They received the Word in much affliction" (v. 6) These were troublous times, as we learn from Acts 17; but the antagonism of the worldly-minded did not hinder them from boldly receiving the Word. It is always a sign of a healthy soul or Church, which gladly drinks in the truth as revealed in God's Word Human philosophies may have their place, but they are the food to build up a model Church. Quickened spirits need the "Word of Life. "

IV. They were **Devoted to the Service of God**. "They turned from idols to *serve the living and true God*" (v. 9). What a change! Serving the *Living God*, instead of dead things that only mocked their needs with a silent indifference. "To whom, O Lord, can we go but unto Thee?" Thou art worthy of the service of every power and passion, every thought and feeling of the soul, which Thou hast redeemed by Thy Blood. "Serve the Lord with gladness. "

V. They were **Looking for the Son of God**. They had made up their minds to *serve*, and "*to wait for His Son from Heaven*" (v. 10). They believed Christ would come again, as all the early Christians did, and as He Himself had promised This was called "*that blessed hope*" (Titus 2. 13). The prophets of old looked and waited for the Coming of the Messiah long ages before He came; but in the fulness of the time He did come. The Church may have waited long, so long that many have lost the vision and the hope. But in the fulness of the time *He will Come* as He said (see John 14. 3; Acts 1. 11; 1 Thess. 4. 16 Rev. 1. 7).

VI. They were **Joyful in the Spirit of God**. They had the "joy of the Holy Ghost" (v. 6). With the Word of God in their hearts, and this glorious prospect before their eyes, and the power of the Spirit resting on them, their service was not a burdensome task, but a happy privilege and a growing delight. This was characteristic of the first Church members. "They were filled with joy, and with the Holy Ghost" (Acts 13. 52). "How are the mighty fallen?"

VII. They were **Examples to Others**. "Ye were ensamples to all that believe" (v. 7). This was certainly a prosperous Church, although there is nothing said regarding their financial position, no reference to their "Annual Balance Sheet." But their *faith in God* was known everywhere (v. 8), and the *influence* of their missionary enthusiasm, in sounding forth the Word of God, had been felt throughout Macedonia and Greece. They honoured Christ as the Head of the Church, and they were honoured by Him in doing things worthy of His great Name. This is what the Church of Christ should do. This is what every Church true to the Word of God is; and this is what every Christian should be—an encouraging example to others. "Believe, and thou shalt see."

COMFORTING WORDS.

1 THESSALONIANS 4. 13-18.

THERE is much food for thought in these verses, closing with this exhortation: "*Wherefore*, comfort one another with these words" (v 18). There is comfort here concerning—

I. The Second Advent. "The Lord *Himself* shall descend from Heaven" (v. 16) The Lord does not promise to send death, or any other messenger, to take His Bride home. He is coming *Himself* for her. It is "this *same Jesus* which was taken up into Heaven, that is coming in *like manner* as He was seen to go" (Acts 1. 11); and "they shall see the Son of Man coming in the clouds of Heaven with power and great glory" (Matt. 24. 30). What a comforting hope this is in these "perilous times."

II. Our Departed Friends. We are not to be in ignorance about them, nor to be in sorrow for them, for we believe that Jesus rose again, and that when He comes He will bring them *with Him* (vv. 13, 14), for in spirit they are with Him now (2 Cor. 5. 8) It is the "dead in Christ" who will *rise first* (v. 16). This rising means the putting on of the incorruptible body, being changed into His resurrection image. They shall lose nothing by being put to sleep before the Coming of the Lord (1 Cor. 15. 52). For we who are alive at the Coming of the Lord shall have no precedence over those who have gone to sleep (v. 15). Comforting words indeed.

III. The Living Saints. "Then we which are alive and remain shall be caught up *together with them* to meet the Lord in the air" (v 17). We are assured, as God's people, that all shall not die before He Comes. "We shall not all sleep (die), but we shall all be *changed in a moment,* in the twinkling of an eye, at the sound of His last trump" (1 Cor. 1 51, 52). When all in every age who have been put to sleep in Jesus have been raised and clothed with immortality, and when all the believers who are alive on the earth, when He comes, are changed in a moment and caught up *together with them* What a host of ransomed souls. "A multitude whom no man can number " Tell me, will any man say on that day that the Church of God has been a failure? "He shall see of the travail of His soul, and shall be SATISFIED." "Comfort one another with these words" (v. 18).

IV. **The Place of Reunion.** "Caught up in the clouds, to *meet the Lord in the air*" (v. 17). The *air* is spoken of as the sphere of Satan's stronghold. He is called "the prince of the *power of the air*, the spirits that are now at work in the hearts of the sons of disobedience" (Eph. 2. 2). Does it mean that the transfiguration and *reunion* of all Christ's redeemed ones will take place right in the heart of Satan's territory? What a triumph this would be for "The Lamb that was slain," and for all those who all their lives were warring against the prince of darkness? And what a shameful defeat for the Devil. "I saw Satan fall like lightning from Heaven" (Luke 10. 18).

V. **Our Final Position.** "And so shall we *ever be with the Lord*" (v. 17). Saved by Him. Made like Him. Then for ever with Him. He has gone to *prepare a place* for His Church in the coming Kingdom. He will come again and receive it unto Himself, that where He is, there shall the Bride be also (John 14. 3). Then the Bridegroom's prayer will be gloriously answered. "Father, I will that *they also* whom Thou hast given Me be *with Me* where I am; that They may *behold* My glory" (John 17. 24); and be *"for ever* with the Lord." Earth's greatest blessing is to *find* Him. Heaven's greatest honour is to be for *ever with Him*. This honour have all the saints. "Comfort one another with these words."

THREE FACTS OF UNIVERSAL IMPORTANCE.
2 THESSALONIANS 1. 6-12.

HERE are events that are sure to come, and will affect all mankind.

I. A New Revelation. "The Lord Jesus shall be
revealed from Heaven *with His angels of might* in flaming
fire" (v. 7). The same Lord Jesus who was forsaken by
His disciples in the time of His greatest sorrow. In the
day of *His humiliation* He could have called "legions of
angels" to His assistance, but now the angels of *His might*
came with His *burning Presence,* to accomplish His long-
delayed purpose of gathering out of His kingdom *all things*
that offend and them that do iniquity (Matt. 13. 40-42).
"The reapers are the angels" (Matt. 13. 39), who are
waiting now till the "harvest of the earth is ripe" (Rev.
14. 15). The Lord has been during this age revealing
Himself as the meek and lowly and merciful Christ; but
He will yet reveal Himself as a "flaming fire" against all
ungodliness. Who shall be able to stand when He so
appeareth?

II. An Unfailing Retribution. "Taking vengeance
on them that *know not God,* and that *obey not the Gospel*
of our Lord Jesus Christ" (v. 8) The day of grace has
now passed; there remaineth no more sacrifice for sin, but
a *certain* fearful looking for of judgment and *fiery indignation,* which shall devour the adversaries (Heb. 10. 27).
The culprits are those who *know not God,* because they have
not obeyed the good news of Jesus Christ. To obey the call
of the Gospel of Christ is the way to *know God,* whom to
know is eternal life. There may be some excuse for
ignorance, but there is no excuse for *neglect.* "How shall
we escape if we neglect so great salvation?" *What is the
punishment?* Everlasting destruction *from the Presence*
of the Lord and the *glory of His power.* Not annihilation,
but eternal *banishment* from the *Presence* of the Lord and
the *glory* of His power. "In His presence there is *fulness*
of joy. At His right hand there are *pleasures for evermore*"
(Psa. 16. 11). Then what will it mean for those who are
eternally exiled from the Kingdom of God and the pleasures

that are ever flowing from His beneficent Presence? Call this state or condition by whatever name you may. There is an awful atmosphere about it. "Escape for thy life."

III. **A Christ-Honouring Reward.** "He shall come to be glorified *in His saints*, and admired *in all them that believe*" (v. 10). *He* shall be glorified in glorifying His saints with His own glorious likeness. He shall be "admired" in the work of grace bestowed upon all them that believe. While the reward will be ours, the glory will be His. "Not unto us, O Lord, but unto Thy Name be the glory." "All principalities and powers in heavenly places shall be made to know by the Church, the manifold wisdom of God" (Eph. 3. 10). *We* shall be satisfied when we shall see Him as He is; and *He* shall be satisfied when He shall see us as we shall then be. The *Church* will be His joy and crown of rejoicing at His Coming (1 Thess. 2. 19, 20), and something to be wondered at through all the coming ages. Its presence with the Christ of God in the glory will mean: "Blessing and glory, and wisdom and thanksgiving, and honour, and power, and might, unto our God for ever and ever" (Rev. 7. 12).

> "Thou shalt see my glory soon,
> When the *Work of Grace* is done."

THE "MAN OF SIN."
2 THESSALONIANS 2: 1-12.

IN the above verses we have a prophetic picture drawn by the inspired apostle, which demands serious attention in these days. and which is also a powerful indictment against the popular doctrine that the "world will be converted" *before* the Coming of the Lord. Paul bases his appeal (vv. 1, 2) on the fact that the Lord Jesus Christ is Coming, and that His people will be gathered together

unto Him on that day. Then gives the warning against
being "shaken in mind" or "troubled" because of false
teaching concerning His Coming. But *His appearing* is
certain; so also is the appearing of that "Man of Sin" (v. 3).

I.—**The Time of His Appearing.** Two conditions
precede "The Day of Christ." First, there will be a
"falling away" from the faith, then the revelation of that
"Man of Sin." This *falling away* must mean the apostasy
of the Church in the denial of those truths once believed or
consented to. No one can fall away from where they have
never been. The *Spirit speaketh expressly*, that in the latter
times *some* will depart from the faith, giving heed to
seducing spirits, etc. (1 Tim. 4. 1-3). "The mystery of
iniquity," or, rather, *lawlessness*, is always in evidence
(v. 7). This is the spirit of Antichrist, which even now
already is in the world (1 John 4. 3), and in these days
abundantly manifest in midst of much preaching and
Bible distribution. *Lawlessness*, which is the practical
denial of Divine and Spiritual authority, is a congenial
moral condition for the appearing and work of this "Man
of Sin." The fulness of the time for his manifestation
may be near (2 Peter 2. 1, 2).

II. **His Character.** He is called "the son of perdition"
(v. 3). As Jesus, the Son of God, was the embodiment of
the Divine character, so the "son of perdition" seems to be
the human embodiment of the satanic character, for "His
coming will be after the working of Satan" (v. 9). He is
also called "that wicked one," whom the Lord will consume with the "brightness of His Coming" (v. 8). Does
this imply that sin and lawlessness will yet find its cul-
mination in a *person*, a man of the world, energised by
satanic power, believed in, and followed by a restless,
sceptical, and Christ-defiant populace, making their last
united attempt to overthrow the faith that was "once for
all delivered unto the saints?"

III. **His Purpose.** Is to oppose everything that belongs to God, and *His Christ* and to *exalt himself* above all that is called God, or that is worshipped (v. 4). Thus showing himself to be *"the Antichrist "* "Exalting himself," this was the sin of Satan at the beginning, but by becoming incarnate in the "Man of Sin," will surely be his last device to seduce a gullible humanity. He has always been the *"Deceiver* of the whole world." If Satan hopes to succeed by this blasphemous pretention of being himself above "all that is called godly," it certainly reveals something of the terrible depths into which humanity has fallen by this departure from the truth. Beware of self-seeking and self-exaltation, it savours of the "Man of Sin." "He that exalteth himself shall be abased." "Not I, but Christ." is the only absolutely safe attitude.

IV. **His Methods.** They are varied and mighty. "With *all power* and *signs,*" and *"lying wonders,"* with all *"deceivableness of unrighteousness"* (vv. 9, 10). That is, with every wicked device *agreeable* to those who are on their way to perdition. This "Man of Sin" looks like the beast that is to *come out* of the earth with the power (horns) of a *lamb,* and the passion and purpose of a *dragon*; and who is able to make fire come down from heaven in the *sight of men* (Rev. 13. 11-13). We have often thought of the *"wiles* of the devil" in relation to our individual life, but here is a *"Man* of Sin," the offspring of perdition (v. 3), endued with the power of Satan, worshipped as God, and leading to the eternal abyss the multitudes of those who *"have not received* the love of the truth that they might be saved" (v. 10). The wonders of the truth were rejected for "lying wonders."

V. **His Hinderer.** There is *One* who is a Hinderer to his diabolical mission. "He that hindereth will hinder, until *He be taken out* of the way" (v. 7).

1. Who is He? This hinderer is not a system, or party, but a Person. He must be mighty and Divine to resist such powerful and delusive work. Who can He be but the Holy Spirit of God, who is still striving with men, and leading many to Jesus Christ.

2. How Does He Hinder? By *opening* the blinded eyes of sinners to see their *need* of a Saviour. By *revealing* to them the things that are Christ's for their salvation. By *guiding* them into *the truth* which satisfies and fortifies against the "wiles of the Devil."

3. When Shall He be "Taken Out of the Way?" Surely when the Church of God is *taken away* from the world, as in 1 Thessalonians 4. 17. The Church, as the Redeemed Body of Christ, is presently the "temple of the Holy Ghost." When He is *taken away* with the Church, then shall He cease to "strive with men." Then who shall hinder Satan in his work of deception and spiritual destruction? "If the salt lose its savour, wherewith shall it be salted?"

VI. **His Temporary Ally.** For once we see God adding His influence to crown Satan's efforts with success. What an awful crisis this is. The people have *rejected His truth* that was given to save them (v. 10). "For *this cause* He sent them strong delusion, that they should *believe a lie*" (v. 11), because they would not believe the truth (v. 12). Thus making their condemnation doubly sure. Brethren, what shall we say to these things? God is not to be mocked. When Israel would not hearken to His voice He gave them up to their own hearts' lusts (Psa. 81. 11, 12). In the reign of the coming "Man of Sin," when men's spiritual indifference has turned into God-defiance, and God's longsuffering mercy turned into loathing and vengeance, then what shall the end be? (1 Thess 1. 8)

VII. **His Destruction.** The Lawless One, "whom the

Lord will *sweep away* with the tempest of His anger, and *utterly overwhelm* by the *awful splendour of His Coming*" (v. 8). Those who have been dazzled and bewitched, and awe-stricken by the lying wonders of this Satanic "man," will be smitten with terrible confusion before the "BRIGHTNESS of His Coming." "They shall see the *Son of Man* coming in the clouds of Heaven, with power and GREAT GLORY" (Matt. 24. 30). The glory of that "Man of Sin" will be discovered as a delusive will-o-the-wisp in the *Presence* of the glorious effulgence of the Man Christ Jesus. But there will be those at His Coming who shall say: "Lo, this is *our God*. We have waited for Him. He will *save us*, and we will rejoice in *His salvation*" (Isa. 25. 9). "Even so, come, Lord Jesus."

A PERFECT PATTERN.
1 TIMOTHY 1. 11-17.

HERE the apostle speaks of *himself* as a pattern to believers (v. 16). A pattern may be given as a specimen of workmanship for exhibition, or as an example for imitation. Paul's experience was both an exhibition of Divine grace and an example to all them "which should hereafter believe." We shall look at him as a pattern or specimen of—

I. **Sin's Delusiveness.** He was "a blasphemer, a persecutor, and injurious" (v. 13). Here is a man so self-deceived that he thought he was doing God service by making havoc of the Church (Acts 26. 9-11). History has furnished us with many examples of the same kind of madness, through the pride and prejudice of unbelieving hearts and sin-blinded minds. But what a disillusion came when this "Jesus of Nazareth" whom he was persecuting, met him and smote him to the earth with the brightness of His Presence, and when he, "trembling and astonished," said, "Lord, *what wilt Thou* have me to do?" (Acts 9. 1-6). Every saved sinner has in some measure made the same discovery.

II. **Abundant Grace.** "I obtained mercy: the *grace of our Lord* was exceeding abundant" (vv. 13, 14). The might and the abounding sufficiency of the grace of Christ to subdue and to save a sinner surely was never more manifest. Here is a pattern of what the "grace of our Lord" can do. "Where sin abounded, grace did *much more* abound" (Rom. 5. 20). He was thankfully speaking the truth when he said: "By the *grace of God* I am what I am" (1 Cor. 15. 10). If the "chief of sinners" was saved by grace, none need despair. "By *grace* are ye saved through faith." But remember that it is the *grace* of GOD.

III. **Believers' Responsibility.** "The Gospel of the glory of the blessed God was *committed unto me*" (v. 14). If we have been made partakers of this same salvation, are we not also partakers in some measure of this responsibility? The *good news* has been given to save us, and also as a *deposit* that we might be a blessing to others. If God, "who commanded the light to shine out of darkness, hath shined in our hearts, giving us the *light of the knowledge* of the glory of God in the face of Jesus Christ," then He has also commanded that we let *our light shine.* "Ye are as *lights* in the world" (2 Cor. 4. 6). "Go ye, therefore, preach the Gospel by lip and life."

IV. **Christian Testimony.** As a brief and perfect pattern of personal testimony, there can be nothing on record more effective than 1 Timothy 1. 15. "This is a faithful saying, and worthy of the acceptation of all, that Christ Jesus came into the world to save sinners, of whom I am chief." This saying is as *faithful* as God Himself is, and the blessing offered meets the most urgent need of humanity "to *save sinners.*" No statement more worthily deserves the acceptation of all. Jesus Christ *came into* the world to save. Where did He come from? What an incidental proof of His pre-existence. Through Him God the Father is *commending His love* to a rebellious race (Rom. 5. 8). Do your friends know what great things God hath done for your soul? (Mark 5. 19). The Psalmist said: "Come and hear, all ye that fear God, and I will declare what He hath done for my soul" (Psa. 66. 16). "Let him that heareth *say, Come.*"

V. Praise and Thanksgiving. What a beautiful pattern this is. "Now to the immortal and invisible KING of *all the ages,* who alone is God, be honour and glory to the ages of the ages. Amen" (v. 17). Often the language of mortals cannot express the deep things the heart may feel; but God judgeth *the heart,* and takes account of every thankful recognition of His mercies. Praise and thanksgiving, adoration and worship, are most fitting when the Majesty of God's goodness becomes overwhelming. "Oh that men would praise the Lord for His goodness" (Psa. 107. 15). In counting your many blessings, do not fail to add your benediction.

INTERCESSORS NEEDED.

1 TIMOTHY 2. 1-6.

IN Isaiah 59. 16 we read that the Lord "wondered that there was no intercessor." He wondered at the folly and unbelief of His people, in neglecting this most effective means of blessing. This is a privilege within the reach of every child of God, a sphere of service open to every believer to make *intercession.*

I. Its Importance. "I exhort, therefore, that *first of all* supplications, prayers, intercessions be made" (v. 1). Here this holy exercise gets the *first* place in his exhortations. It is possible that an intercessor's reward may be greater than a preacher's. Samuel knew how this honoured the Lord when he declared: "As for me, God forbid that I should sin *against Jehovah* by *ceasing to pray for you*" (1 Sam. 12. 23). Prayerlessness is n'ot only a sin against our own souls, but our fellowmen, and against God.

II. **Its Scope**. "For *all men* and for *all in authority*" (vv. 1, 2). If ye know not *what to pray for* as ye ought, here at least is a wide field for its operation. Those of the Captivity were exhorted to "seek the peace of the city wherever they were, and to *pray unto the Lord for it*" (Jer. 29. 7). Our modern cities are in desperate need of intercessors, and perhaps our modern Churches not less. In praying for "all men," don't forget *the all* in your own home, all in your fellowship, city, and nation. Remember the great ALL for whom Christ died.

III. **Its Incentives**. As an encouragement for intercession, think of—

1. THE WILL OF GOD. "Who *will have all men* to be saved, and to come unto the knowledge of the truth" (v. 4). By His own *power* God could save all men whether they will or not. But *in grace* He is willing to save all that *come* unto the knowledge of the truth. In praying for "all men" we are in line with the Divine will, and helping the fulfilment of His purpose.

2. THE RANSOM PRICE. "Christ gave *Himself* a ransom *for all*" (v. 6). There is ample provision in the death of Christ, and in the will of the Father for the salvation of all men. "Behold the *Lamb of God* which taketh away the sin of the world" (John 1. 29).

3. THE MEDIATOR. "There is one Mediator between *God and men*, the *Man* Chirst Jesus" (v. 5). What an incentive to prayer this is, when we realise that the Eternal

Son of God in the likeness *of men* is our Mediator before the throne, and He ever liveth to make intercession. Ponder also——

IV. **The Examples** set before us. Abraham interceded for the doomed city of Sodom (Gen. 18. 24), Moses on the hill top with uplifted hands silently pleading for victory (Exod. 17), Elijah praying for a Divine manifestation that the nation might be rescued from idolatry (1 Kings 18. 37), Job in midst of his sorrow and sufferings making intercession for his mistaken friends (Job 42. 10). Think also of "the Man of Sorrows," who was wounded and bruised for our iniquities, yet *He made intercession for the transgressors* (Isa. 53. 12), and His last prayer on earth was for His murderers. "Father, forgive them." Well may we pray. "Lord, *teach us* to pray." The need for intercessors is a great and *growing need*, for the harvest *is plenteous*, but the divinely equipped labourers are few. *Pray ye therefore* (Matt. 9. 37, 38).

THE FOUNDATION, THE HOUSE, AND ITS VESSELS.
2 Timothy 2. 19-21.

Timothy is being warned against a cankerous error that had overthrown the faith of some; but no amount of error can alter the "foundation of God."

I. **The Foundation.** It is "the foundation *of God*" (v. 19).

1. It is Sure. "It standeth sure." This Rock, as a foundation for God's building, is as firmly established as His own Eternal Throne, for that Rock is Christ (Matt. 16. 16), and He liveth and abideth for ever (1 Cor. 3. 11).

2. It is Unmistakable. Having this inscription: "The Lord knoweth them that are His." Every individual

soul that is trusting in Christ is known *personally* by Him. This is not true of any other religion under Heaven. Multitudes bow to dead prophets and false gods, but the worshippers are individually unknown by the objects of their adoration. "I *know My sheep*" (John 10. 14).

II. **The House,** "In a *great house* there are different vessels" (v. 20). This "great house" doubtless refers to the "Church of God" (1 Tim. 3. 15). Which is the *biggest* and most *self-evident* concern in the world, because it is the *strongest*, built on Jesus Christ, who is the embodiment of Eternal Truth. It is great, because it is occupied by a great tenant, the Holy Spirit, who is through Christ's Body, the Church, seeking to fulfil the great purpose of God in the salvation of men. It is a great house, has been abuilding for over 1900 years, and is still being "added to "

III. **The Vessels.** In every great house there are vessels of different value and design, suited for all useful purposes. "Some gold and silver, some wood and earthenware" (v. 20). Some to honour and some for common use. Those of gold and silver get the position of honour, because of their more *perfect character* and special fitness for the higher and more conspicuous service. Those servants who may be classed with the "wood and earthenware" types may be just as *useful* in their own sphere as their more honoured brethren. The gold and silver vessels are not looked for in the lowly but indispensable work of the kitchen. God's servants have all their own place in the great house of God. Some prophets, some apostles, some pastors, some teachers, some evangelists, and some who may be the "wood and earthenware," who are taken no special notice of, but who are waiting and ready to be used for *anything* that the Master appoints. These vessels, though different in character, *all* belong to the same great

house, and owned by the same Master, and are all needed
for the one purpose, the fulfilling of their Lord's will.
All have not the same gifts and qualifications, but all are
partakers of the same grace. There is no occasion for envy
or jealousy. Each one might say: "By the grace of God
I am what I am."

But the alchemy of Divine grace is suggested here. It is
possible for a common vessel to be transformed into a
vessel of honour. "If a man purge himself from all that is
false and unclean, he shall be made a vessel unto honour,
sanctified and made meet for the Master's use, *fully
equipped* unto *every good work*" (v. 21). "Behold, as the
clay is in the hand of the potter, so are ye in Mine" (Jer.
18. 6). "We are His workmanship, created in Christ
Jesus unto good works" (Eph. 2. 10). "Lord, what wilt
Thou have me to do?"

A DYING CHRISTIAN'S TESTIMONY.
2 TIMOTHY 4. 6-8.

THIS joyful testimony was written by Paul the prisoner,
while lying in a dungeon at Rome, waiting the hour of
his doom. It speaks of—

I. A Victorious Past.

1. As a SOLDIER. He had "Fought a good fight" (v. 7).
He had gone through a glorious contest. He had fought
"the good *fight of faith*" against all the principalities and
powers of evil, seen and unseen. It was a *good* fight,
because it was for the *goodness* he had discovered in his
God and Saviour.

2. As a RACER. He had "finished his course." His
course was specially marked out for him (Acts 9. 15, 16).
The track Divinely ordained for this runner had many
obstacles, which proved hard for flesh and blood. "The
Holy Ghost witnesseth in every city saying that bonds

and afflictions abide me" (Acts 20. 23). It is ours "to run *in the way* of His commandments;" it is His to help us to finish.

3. As a BELIEVER. He had "kept the faith." He had guarded the truth revealed to him, and preached and presented the Gospel of God's grace as revealed in Jesus Christ. If any man "preach any other Gospel let him be accursed" (Gal. 1. 8).

II. A Peaceful Present. "I am *now ready*, and the time of my departure is at hand" (v. 6). He was ready, like *ripe* fruit, to fall into the hand of Him to whom he belonged. Death to him had no sting or terrors; to him the grave had no victory. To *depart* was to be "*with Christ*, which is far better" (Phil. 1. 23). "Be ye also ready." Our readiness does not consist in the amount of good works we may have done, or the number of years we have lived, but in that "quietness and confidence" in Jesus Christ which brings the strength of His prevailing peace into the heart, and that calmly whispers: "Father, not my will, but Thine be done. Thou hast redeemed me, O Lord. Into Thy hands I commit my spirit." A Scotsman lay dying in a country home, while a snow storm was on. His daughter said: "Father, will I read to you." He answered: "Na, my lassie, don't trouble. I thatched my house in calm weather."

III. A Blissful Future. "Henceforth there is *laid up for me* a crown of righteousness, which the Lord will give me" (v. 8). The *crown* of righteousness is the reward that is kept for and bestowed upon those who have lived the righteous, God-pleasing life. It is not only for an apostle, but for "all them that *love* His appearing." Does not this imply that *loving* His appearing has a gracious and inspiring influence on the life? This faith in, and this *looking for*, the Coming of the Lord is no vain and fruitless imagination, but an holy incentive to a righteous life. "He that hath this hope in him purifieth himself. " "When the Chief Shepherd shall appear, ye shall receive a crown of glory that fadeth not away" (1 Peter 5. 4). The Second Coming of Christ is the enlightened believer's perennial expectation and the world's only hope of deliverance (Rom. 11. 26).

"Behold I come quickly: and *My reward is with Me,* to give every man according as his work shall be" (Rev. 22. 12).

SEVEN WONDERS.
Titus 2. 11-14.

THE novelty hunters are very numerous; like the Athenians they are always grasping for something new. But the greatest wonder in the world is the Bible. Its origin, teaching, and power are all superhuman.

I. A Wonderful Exhibition. "The grace of God that bringeth salvation to all men hath appeared. " This is an exhibition of the grace of God. This means all the attributes of God, flowing out in order to save men. An exposition of the goodness of God. This is seen at the Cross of Calvary, in the Son of God's love, bleeding and dying for guilty men. The great "World's Fair" was only a heap of rubbish compared with this.

II. A Wonderful Character. Jesus is here called "The Great God and our Saviour. " You may say Jesus Christ was only a man. Paul declares that He was the Great God. "His Name shall be called Wonderful—the Mighty God. " What consolation is here for the Christian! Your Saviour is the Great God—fear not. What encouragement is here for the anxious! The great God is a Saviour—fear not to trust Him. What consternation is here for the self-righteous. You hope to save yourself, how fruitless your effort. It takes the Great God to save a soul.

III. A Wonderful Gift. "He gave *Himself* for us."
For a man to lay down his life for his friend is wonderful.
This is man at his best. But while we were yet enemies,
Christ died for us. This is Divine. This is the only
example the history of the world has ever given us of one
willingly dying for his own murderers. He gave Himself
for you. What hast thou given for Him? Oh, you say,
"I have no time." What, no time to thank thy God for
such a Gift.

> Room and time now give to Jesus,
> Soon will pass God's day of Grace;
> Soon thy heart be cold and silent,
> And thy Saviour's pleadings cease.

IV. A Wonderful Work. The work of Christ as here
stated was to redeem and to purify, to purchase and to
cleanse. When a woman buys a set of china, she does not
think them fit for use until they are washed. They are
bought, then washed. The Lord uses us, not because we
are great and gifted; not because we are clever, but because
we are clean. It is not enough that we be redeemed. If
God is to be glorified in us we must be cleansed.

V. A Wonderful People. The redeemed and the
purified are to be "a *peculiar* people." Some Christians
are afraid of being peculiar, lest they should be talked
about. They wish to mar the very works by which they
ought to be known. Christians are a peculiar people.
They have a peculiar citizenship. Their citizenship is in
Heaven, because they have been born from above. Such
a birth is not a thing to be ashamed of. They speak a
peculiar language. The ungodly don't care about their
conversation any more than for one speaking in a foreign
tongue.

VI. A Wonderful Life. The life of the redeemed man
is to be a *resisting* life. "A denying of ungodliness." It
is to be a *sober life*, not only a teetotal life. This is

implied, but much more. Be sober in your eating, in your clothing, in your speech. It is to be a *righteous* life. The Christian should be the most punctual business man, the most trustworthy of all men. It is to be a *godly* life. A life beaming with the gentleness and truthfulness of Jesus, reflecting back on a dark world the image of the invisible God. It is to be an *active* life, "zealous of good works. "

VII. **A Wonderful Prospect.** "Looking for His glorious appearing. " That the sun will rise to-morrow is not more certain than that Christ will come again. It may seem strange that He should say, "Behold, I come quickly, " nineteen hundred years ago, and not to have come yet. But we must remember that 1000 years are with the Lord as but one day, so that two days have not yet passed according to His reckoning. He will come. Are you ready for His appearing? God grant that you may be prepared for that great day.

FULL SALVATION.
Titus 3. 3-7.

It is easy to say that there is fulness of water in the ocean, fulness of wealth in the earth, and fulness of light in the sun; but can the *richness* of this fulness be reckoned up? So there is fulness of salvation in the grace of God, but that *fulness* can only be realised in the ages of the ages. In the above Scripture we see what might be termed seven steps into a full salvation.

I. **An Honest Confession.** "We ourselves also were sometimes foolish, disobedient, deceived, and slaves of sin" (v. 3). Confession is the opening of the windows of the heart to the light of Heaven: an acknowledgment before God of our guilt and need of His mercy. God is faithful and just to forgive every sincere confessor (1 John 1. 9).

II. **A Divine Revelation.** Of the "kindness and love
of God our Saviour toward men" (v. 4). God's *kindness
and love*, as revealed in Christ Jesus, is the greatest and
most precious discovery any sinful man ever made. To
him it is a fountain opened, where streams of mercy flow
for all his sin and uncleanness. When seen and trusted,
constraining him to make this other confession: "Herein
is love, not that we loved God, but that He loved us, and
sent His Son to be the propitiation for our sins" (1 John
4. 9, 10).

III. **A Complete Justification.** "Being justified
by His grace" (v. 7). As we have sinned *against God*, God
alone can justify. This He does by His own free, unmerited favour, through Jesus Christ. "It is not by
works, lest any man should boast" (Gal. 2. 16). When
God justifies the believer in Jesus it is an evidence that
his forgiveness has been full and complete.

IV. **An Entire Regeneration.** "He saved us by the
washing of regeneration" (v. 5). Suppose it were possible
to be justified from all sin, and yet not be changed in
heart, or made a new creature How soon this justified one
would·be like the sow that was washed returning again to
the mire. "Whom God justified, them He also glorified"
(Rom. 8. 30). Justification sets us right with God for
further blessing. Regeneration makes us like God in
character for holy service. It would not be a *full* salvation
without being "born from above. "

V. **A Daily Renovation.** To meet this need there is
"the *renewing of the Holy Ghost* which He shed on us
abundantly" (vv. 5, 6). This is the Divine remedy for
spiritual staleness. "Be *renewed* in the spirit of your
mind" (Eph. 4. 23). Along life's rough path there is
much to tear and wear the energy of the soul; but the
Holy Spirit can *renew* our freshness and fitness by His

quickening influence. "It is the Spirit that quickeneth." Here the flesh profiteth nothing. *Where* the Spirit of the Lord is, *there is* liberty. Our Lord said: "He that believeth on Me out of his inner man shall flow rivers of *living* water: this spake He of the Spirit" (John 7. 37). "Believe and thou shalt see."

VI. An Eternal Possession. "Made heirs of the life of the ages" (v. 7). Our Heavenly Father has such vast possessions that every child "born of God" becomes an *heir*—not merely of eternal *existence*, that is seen, without being "born again;" but of the *abundant life* that is in Jesus Christ, throughout all the coming ages. Thus we have fulness of mercy to begin with, fulness of grace to continue in, and at last fulness of life to glory in through all eternity. "He that hath the Son hath life" (1 John 5. 11). "He is able to save to the UTTERMOST."

ALMOST A CHRISTIAN.
ACTS 26. 28.

1. **What you Might Be, and Not Be a Christian.**
   Born in a Christian country.
   Brought up in a Christian family (Judas).
   Educated in a Christian fashion.
   Connected with a Christian Church.
   Buried in a Christian manner.

2. **What is a Christian?**
   One who has *received* Christ.
   One who *belongs* to Christ.
   One who is *like* Christ.
   One who *serves* Christ.

3. **What is it to be an Almost Christian?**
   It is to *see* your need and not confess it.
   It is to *wish* to be saved and remain undecided.
   It is to be *at the door*, but still outside.

BIBLE READINGS.

THE POWER OF PRAYER.

WE have more need to be taught to pray than to preach. "Wireless" communication may be a mystery to many, but it is a great reality to those who make use of it. With regard to prayer, there is need for a rediscovery of the possibilities that have always existed, that of direct communication with eternal personalities.

I. Conditions of Power in Prayer.

1. THE WILL OF GOD. "This is the confidence that we have in Him, that if we ask anything *according to His will*, He heareth us, and if we know that He hears us we know that we have" (1 John 5. 14, 15). The supreme source of all power in prayer belongeth unto God.

2. THE NAME OF JESUS. "Whatsoever ye shall ask *in My Name*, that will I do; that the Father may be glorified" (John 14. 13, 14). His "Name" stands for all that Jesus Christ is in the eyes of His Father. When praying in *His Name*, think of His character and work. "No man can come unto the Father but *by Me.*" "Abide in Me, then ask what ye will" (John 15. 7).

3. THE MINISTRY OF THE HOLY SPIRIT. When we do not know how to *pray as we ought*, the Holy Spirit Himself maketh intercession for us (Rom. 8. 26). When we cannot frame our words to express the deep yearnings of the soul, the Holy Spirit, who is a "discerner of the *thoughts of the heart,*" helps our infirmities by making intercession for us

4. THE FAITH OF THE HEART. With the *heart* man believeth. "Let him ask *in faith*, nothing wavering" (James. 1. 5, 6). It is the *desire* of the heart that is to be

made known unto God (Mark 11. 24), and the Word of God must be trusted. Asking in faith means receiving with joy (John 16. 24). Thus we have a fourfold secret of power.

II. **Hindrances to Effectual Prayer**. These are numerous. Here are some that are common.

1. SELFISHNESS. "Ye ask and receive not because ye ask amiss: that ye might use it for your own pleasures" (Jas. 4. 3). We ask amiss when we ask anything for the honour and exaltation of self. "God will not give His glory to another." To many this is a subtle and powerful temptation.

2. SECRET SIN. "If I regard iniquity in my heart, the Lord will not hear me" (Psa. 66. 18). Let us see that, first of all, our own souls are "cleansed from secret fault." Remember the wandering, "searching eyes of the Lord" (2 Chron. 16. 9).

3. UNBELIEF. "He that cometh to God *must believe*" (Heb. 11. 6). "Let not that man that wavereth in his trust think that he shall receive anything of the Lord" (Jas. 1. 7).

4. FORMALITY. Jesus said, "If ye ask anything in My Name, I will do it" (John 14. 14). We may end our prayers with, "For Christ's sake, Amen," when there has been nothing for *Christ's sake* in the prayer. This holy and almighty NAME is often used in heartless flippancy. This was the condemnation of the leading Pharisees. The angel prayers ascend and descend *upon the Son of Man*.

5. AN UNFORGIVING SPIRIT. When ye pray, forgive; if *you do not forgive*, neither will your heavenly Father forgive you (Mark 11. 25, 26). No use praying if harbouring a grudge against any one. We must forgive one another, as Christ forgave us (Col. 3. 13).

6. IMPATIENCE. "He is the Rewarder of them that

diligently seek Him" (Heb. 11. 6). The reward may be
lost for lack of perseverance. Abraham prevailed because
he *staggered not* at the promise of God (Rom. 4. 20).
Jacob prevailed because he would not *let go.* Elijah
prevailed in Mount Carmel because he *continued* in prayer
when there was no sign of rain, saying, "Go again seven
times." The widow prevailed with the unjust judge
because of her *importunity,* and Jesus added: "Shall not
God avenge His own which cry day and night unto Him,
though He bare long with them?" (Luke 18. 1-7). *I tell
you that He will* (v. 8).

THE MIND OF CHRIST.

"LET this mind be in you which was also in Christ Jesus"
(Phil. 2. 5). The *mind* of Christ has been a mystery in
every age. It is expected that all Christ's followers
should have the same disposition as their Master. "I
have given you an example, that ye should do as I have
done to you" (John 13. 15). Features of Christ's mind.

I. **Resignation.** "Not My will, but Thine be done"
(Luke 22. 42). This is the foundation of true Christian
character. Willing to be absent from the body of self-
interest and to be present with the will of God. Seeking
not our own will, but the will of our Father (John 5. 30).
"Even Christ pleased not Himself" (Rom. 15. 3). "I
delight to do Thy will, O my God." Submit *thyself* unto
God.

II. **Devotedness.** "Wist ye not that I must be about
my Father's business?" (Luke 2. 42). His Father's
business was the highest and most important concern in
the world. He was fully devoted to "work the works of
Him that sent Me." His meat was to do His will and to
finish His work (John 4. 34). What a privilege to be a
partner in such a business and to be "workers together"

with Him in the fulfilling of the Father's purpose. Let this mind be in you which was also in Him.

III. **Meekness.** "I am meek and *lowly in heart*" (Matt. 11. 29). Where this Christ-likeness is lacking there is suitable soil for the growth of pride and presumption, selfishness, envy, covetousness, high-mindedness, and the love of pleasure more than the love of God. We find Paul beseeching believers *by the meekness and gentleness of Christ* (2 Cor. 10. 1). He made Himself of *no reputation*, and took upon Him the form of a servant (Phil. 2. 7). Let this mind be in you. "Blessed are the meek," they shall *inherit* (Matt. 5. 5). They shall be guided and taught His way (Psa. 25. 9). They shall increase their joy in the Lord (Isa. 29. 19). They shall find rest in His service (Matt. 11. 29).

IV. **Prayerfulness.** Christ was the busiest man on earth, but He always found time to pray, and sometimes continued all night in prayer (Luke 6. 12). He was emphatically *"the Man of Prayer."* He prayed (Mark. 1. 35; Luke 5. 16; 6. 12; 9. 28, 29; John 11. 41; 17. 1; Matt. 26. 36-39; Heb. 5. 7-9). These are only recorded prayers. He never was out of fellowship with His Father. His whole life was one long, unbroken intercession. "Let this mind be in you." "Pray without ceasing."

V. **Sympathy.** "Jesus wept." He saw Mary weeping. He also wept (John 11. 33-35). When He beheld the city He wept over it (Luke 19. 41). He, as our High Priest, is *touched* with the feeling of *our infirmities* (Heb. 4. 15). We are also taught to "weep with those that weep, and rejoice with those that rejoice." The grace of God never saves us from human brotherliness. Let this mind be in you.

VI. **Grief at the Unbelief of Others.** He looked round about on the staring and sceptical crowd, and was "grieved for the hardness of their hearts" (Mark 3. 5). He knew *their need* and also *His own ability* to help them, and grieved at their madness in committing spiritual suicide. As Christian workers we know the need of the unsaved, and we also know the remedy. Does this unbelief touch our hearts with real sorrow? Is this disposition in us?

VII. **Benevolence.** God anointed Jesus of Nazareth with the Holy Ghost, who *went about doing good"* (Acts 10. 38). The great purpose of His life was to show kindness and to offer help. To accomplish this He was constantly *"going about"* looking for opportunities to show the "kindness of God." What a power the Church of God would be if all belonging to it were possessed with this mind. Let *this mind* be in you for this is the highest ideal in Christian living.

THE GOSPEL, A DIVINE REVELATION.

A SIMPLE definition of the term "Gospel" is "good news," "glad tidings of good things," but the Biblical definition is not quite so elementary. What is this good news? What are these glad tidings? To include all that the New Testament teaches as embodied in the Gospel is to take in the whole universe of grace. The seven prismatic colours in nature are all visible in the rainbow. The sevenfold character of the Gospel is revealed in the gracebow of Divine promise.

I. **What this Gospel Is.** It is called—

1. THE GOSPEL OF GOD (Rom. 1. 1). It is the good news of God's merciful attitude toward the world. "God so loved the world that He gave His Son" (John 3. 16). He who declared, "All souls are mine," now reveals Himself as seeking to save all through the sacrifice of His own Son.

2. THE GOSPEL OF CHRIST (Rom. 1. 16). Paul declared: "I am not ashamed of the the good news; it is God's power which is at work for the salvation of every one who believes. " Christ's character and work, including His life, death, and resurrection is the brightness, or the flashing out, of the glory of Divine love and power.

3. THE GOSPEL OF THE GRACE OF GOD (Acts 20. 24). Can we realise what *grace* really means as offered by the Almighty God? It is favour bestowed on us, with all the Almightiness of God in it. The *grace of God* is God's power operating in love and mercy on our behalf. This grace was manifested in Jesus Christ, His Son. Surely this is "good news. "

4. THE GOSPEL OF YOUR SALVATION (Eph. 1. 13). Good news for your own individual soul. Something to meet our own *personal needs*, to call forth our own heart's trust, thanksgiving, and grateful service. "Of *His own will* begat He us with the word of truth" (Jas. 1. 18). Thanks be unto God for such joyful tidings.

5. THE GOSPEL OF THE KINGDOM (Mark 1. 14). The good tidings of a kingdom yet to come, when Jesus shall reign from sea to sea, and the uttermost parts of the earth shall become His possession. Meanwhile this "Gospel of the Kingdom is to be preached in all the world *for a witness* unto all nations, and *then* shall the end come" (Matt. 24. 14).

6. THE EVERLASTING GOSPEL (Rev. 14. 6). This is the good news of the ages. Here is something that shall never lose its freshness. It is eternally good, and growingly precious to every believer. What a contrast to the delusive pleasures of the worldlings. Pleasures for *ever more* at God's right hand.

7. THE GOSPEL OF THE GLORY OF CHRIST (2 Cor. 4. 4). The Gospel is truly "glorious, " but here it is the "good

news" of the *glory of Christ*. The Christ who gave Himself
to the "accursed death of the Cross" is now glorified, and
has become our Mediator before the Throne of God. Glad
tidings indeed, that our Lord is now "exalted above every
name that is named."

II. **This Gospel is a Revelation**. Manifold and in-
tensely Divine. It is a message from the Father of spirits
to human spirits. The four evangelists never attempt to
describe Christ, or even to give their own opinions of Him.
They simply "declare Him." In this Gospel, then, we
have—

Something that could not be *invented* by man, because
the natural mind could never *conceive* what it is not able
to *receive*, apart from the Holy Spirit.

Something that man could never *discover*, but by the
revelation. This is the mystery of Godliness.

Something for which civilisation has no substitute.

Something amid all the advancements of the ages which
can *never be improved*.

Something that neither God nor man will never be
ashamed of.

Something which alone can solve the mystery of human
guilt and the righteousness of God. This is the Gospel
of peace (Rom. 10. 15).

Something that the "angels desire to look into," as a
new manifestation of the Divine character (1 Peter 1. 12).
Is it nothing to you, all ye that pass by?

THE CHRISTIAN'S RELATIONSHIP TO THE WORLD.

IT is important to note that the word "world" in the New
Testament does not always mean "people," as in John
3. 16 and 1 John 2. 2, but frequently means "age;" as
when we read, "The god of this world (age)," "Be not

conformed to this world (age)," "The harvest is the end of the world (age)," "The world to come," lit., the age, or ages, to come.

I. Its Character. This world, then, is represented as governed by principles that are not in harmony with the revealed will of God; for "the god of this age hath blinded the minds of them which believe not" (2 Cor. 4. 4). What can be expected from an age that has been blinded by Satan to the glories of the risen Christ? "We know that we are of God," said John, and that "the whole world lieth in wickedness" (1 John 5. 19). When we mediate on the fact "that every spirit that *confesseth not* that Jesus Christ is come in the flesh *is not of God*" (1 John 4. 3), but savours of the spirit of Antichrist, well may we wonder and adore the God of Love, who gave His Son to die for a world like this.

II. How this Character is Manifested. It is expressed—

1. IN THE LUST OF THE FLESH. They that are after the flesh—controlled by their earthly nature—do mind the things of the flesh (Rom. 8. 5), the things they can touch, and taste, and boast of. The *lust* of the flesh is the antagonist of the Holy Spirit (Gal. 5. 24).

2. IN THE LUST OF THE EYE. Cravings for things which minister to sight and the desire of the mind. This is seen in the love of fashion and the greed of gain.

3. IN THE PRIDE OF LIFE. If the lust of the flesh is the bud, the lust of the eye the blossom, then the pride of life is the matured fruit of conceit and self-satisfaction. Alienated from the life of God, such things are *not of the Father*, but of the world (1 John 2. 16).

III. What is Our Relationship to this World.

1. DELIVERED FROM IT. "He gave Himself for our sins,

that He might rescue us from this present wicked age"
(Gal. 1. 4). Being rescued from *our sins*, the link of connection with this evil age has been broken, and a new
centre of attraction formed. We *love Him* because He
first loved us. "They overcame the world who believe in
the Son of God" (1 John 5. 5).

2. CRUCIFIED TO IT. "I glory in nothing except the
Cross of our Lord Jesus Christ, upon which the world is
crucified unto me, and I am crucified to the world" (Gal.
6. 14). Here is a double crucifixion. "Our old man
(nature) is crucified with Him, that the *body of sin* might
be destroyed" (Rom. 6. 6), and when the body of sin,
that was subject to, and served the world, is destroyed,
then it also becomes to us a dead thing.

3. UNKNOWN BY IT. "Behold, we are the sons of God,
therefore the *world knoweth us not*, because it knew Him
not" (1 John 3. 1). Godliness separates from the world
and is foreign to it. "The world loves *its own*, but because
ye are not of the world, *therefore* the world hateth you"
(John 15. 19). Jesus said, "Marvel not if the world *hate
you*, because it hated Me." "Be not conformed to this
age" (Rom. 12. 2).

4. WITNESSING IN IT. "I pray not that Thou shouldest
take them out of the world, but that Thou shouldest *keep
them from the evil*. As Thou hast sent Me into the world,
even so have I *also sent them into the world*" (John 17. 18).
Believers are *called out* of the world into fellowship with
Himself, then gifted with His Spirit, are *sent into it* as
witnesses for Him and His saving Gospel (John 20. 21).
Now then we are *"ambassadors* for Christ to beseech men in
Christ's stead to be reconciled to God" (2 Cor. 5. 20).

5. VICTORS OVER IT. "Because *"greater* is He that is
in you, than he that is in the world" (1 John 4. 4). He
that is in the world is *great*. He has all the wisdom of a

fallen angel, all the venom of the serpent, all the ferocity of the dragon, all the resources of Hell, and all the uncleanness and deceivableness of a sinful humanity in his favour. But *greater* is He that is *in you*, the Almighty Spirit of God and the victorious Christ is with you. "Lo, I am with you alway, even to the end of the age. " This is the victory that overcometh the world, even our faith (1 John 5. 4). "Thanks be unto God, who giveth us the victory, through our Lord Jesus Christ" (Rom. 8. 37).

WHAT ARE WE WAITING FOR?

THE Thessalonian Church had turned to God from idols to serve the living God, and to *"wait for His Son for Heaven"* (1 Thess. 1. 10). On the Great Day of Atonement the High Priest went within the veil—not without blood, and the congregation *waited* without looking for his reappearing. Now Christ, our Great High Priest, has gone within the veil by His own blood, and the Church without is waiting and looking for His appearing according to His promise (John 14. 3).

1. **For His Son from Heaven.** "Our citizenship is in Heaven, *from whence* also we look for the Saviour, the Lord Jesus Christ" (Phil. 3. 20). We are not waiting for death, nor for the Holy Spirit, who has already been given; nor for the conversion of the world, before He comes, for "as it was in the days of Noah, *so shall it be* in the days when the Son of Man is revealed" (Luke 17. 30). Certainly the world was not converted before the flood came.

2. **For the Completion of Our Salvation.** "He shall appear the second time to make their salvation complete" (Heb. 9. 28). Our salvation now, great as it is, is but the *foretaste* of what is yet to come. We have been

saved from the penalty and power of sin, but not from its *presence*. Suffering and sorrow are still associated with our present condition. He who hath begun this good work will perfect it in His day.

III. For the Redemption of the Body. "We look for the Saviour, who shall change our mortal body that it may be fashioned *like unto His glorious body*" (Phil. 3. 20, 21). This will indeed be "a new fashion" for the redeemed. The transfigured soul, with a transfigured body. It has been good to *hear* His Word; it will be better to *see* Himself, but best of all to be made *like Him*. This is the eternal life.

IV. For the Bridegroom of the Church. It was at *midnight* when the cry was raised: "Behold the Bridegroom cometh" (Matt. 25. 6). He is coming to receive His Bride unto Himself (John 14. 3). She is a cold-hearted bride who is not lovingly longing for the coming of her betrothed. If He tarry, wait for Him. He is faithful that hath promised. "Be ye also ready, for in such an hour as ye think not, the Son of Man cometh" (Matt. 24. 44).

V. For the Consolation of Israel. "Simon waited for this, and the Holy Ghost was upon him" (Luke 2. 25). But Israel was not consoled by the coming Jesus. They hated Him, saying, "We will not have *this* man to reign over us," and clamoured for His crucifixion. So Israel is still unconsoled. But there shall come out of Zion their Deliverer, and so all Israel shall be saved (Rom. 11. 26). A saved nation will mean world-wide testimony and blessing.

VI. For the Reward that is to be Ours at His Coming. "Be like unto men that wait for their lord" (Luke 12. 36). Not in idleness, but with girded loins and burning lights, looking for the grace that is to be

brought *unto you at the revelation* of Jesus Christ (1 Peter
1. 13). "Lo, I come, and *My reward is with Me,* to give
to every man according to his works." "Therefore, let us
not sleep, as do others; but let us watch and be sober"
(1 Thess. 5. 6). "Watch, therefore, for ye know not when
the *Master of the House* cometh" (Mark 13. 34).

VII. **For the New Heavens and the New Earth**.
"Nevertheless we, according to His promise, look for new
heavens and a new earth, wherein dwelleth righteousness"
(2 Peter 3. 13). Or, as this same apostle declared in his
great speech: "Even Jesus, whom the Heaven must
receive until the times of the *reconstitution of all things*"
(Acts 3. 21). These new conditions in the elements of the
heavens and in the principles prevailing on the earth, will
be perfectly congenial to righteousness. God's testing
fire will only purify (2 Peter 3. 10). The new heavens and
the new earth will be made meet for His new creatures in
Christ Jesus. "Seeing then that all these things shall be
dissolved, what manner of persons ought we to be...life
and godliness? (2 Peter 3. 11). See that ye don't fall
behind in this gift of waiting for the Coming (1 Cor. 1. 7).

THE BELIEVER'S PRESENT PRIVILEGES.
JOHN 14.

THESE words of our Lord, spoken at His last Passover,
contains a revelation of the precious privileges conferred
on His believing people. There is—

I. **A Cure for Trouble.** "Let not *your* heart be
troubled, ye believe in God, believe also *in Me*" (v. 1).
It is possible to believe in the *existence* of God, and yet
know nothing of His power to heal heart-trouble. Jesus
says, "believe also in Me. I died to put away your sins.

I rose again to give you peace. " "Cast all your care upon Him, for He careth for you. " "Fear not, for I am with you. "

II. **A Blessed Hope.** "I go to prepare a place for you. I will come again and *receive you unto Myself*" (v. 3). These words were spoken to the Church that then existed, and are applicable to the Church that now is; and will be perfectly fulfilled as recorded in 1 Thessalonians 4. 17. Jesus prayed for this. "Father, I will that *they also* whom Thou hast given me be with Me where I am: that they may behold My glory" (John 17. 24). What an outlook this is for hearts that may at times be troubled because of the way.

III. **A Vision of the Father.** "Philip saith unto Him, Lord, shew us the Father and it sufficeth us. " Jesus answered: "He that hath seen Me hath seen the Father" (v. 9). The invisible Father of all has revealed Himself in and through Jesus Christ the Son. The more we know of Christ, the more we know of the Eternal Father. "GOD hath in these last days spoken unto us by His Son, who is the express image of His Person" (Heb. 1. 3). In Him the pure in heart see God. Believe and thou shalt see.

IV. **A Great Opportunity.** "Whatsoever ye ask in My Name, *that will I do, that the Father may be glorified in the Son*" (v. 13). What a wide and effectual door this is for believing prayer. "My Name" and the "Glory of the Father. " What a powerful plea! "I have chosen you and ordained you...that whatsoever ye shall ask of the Father in My Name, He may give it you" (John 15. 16). How shall we escape poverty of soul and shameful defeat if we neglect so great an opportunity?

V. **A Personal Comforter.** "I will pray the Father, and He shall give you another Comforter, that He may *abide with you for ever*" (v. 16). This Comforter, which is the Holy Ghost, He shall *teach* you all things" (v. 26). He is the "Spirit of Truth" (v. 17). He helpeth our infirmities (Rom. 8. 26). He sheds the love of God abroad in our hearts (Rom. 5. 5). He makes us to abound in hope (Rom. 15. 13). He anoints with power (John 2. 20). Through us He testifies of Christ (John 15. 26). He is the Source of all God-honouring fruit (Gal. 5. 22). He seals the believing soul until the final redemption (Eph. 1. 13).

VI. **A Double Assurance.** "He that hath My commandments and keepeth them, shall be *loved of My Father*, and I will love him, and *will manifest Myself to him*" (v. 21). In the keeping of His word, the love of God is perfected in the heart (1 John 2. 5). What comforting assurance this is. Loved by the Father, loved by the Son, who has promised to give us a growing manifestation of Himself. Love delights to give. Christ gives us His best when He vouchsafes to us a fuller revelation *of Himself*. This is eternal life to know Him.

VII. **An Abiding Bequest.** "Peace I leave with you, *My peace* I give unto you." "Let not your heart be troubled, neither let it be afraid" (v. 27). What a neglected heritage this is. "In the *world* ye shall have tribulation," but ye need not have this tribulation in "your *heart*, for in ME ye might have peace" (John 16. 33). Then "let the peace of God *rule* in your hearts, to the which also *ye are called*" (Col. 3. 15). Called to a life of peace, as well as of faith. And what a peace this is. "My peace." "The peace of God which passeth all understanding shall *keep* your hearts and minds, through Jesus Christ" (Phil. 4. 7). "Peace, be still."

THE BELIEVER'S THREEFOLD RELATIONSHIP.
JOHN 15.

THIS chapter is a continuation of our Lord's last words to His bewildered disciples, and reveals—

I. **Our Relationship to Christ.** Our union with Him implies—

1. ONENESS OF LIFE. "I am the Vine, ye are the branches" (v. 5). The life that is in the branch is the same life that is in the vine. It is the sap of the vine that worketh in the branch. So it is God which worketh in you both to will and to do of His good pleasure (Phil. 2. 13).

2. ENTIRE DEPENDENCE. "Without the vine the branch can do nothing, but wither and die" (v. 6). "If a man *abide not in Me*, he shall become like a branch broken off and withered." Fruitlessness in the Christian life is the evidence of a broken relationship. Grapes will not grow on a sapless branch. Paul knew the power of this inworking Spirit. "I can do all things *through Christ* which strengtheneth me" (Phil. 4. 13). Being filled with His Spirit is the prime condition of fruitbearing.

3. CO-OPERATION. "Herein is My Father glorified, that ye bear much fruit" (v. 8). The vine might say to the branch: "Without me ye can do nothing." The branch might also say to the vine: "Without me ye can do nothing." But in united effort both can accomplish their destined purpose. Without Christ the Church can do nothing that will glorify the Father But we dare not say that without the Church Christ can do nothing, for He could easily send legions of angels as heralds of the Gospel; but He hath chosen those redeemed by His Blood and saved by His grace to be His witnesses. Herein lies the Church's responsibility.

II. **Our Relationship to One Another.**

1. ALL ONE IN CHRIST. The branches are all in the one vine. "I have chosen you and ordained you, that ye should go and bring forth fruit" (v. 16). We are His workmanship. Created in Christ Jesus unto good works

(Eph. 2. 10). Every single believer is a member of His Body, and, as such, members one of another.

2. ONE IN LOVE. "Love one another *as I have* loved you" (v. 12). This is Christ's *new* commandment to His new born people (John 13. 34). It was the message they heard *at the beginning* of their Christian life (1 John 3. 11). Alas, that we are so slow to learn it. One may have gifts, great wisdom, and faith; but *without love*, nothing (1 Cor. 13. 2).

3. ONE IN WORK. We have but one Master, and one purpose in life: that is, to bring forth fruit that shall remain (v. 16). For this end He gave this gracious promise: "Whatsoever ye shall ask of the Father in My Name, He may give it you" (v. 16).

III. **Our Relationship to the World.** Our position in the world is one of—

1. SEPARATION. "Ye are *not of the world*, but I have chosen you *out of the world*" (v. 19). Having been made new creatures in Christ Jesus, we are now, *in character*, strangers and foreigners in the world. Separated unto God, and saved from the wrath that is coming upon a world that "lieth in wickedness" (1 John 5. 19).

2. OPPOSITION. Because ye are not of the world, *therefore* the world hateth you (v. 19). This is the hatred of Cain, who slew his brother because his own works were evil and his brother's righteous (1 John 3. 12). The believer's *life* is opposed to the spirit that is in the world. He cannot hate ungodly men, but he can, and does, *resist* all that savours of the Devil. To pray for our enemies is Christ's example of passive resistance. It is enough for the disciple that he be as his Master (Matt. 10. 25).

3. WITNESSBEARING. "The Spirit shall testify of Me, and *ye also* shall bear witness" (vv. 26, 27). We are His witnesses, and *so is also* the Holy Ghost (Acts 5. 32). On

the testimony of these *two* witnesses shall His Word be established. When His Word burns in our hearts like "fire shut up in our bones," then, like Peter and John, we will be constrained to say: "We cannot but speak the things which we have seen and heard" (Acts 4. 20). "Ye are My witnesses." There is a woe unto those who hide their light (1 Cor. 9. 16, 17).

THE BELIEVER'S EQUIPMENT.

JOHN 16.

THE Lord is here warning His disciples that times of trial and suffering were before them. "These things have I told you, that when the time shall come ye may remember" (vv. 1-4). But He did not leave them with their "sorrow-filled hearts," without giving them many encouraging promises, which we may regard as their equipment for life's work. There was—

I. **The Promise of a Comforter.** "If I go not away, the Comforter will not come unto you; but if I depart I will send Him unto you" (v. 7). He does not say, I will sent *it*, but HIM. Christ never dishonours the Holy Spirit by speaking of Him as a mere thing. As a companion, the Holy Spirit was to be to them all that Christ had been. This was abundantly proven after Pentecost. This is what the Spirit can be to us in our times of suffering for His Name. His invisible Presence is here as really as the visible Presence of Christ is departed.

II. **The Promise of Guidance and Teaching.** "He will guide you into *all truth*, and He will shew you *things to come*" (vv. 13, 14). John says that ye need not any man teach you, for this anointing teacheth you all things (1 John 2. 20-27). This is the Spirit that searcheth all things (1 Cor. 2. 9, 10). Why should we not expect the Holy Spirit to do His work *in us* just as effectively as

Christ has done His work *for us*? Don't grieve the Spirit
by refusing His teaching regarding these "things to come."

III. **The Promise of His Coming Again.** "You
now have sorrow, but I will see you again, and your heart
shall rejoice" (v. 22). This was literally fulfilled when He
rose from the dead. "Then were their hearts glad when
they saw the Lord." But is there not a wider fulfilment
awaiting for His suffering, sorrowing disciples in these
latter days? When He promised: "I will come again and
receive you *unto Myself*, that *where* I am, *there* ye may be
also" (John 14. 3).

IV. **The Promise of Answered Prayer.** "Whatsoever ye shall ask of the Father in My Name, He will give
you; ask and ye shall receive that *your joy may be full*"
(vv. 23, 24). Having, therefore, brethren, such good and
sure promises, let us come with boldness into the holiest
by the Blood of Jesus and confidently make our requests
known (Heb. 10. 19). "Open thy mouth wide and I
will fill it" (Psa. 81. 10).

V. **The Promise of Christ's Intercession.** "I will
pray the Father *for you*, for the Father Himself *loveth
you*" (vv. 26, 27). What thanksgiving and confidence
this should bring to our hearts, that Christ is pleading for
us with the Father who loves us. What then in Heaven,
earth, or Hell can hinder His will being done in us? Only
our own unbelief.

VI. **The Promise of Peace.** "These things have I
spoken unto you, that in *Me* ye might have peace" (v. 33).
He hath made peace by the Blood of His Cross. He hath
spoken peace by the power of His resurrection. This
peace is not of ourselves, not the result of anything we
can do. It is not conditioned by our circumstances. Not
affected by our disappointments or tribulations. The
world cannot give it nor take it away. It is *in Himself,*

and all that *He is* to His own people. It is as real as abiding and as eternal as He Himself is. "In *Me* ye shall have peace."

VII. **The Promise of Victory.** "In the world ye shall have tribulation; but be of good cheer, I have overcome the world" (v. 33). "All that will live godly in Christ Jesus shall suffer persecution" (2 Tim. 3. 12). But persecution, mockery, or death does not mean defeat, for out of their tribulation they shall come with washed robes (Rev. 7. 14). Nothing can "separate us from the *love* of Christ, and where His *love* is, His *power* also is there to make us *more than conquerors*" (Rom. 8. 35-37). The powers of the world are impotent when the "Greater is He that is in you" is with us (1 John 4. 4). Christ has already overcome the world, and your life is hid with Christ in God. To God be the thanks, who in Christ ever heads our triumphal procession (2 Cor. 2. 14).

THE BELIEVER'S RESPONSIBILITIES.

JOHN 17.

HERE we have what is emphatically "The Lord's Prayer" offered at the close of that solemn meeting with His disciples, before He went out to face the last great storm of human and diabolical hatred. The words are simple, but the thoughts are perhaps the most profound in all Scripture. They reveal many high and holy privileges belonging to His own loved ones. But we wish to point out some of the responsibilities that are ours in consequence of our privileges. We have responsibilities—

I. **As Those to Whom His Name has been Revealed.** "I have manifested *Thy Name* unto the men which Thou gavest Me out of the world" (v. 6). Or as it might be read: "I have revealed the perfections of Thy character to those which Thou hast given Me." The character of that great and holy NAME is seen in Exodus 34. 5-7. Through the grace of Christ that Name has become the *practical experience* of every true believer. "My name is in *Him*" (Exod. 23. 21). What manner of persons, then, ought we to be with such a possession?

II. **As Custodians of His Words.** "I have given unto them the words which Thou hast given Me" (v. 8). The truths which the Father committed to the Son, the Son has committed to us, who are His own. What a treasure this is, and what a responsibility rests on us to pass on to others what we by faith have received. How many are burying this treasure in the grave of their own personal interests. This *Word* of the Gospel never gets beyond their own need. His words are the words of "eternal life." Let your light *so shine* that *others* may see, and believe, and glorify your Father.

III. **As God-given Ones, for the Glory of His Son.** "I pray for them which *Thou hast given. Me*, for they are Thine, and Thine are Mine; and *I am glorified in them*" (vv. 9, 10). If Christ is to be fully glorified in His people, surely His redeemed ones must glorify Him while here as witnesses for Him. As Paul said: "Christ shall be *magnified in my body*, whether it be by life or by death" (Phil. 1. 20). Ye see your calling, brethren, let us walk worthily of it, for the glory of His Name.

IV. **As Separated Ones.** "They are *not* of the world, *even as I am* not of the world; keep them *from the evil one*; *sanctify them* through Thy truth" (vv. 14-17). The Lord further adds: "And for *their sakes* I consecrate Myself, in order *that they* may become perfectly consecrated in truth" (v. 19). The Lord set Himself apart for our salvation, and expects us to set ourselves apart for His service in the truth. Ye are not your own, *therefore* glorify God in your body and spirit, which *are His*.

V. **As Sent Ones.** "As Thou hast sent Me into the world, *even so* have I also sent them into the world"

(v. 18). This commission was repeated after He rose from the dead (John 20. 21). For what purpose did the Father send Him? Briefly, it was this: "I came down from Heaven, not to do Mine own will, but *the will of Him* that sent Me" (John 6. 38). "As the Father sent Me, so have I sent you." Not to do your own will, but the *will of Him* that sent you. Herein lies our God-given privilege and our God-given responsibility. Surely our motto should be: "Thy will be done."

VI. As Brethren. Christ prayed "for them also which shall believe on Him through their word. That they all may *be one*, as the Father and the Son are, and that they may be made perfect *in one*, that the world may know that Thou hast sent Me" (vv. 21-23). This union is not limited to any ecclesiastical system, nor to any religious creed or nation. In Christ there is neither Jew nor Gentile; neither bond nor free, neither male nor female; but ye are *all one in Christ Jesus* (Gal. 3. 28). All given by the same Father to the Son. All redeemed by the same price. All quickened by the same Spirit. All obedient to the same Word. All heirs of the same inheritance, and their names all written in the same "Book of Life." It is ours to *keep this unity* of the Spirit in the bond of peace (Gal. 4. 3).

VII. As His Eternal Companions. "Father, I will that *they also* whom Thou hast given Me, be *with Me* where I am; that they may behold My glory" (v. 24). What grace is this. "Where I am there shall also *My servant be*" (John 12. 26). *Servants* sharing their Master's honour. "So shall we *ever* be with the Lord" (1 Thess. 4. 17). By faith we company with Him now. He says: "I have called you *friends*" (John 15. 15). Let nothing mar your fellowship with Him. Remember, this is to be for ever and ever. Amen.

JOSHUA'S CONQUEST.

JOSHUA 10. 7-14.

THE whole land of Canaan was the gift of God to His people Israel, but they were slow to go in and possess. God is ever more ready to give than we are to take—

I. **The Work to be Done.** Five kings of the Amorites, with all their hosts, had encamped before Gideon, with whom Joshua had lately made a league. They sent an urgent message to him saying: "Slack not thy hand from thy servants; come up to us quickly and save us." As soon as the Gideonites became the allies of Israel they became the enemies of the Amorites. Joshua feels in honour bound to help his weaker brethren to maintain their stand against the common foe. They had enemies, and so have we, with which compromise is impossible.

II. **The Encouragement Given.**—"Fear them not: for I have delivered them into thy hand" (v. 8). So said the Lord to Joshua, as he prepared himself for the battle. Those who have purposed in their heart to do the *will* of God may confidently expect the *help* of God. Everything depends upon the attitude God takes towards our enterprises, whether they shall prosper or end 'in confusion (Gen. 11. 4-8). His promise, "Lo, I am with you," may be claimed by every one who fights against all evil principles and habits, which hinder souls from the enjoyment of the gift of God's grace.

III. **The Method Adopted.** "Joshua went up from Gilgal all night, and came upon them suddenly" (v. 9). He lost no time. Whatsoever ye do, do it heartily as unto the Lord. "Going up *all night*" meant some personal sacrifice, but great victories in the Name of God are very seldom won without this. Those who attempt great things on the authority of the Divine Word know what it is to be "a night and a day on the deep."

IV. **The Weapons Used**. There was, of course, the sword, but our weapons are not carnal, but spiritual and mighty, to the pulling down of the strongholds of Satan.

1. The sword of the SPIRIT is also our sword, which is the "WORD OF GOD." If the Spirit has infallible confidence in this double-edged blade as unbreakable, and effective for the overcoming of the enemy and the establishing of the Kingdom of God, so well may *we*. They had another weapon called "hailstones from Heaven." Those who war against the revealed purposes of God have more to reckon with than they dream of. This destructive shower of hailstones were the arrows of the Almighty, shot from the unerring bow of judgment (Isa. 30. 30). The battalions of Heaven are on the side of those who believe God's Word and do His will (Job 38. 22, 23).

2. The next weapon brought into action was DARING FAITH. When Joshua said to the Lord in the sight of Israel, "Sun, stand thou still upon Gideon," it was not only an unprecedented, but, we would have thought, an unimaginable, venture of *faith*. At that moment he seemed to feel the presence of the Almighty so near and real that "all things were possible to him that believeth." There and then he asked a "great thing, and got it." It was not demanded for his own sake, but for the fulfilment of that commission given him by God.

3. All POWER in Heaven and on earth is still at the disposal of those consecrated to His service (Matt. 28. 18-19). If need be, it was as easy for God to stop the whole Solar system and start it again without the slightest dislocation of any part, as it is for a railway driver to stop his engine. It is of the nature of faith to expect miracles, and when it is definitely exercised it is not disappointed. The Lord still "hearkens unto the voice of a man," and does memorable things for him (v. 14).

GOSPEL OUTLINES AND SEED THOUGHTS.

THE ROOT OF THE MATTER.
Job 19. 25-28.

I. **What is the Root?**
 1. Faith. "My Redeemer liveth."
 2. Assurance. "I know that," etc.

II. **How is Christ like a Root?**
 1. Because He is Indispensable to *Life.*
 2. Indespensable to *fruitfulness.*

III. **Where this Root should Be.**
 1. "*In* me," as a new principle.
 2. "*Found* in me." Testimony.

INVITED TO CONFERENCE.
Isaiah 1. 18.

1. The **Invited**. The rebellious (v. 2), thoughtless (v. 3), burdened and corrupters (v. 4), sick (v. 5), diseased (v. 6).

2. The **Invitation**. To "come," to "reason." This reveals the division, condescension, and anxiety.

3. The **Promise**. "Though sins be as scarlet...be as white as snow."

THIS MAN RECEIVETH SINNERS.
Luke 15. 2.

1. **Who?** "This Man." The Man Christ Jesus.
2. **Whom?** "Sinners." Guilty, helpless.
3. **How?** Heartily, and just as they are.
4. **When?** "Now." "Behold, now is the accepted time."
5. **Why?** Because He *loves* them and *died* for them.

THE FORGIVING GOD.
ISAIAH 43. 25.
1. **The Blessing Spoken Of.** "Forgiveness."
2. **The Persons Forgiven.** "Sinners."
3. **The Great Forgiver.** "I, even I."
4. **The Ground of Forgiveness.** "For Mine own Name's sake."

WITHOUT CHRIST.
EPHESIANS 2. 12.
To be without Christ is to be—
1. **Without God.** "God was in Christ" (2 Cor. 5. 19).
2. **Without Life.** "I am the Life" (John 14. 6).
3. **Without Light.** He is "The Light of the World.".
4. **Without Salvation.** "None other name."
5. **Without Promise.** "All the promises are in Christ."
6. **Without Hope.** "Without hope in the world."

UNDER HIS WINGS.
MATTHEW 23. 37.
THESE words are suggestive, and imply—
1. **Danger.** His wings are needed.
2. **Opportunity.** His wings are spread.
3. **Power.** His wings are Almighty.
4. **Compassion.** His wings offered.
5. **Salvation.** His wings save.
6. **Responsibility.** Refusing the wings of His shelter is to perish.

THE HOPE OF THE WORLD.
JOHN 12. 46, 47.
1. The **Condition** of the World. "In darkness."
2. The **Character** of Christ. "A Light."
3. The **Sphere** of His Shining. "In the world."
4. The **Purpose** of His Coming. "To save the world."
5. The **Condition** of Salvation. "Believeth on Me."

A WORD FOR ALL.

1. To the **Unconverted**, ... John 3. 7
2. To the **Anxious Inquirer**, .. John 1. 12
3. To the **Doubting**, ... 1 John 5. 12, 13
4. To the **Despairing**, ... Hebrews 7. 25
5. To the **Young Convert**, ... 1 Peter 2. 2
6. To the **Aged Christian**, ... Isaiah 46. 4
7. To the **Weary Worker**, .. 2 Cor. 12. 9

REPENTANCE.

THE law does not demand it, because it cannot offer forgiveness.

1. **Christ Declared the Need of It**, ... Matt. 4. 17
2. **Christ Exalted to Give It**, .. Acts 5. 31
3. **Offered in His Name**, ... Luke 24. 17
4. **Commanded by God**, ... Acts 17. 30
5. **Produced by the Goodness of God**, Rom. 2. 4
6. **Necessary to Forgiveness**, .. Acts 3. 19
7. **Accompanied with Faith**, ... Mark 1. 15
8. **Joy in Heaven Over It**, ... Luke 15. 10
9. **May be Sought Too Late**, ... Heb. 12. 17

THE TIME IS SHORT.
1 CORINTHIANS 7. 29.

1. For **Study**: Be Decided, ... 1 Kgs. 18. 21
2. For **Salvation**: Be Instant, .. 2 Cor. 6. 2
3. For **Service**: Be Diligent, ... Col. 3. 23
4. For **Suffering**: Be Patient, ... Jas. 5. 7

ETERNITY.
ISAIAH 57. 15.

1. The Soul (spirit) has been **made for Eternity**, ... Gen. 2. 7
2. Life is the **seed-time of Eternity**, Gal. 6. 7, 8

3. **Time** is given to **prepare** for Eternity, 2 Cor. 6. 2
4. **Death** is the gate of Eternity,   ..   Luke 16. 22
5. **No Redemption** in Eternity,   ..   Luke 16. 26
6. You may be **Saved** for Eternity, ..   Heb. 9. 12
7. Where will **you** spend Eternity?

IS THE YOUNG MAN SAFE?
2 SAMUEL 18. 32.

1. **What a Young Man may be, and not be Safe.**
   Good looking.   As Absalom was.
   Highly Gifted.   So was Absalom.
   Greatly Esteemed.   So was Absalom.

2. **What Every Young Man should be—Safe.**
   Think of his Capabilities.
   Think of his Opportunities.
   Think of his Temptations and Dangers.

3. **What Every Young Man may be—Safe.**
   The Love of God declares it,   ..   John 3. 16
   The Atonement of Christ assures it, ..   1 John 2. 2
   The Word of the Gospel invites it, ..   Rom. 10. 13

WONDERFUL.
ISAIAH 9. 6.

1. A Wonderful **Gift.** "A child...a Son."   John 3. 16
2. A Wonderful **Possession.** "Unto *us*...born...Unto *us given.*"
3. A Wonderful **Name.** Called—
   The Wonderful Counsellor,   Wisdom.
   The Mighty God, ...   Power.
   The Father of Eternity (R. V., *margin*), Eternal.
   The Prince of Peace, ...   Grace.
4. A Wonderful **Promise.**
   "The Government shall be upon
   His shoulders,"   ..   ..   ..   King.

IS IT NOTHING TO YOU?
LAMENTATIONS 1. 11, 12.

THINK of these words as coming from the lips of the rejected Son of God.

1. **An Awful Confession.** "I am become vile." Think of *who* He is, and *why* He became vile.

2. **An Urgent Appeal to God.** "See, O Lord, and consider." Consider who I am: "Thy Son." Consider *for whom* I am vile (Gal. 3. 13).

3. **A Pathetic Appeal to Men.** "Ye that pass by: behold and see if there be any sorrow like unto My sorrow." Any sorrow so deep, so undeserved, so effective.

4. **A Mournful Entreaty.** "Is it nothing to you?"

THE AUTHOR OF SALVATION.
HEBREWS 2. 10-11 (R.V.).

1. The **Purpose** of God. "To bring many into glory."

2. The **Character** of those He brings. "Sons."

3. The **Method.** "Through One *made perfect* as a Saviour."

4. How Christ was **Perfected** as a Saviour. "Through suffering."

5. The God-becoming **Act.** "It *became* HIM." It was just like Him.

6. The Blessed **Result.** "*He* that sanctifieth and *they* who are sanctified all of ONE." Oneness in nature and purpose.

A GOOD STRONGHOLD.
NAHUM 1. 7.

1. What the Lord is in **Himself.** "Good."

2. What He is **to His People.** "A Stronghold."

3. When He is a **Stronghold.** "In the day of trouble."

4. To whom He is a **Stronghold.** "Them that trust Him."

5. Consolation for them that **trust Him.** "He knoweth them."

ASK FOR THE OLD PATHS.
JEREMIAH 6. 16.

1. Why ask for the **Old Paths**? Because the *New* ones are delusive and deceptive (Gal. 1. 8).

2. What are the **Old Paths**? Those revealed in God's Word, in which "holy men of old" walked.

3. Why should **we walk** the Old Paths? Because there the pilgrims experience—

>   The Blood of Christ to Justify.
>   The Love of God to Satisfy.
>   The Spirit of Power to Sanctify.

"NO MAN BUT BY ME."
JOHN 14. 6.

To come to the Father three things are absolutely needed. We need—

1. **The Way.** "I am *the Way*. No man cometh unto the Father but by ME."

2. **The Truth.** "I am *the Truth*...No man cometh unto the Father but by ME."

3. **The Life.** "I am *the Life*...No man cometh unto the Father but by ME." "There is *One* Mediator."

PROVOKING GOD.
HEBREWS 3. 15.

1. **A Privilege.** "Hear ye His voice."

2. **A Warning.** "Harden not your hearts."

3. **An Example.** "As in the provocation" (Num. 14. 1-11). Unbelief.

4. **A Responsibility.** "If ye will."

5. **An Opportunity.** "*While* it is said, To-day."

CRIES TO CHRIST IN MATTHEW.

1. The Cry of **Despair,** 8. 29
2. The Cry of **Need,** 9. 27

3. The Cry of **Fear**, ... 14. 26
4. The Cry of **Danger**, ... 14. 30
5. The Cry of **Intercession**, ... 15. 22
6. The Cry of **Importunity**, ... 20. 31
7. The Cry of **Delight**, ... 21. 9
8. The Cry of **Derision**, ... 27. 23

HE IS ABLE.
HEBREWS 7. 27.

1. He is Able to **Save**.

2. He is Able to Save **those that come**.

3. He is Able to Save those that come **unto God**.

4. He is Able to Save those that come unto God **by Jesus Christ**.

5. He is Able to Save them to the **uttermost**.

6. He is Able to Save them to the uttermost **because He ever liveth**.

THE CLEANSING FOUNTAIN.
ZECHARIAH 13. 1.

1. **What was Opened?** "A Fountain." *Deep* as Eternity. *Full* as the Heart of God. *Free* as the air you breathe.

2. **When it was Opened.** "In that day." The day that Christ was "pierced" (12. 10). The day that man committed his greatest sin in "killing the Prince of Life."

3. **Why it was Opened.** "For *sin* and *uncleanness.*" Guilt and pollution. "Ho, every one that thirsteth, come."

REFUGES OF LIES.
ISAIAH 28. 17.

1. **Universalism**, ... Mark 16. 16
2. **Free Thought**, ... Isa. 55. 7, 8
3. **General Mercy of God**, ... 2 Thess. 1. 7-9
4. **General Morality**, ... Heb. 11. 6

5. **Doing the Best,** .. .. .. Rom. 3. 19, 20
6. **General Belief,** .. .. .. John 3. 36
7. **A Good Heart,** .. .. .. John 3. 5

THE TRIAL OF FAITH.
1 Peter 1. 7.

1. **What is to be Tried?** Your faith? Some have "no faith." Some have "little faith." Some have "great faith."

2. **How is Faith Tried?** Our faith may be tried—
Like Job's, by prolonged adversity.
Like Abraham's, by a call to sacrifice.
Like Joseph's, by a temptation to sin.
Like Daniel's, by evil workers.

3. **Why is Faith Tried?** Because, like silver and gold, it becomes more *precious* (2 Peter 1. 1). Because it makes it more *fruitful*. "Praise and honour and glory."

FAITH.
Mark 11. 22.

1. The **Nature** of Faith, ... Heb. 11. 1
2. The **Object** of Faith, ... "God."
3. The **Ground** of Faith. What the
  "Scriptures hath said," .. .. John 7. 38
4. The **Need** of Faith, ... Heb. 11. 6
5. The **Example** of Faith, ... Mark 14. 16
6. The **Results** of Faith, ... Heb. 11.

PLENTY FOR THE PENNILESS.
Isaiah 55. 1-3.

1. **Foolishness Exhibited.** *"Spending* for that which is not bread...*Labouring* for that which satisfieth not."

2. **Counsel Offered.** "Hearken unto Me." "Eat that which is good," etc.

3. **Provision Made.** Waters to cleanse. **Wine to** refresh. Milk to nourish.

4. **Invitation Given.** To the *thirsty*. To the **penniless**: "He that hath no money."

WHAT SHALL THE END BE?
1 PETER 4. 17.

1. What is the **Gospel of God**? It is the good **tidings** of Divine love, mercy, and power seeking to save.

2. What is it to **Obey the Gospel**? It is to **believe** its message, accept its offer, and follow its teaching.

3. What shall the end be of **those who obey not?** The end will be destruction (2 Thess. 1. 8).

SIN.
1 JOHN 3. 4 (R.V.).

1. Its **Character.** Pollution (Isa. 1), rebellion (Eph. 2. 2), bondage (Rom. 5. 21; 6. 17), death (Eph. 2. 1).

2. Its **Course.** (Rom. 5. 12; Gal. 3. 22).

3. Its **Curse** (Rom. 6. 23). Ground cursed.

4. Its **Cure** (2 Cor. 5. 21; Gal. 3. 13).

THE SALVATION OF GOD.
2 TIMOTHY 1. 8-10.

THIS is the testimony of a prisoner for Christ, of the great salvation.

1. It is "according to the **Power of God**" (v. 8).

2. It is "**Given** us in Christ Jesus."

3. It is "Not according to **our works.**"

4. It is "According to **His own purpose** and grace."

5. It is "Now made **manifest by the Appearing** of our *Saviour* Jesus Christ."

6. It implies the "**Abolishing of death.**"

7. It assures "**Life and Immortality.**"

WHAT OF THE NIGHT?

Isaiah 21. 11, 12.

1. To **Whom** the Call Came. "Watchman."
2. The **Question Asked.** "What of the night?"
Night of sin and the life of godlessness. The night of
sorrow, suffering, and testimony.
3. The **Answer Given.** To two classes.
> The *Morning Cometh.* Morning of eternal day.
> The *Night* Cometh. The night of eternal doom.
4. The **Advice** Offered. "Inquire, return, come."

FEARFUL THINKING.

"And when he thought thereon, he *wept*" (Matt. 14. 72).
We may learn from this—

1. That it is a great privilege to **hear the words of
Jesus.** Peter had heard something worth thinking about.
2. That **circumstances may call to mind** the words
of Jesus. Cock crowing. Sin remembered. "He thought
thereon"—on his *sin,* on his broken *promise* (v. 29), the
Person denied.
3. That **serious thought** is sure to have some definite
result—
> He went out (Matt. 26. 75). Separation.
> He wept. Conscience aroused. Heart melted.
> Contrition.
4. That **such mourners** are sure to be comforted.
"He is risen...tell Peter" (Mark 16. 6, 7). Restoration.

"THE WATERS PREVAILED."

Genesis 7. 18: Matthew 24. 37-39.

The waters of judgment shall ultimately prevail against
all ungodliness. See here an example of—

1. The waters prevailing over their **unbelief.**

2. The waters prevailing over all their **indifference.**

3. The waters prevailing over all their **pleasures.**

4. The waters prevailing over all their **efforts** to save themselves.

A STRANGE CURE.
Exodus 15. 23-25.

1. **A Sad Discovery.** "The waters were bitter."

2. **An Appointed Remedy.** "The Lord showed him a tree." Cross.

3. **A Perfect Cure.** "When cast in, the waters made sweet."

THE MEETING PLACE.
Exodus 25. 22.

1. **Where?** "At the Mercy Seat." The place where God rests in mercy. The Cross.

2. **Why?** Under the "Mercy Seat" was the "Testimony—the Law." Atonement.

3. **Whom?** "I will meet with *thee.*" Mercy.

4. **How?** "I will *commune* with thee there." Fellowship.

MANASSEH'S CONVERSION.
2 Chronicles 33. 1-13.

1. He was **Honoured.** Son of a godly man.

2. He **Sinned.** "Did evil in sight of the Lord" (v. 2).

3. He was **Warned.** "Lord spake to Manasseh" (v. 10).

4. He was **Humbled.** "Bound with fetters" (v. 11).

5. He **Prayed** (v. 12).

6. He was **Saved.** "The Lord heard his supplication and brought him... into his kingdom" (v. 13).

PRAISE THE LORD.
PSALM 147. 1-6.

PRAISE Him for His wonderful works of grace.

1. He **Gathereth** the Outcasts.
2. He **Healeth** the Broken-hearted.
3. He **Bindeth** up Wounds.
4. He **Numbereth** the Stars.
5. He **Calleth** them by Names.
6. He **Lifteth Up** the Meek.
7. He **Casteth Down** the Wicked.

LIFE AND ABUNDANCE
JOHN 10. 10.

1. **A Great Need.** "Life." "Alienated from the life of God."
2. **A Great Offer.** "I am come that ye might have life in abundance."

    (1) A Life of FREEDOM from sin and
    death, ... John 8. 32
    (2) A Life that is DIVINE, ... 2 Peter 1. 4
    (3) A Life that is ETERNAL, ... John 10. 28
    (4) A Life that is in ABUNDANCE, .. R.V., *margin*

A SOUL-SAVING SIGHT.
HEBREWS 2. 9, 10.

"BUT we see Jesus." We see Jesus—

1. **Humbling** Himself. "Made lower than the angels."
2. Suffering **death**.
3. Suffering death, **by the grace of God.**
4. Suffering death **for every man.**
5. **Crowned** with glory and honour.
6. **Bringing many** sons unto glory.
7. **Perfected as a Saviour** through sufferings.

GOODNESS AND SEVERITY.
ROMANS 11. 19-22

GOD is Good, but God is also Severe. God is Love, but God is also Light.

1. **The Severity of God.** He severs from Himself the unbelieving and the defiled (v. 17).

2. **The Goodness of God.** "Toward *thee* goodness," because you have *believed Him* (v. 22).

3. **The Solemn Lesson Taught.**

(1) That UNBELIEF SEVERS from the goodness of God (v. 20; Heb. 3. 19).

(2) That salvation is only by THE GRACE OF GOD. The *goodness* of God can never be merited by man.

(3) That FAITH UNITES to the goodness of God (v. 23).

(4) That we STAND only by faith (v. 20).

(5) That God is able and willing to save ALL THAT BELIEVE (v. 23).

THE SAVIOUR'S LAMENT.
LUKE 13. 34.

THIS lament was over a *guilty* city, and reveals—

1. **A Gracious Purpose.** Not judgment, but salvation. "As a hen gathereth."

2. **Infinite Mercy.** Gathered under *His wings*. Persecutors, murderers, etc.

3. **Almighty Power.** "How often would I."

4. **Longsuffering Compassion.** "How *often.*"

5. **Heart - Rending Anguish.** "O Jerusalem, Jerusalem."

6. **Wilful Resistance.** "But ye would not."

7. **Wounded Love.** "Your house *is left* to you desolate"

WHAT IS A CHRISTIAN?
ACTS 26. 19-28.

ONE who has—

1. **Seen** a Vision. "I was not disobedient to the *heavenly vision.*"

2. **Received** a Commission. "To open eyes and to turn from darkness to light."

3. **Performed** a Consecration. "I was not disobedient."

———

THE HEART

WHAT is meant by it? The seat of the affections and the centre of the moral man.

1. **Its Inherent Character.** "Deceitful and wicked,"   ..   ..   .. Jer. 17. 9

2. **Its Natural Outcome.** "Evil continually,"   ..   ..   .. Gen. 6. 5

3. **What should be Done with it?** "My son, *give me* thine heart,"   ..   .. Prov. 23. 26

4. **What God can Do with it.** Remove and renew, ... Ezek. 11. 19

5. **The Purpose of the New Heart.** "To know ME,"   ..   ..   .. Jer. 24. 7

6. **The Vision of the New Heart.** "See God,"   ..   ..   .. Matt. 5. 8

7 **The Privilege of the True Hearted.** Nearness, full assurance, worship,   Heb. 10. 22

———

CUT IT DOWN: LET IT ALONE.
LUKE 13. 7, 8.

THIS may be regarded as the language of justice and mercy, of law and grace. Note—

1. **Some Reasons why it Should be Cut Down.**

(1) It was the EASIEST WAY of getting rid of it.

(2) It had had SUFFICIENT TIME for trial.

(3) It showed NO SIGNS of improvement.

(4) It had never done ANY GOOD.

(5) It was filling a place that might be BETTER OCCUPIED by another.

(6) It was having a BAD INFLUENCE on others. A "cumberer."

2. Some Reasons why it Should be Let Alone. What are they? Well, WHAT ARE THEY?

NOT FAR FROM THE KINGDOM.
MARK 12. 34.

1. What is the Kingdom of God? It is not meat and drink—Material things. It is "Righteousness, peace, joy in the Holy Ghost."

2. What is it to be Not Far from the Kingdom? Many are not far from the kingdom—

(1) As regards their KNOWLEDGE. Young Ruler.

(2) As regards their MORALS. Pharisees.

(3) As regards their INTENTIONS. Foolish Virgins.

3. The Position of Those Not Far from It. Still *outside*. *Ill.* Cities of Refuge. Outside God's righteousness, God's peace, and God's joy.

THE SUFFERER AND HIS SEED.
ISAIAH 53. 10-12.

1. The **Sin**. "An Offering *for sin*."

2. The **Substitute**. "Him."

3. The **Sacrifice**. "His soul."

4. The **Saved**. "His seed."

5. The **Success**. "Prosper in His hands."

6. The **Satisfaction**. "See of the travail of His soul:"

7. The **Spoil**. Divided (v. 12).

WITHOUT ME.
JOHN 15. 5.

WITHOUT Christ a man is—

1. In danger, like **a lost sheep**,   ...   Luke 15. 4-6
2. As black as **an Ethiopian**,   ..   Jer. 13 23
3. As wretched as a **forsaken infant**,   Ezek. 16. 5-8
4. As loathsome as **a leper**, ...   Mark 1. 40
5. As powerless for good as **a corrupt tree**, ...   Matt. 7. 18
6. As poor as **a bankrupt**, ...   Matt. 18. 24-27
7. As hopeless as **a severed branch**,   John 15. 5

SEEK YE THE LORD.
ISAIAH 55. 6, 7.

1. The **Object** to be sought. "The Lord."
2. How the Lord is to be **Found**. "Seek."
3. Some **Encouragements** to seek. He *may* be found. He *is* near.
4. The **Time** to seek. "While."
5. The **Manner**. "Forsaking his way—thoughts."
6. The **Blessings** found in the Lord. "Mercy, Pardon."

SPIRITUAL LIFE.
EPHESIANS 2. 1.

1. The **Need** of it. "Dead."
2. The **Nature** of it. "Quickened."
3. The **Author** of it. "You hath HE quickened."
4. The **Joy** of it. Newness of life.

TEMPORARY RELIGION.
HOSEA 6. 4.

THEY had—

1. A **Sense** of need. "He hath torn."
2. A **Desire** to be saved. "Come, let us."

3. A **Prospect** of new life.   "After...we shall **live.**"
4. A **Knowledge** of the way (v. 3).
5. A **Belief** in His mercy (v. 3, *l.c.*).
   Yet all was as a morning cloud.

SALVATION.
Titus 2. 11-14.

1. Its **Need**.   "Ungodliness and worldly lusts"
2. Its **Source**.   "The grace of God."
3. Its **Extent**.   "To all men."
4. Its **Fulness**.   There is in it—
   (1) Substitution.   "He gave Himself for us."
   (2) Redemption.   "That He might redeem us from all iniquity."
   (3) Purity.   "Purify unto Himself."
   (4) Service.   "Zealous of good works."
   (5) Hope.   "Looking for that blessed hope," etc.

FREEDOM.
John 8. 36.

1. The **Privilege** spoken of.   "Make you *free.*" What from?
2. The **Nature** of this freedom.   "Free *indeed.*" What for?
3. The **Character** of the Deliverer.   "If the *Son,*" What by?

SEVEN WONDERS.
Titus 2. 11-14.

1. A Wonderful **Exhibition**.   "The grace of God hath appeared."
2. A Wonderful **Character**.   "The great God and our Saviour."
3. A Wonderful **Gift**.   "Gave Himself."
4. A Wonderful **Work**.   "Redeem...**purify.**"

5. A Wonderful **People**.   "A peculiar people. "

6. A **Wonderful Life**.   "Soberly, righteously, and Godly. "

7. A Wonderful **Prospect**.   "Looking for the glorious appearing of the great God our Saviour. "

HIS WORK IS PERFECT.
DEUTERONOMY 32. 4.

THIS can be proved by testing it—

1. As seen in **Creation**.
2. As seen in **Revelation**.
3. As seen in **Redemption**.
4. As seen in **Salvation**.
5. As seen in **Providence** (with regard to His own people) (Rom. 8. 28).

THINGS WHICH CANNOT BE SHAKEN.
HEBREWS 12. 27.

I. **Things which Have Been Shaken.**

1. The Opinions of Men.
2. The Kingdoms of this World.

II. **Things which Will be Shaken.**

1. False Foundations (Matt. 7. 27).
2. Physical Bodies.
3. Tombs of the Dead.

III. **Things which Cannot be Shaken.**

1. The Word of God.
2. The Foundation of Christ.
3. The Kingdom of God.
4. The Hope of the Christian.

WHY WILL YE DIE?
EZEKIEL 33. 11.

1. His **Displeasure** at it.   "I have no pleasure in the death of the wicked. "

2. His **Pleasure** in it. "But that the wicked turn from his way and live."

3. His **Affirmation** about it. "As I live, saith the Lord."

4. His **Exhortation** against it. "Turn ye, turn ye."

5. His **Question** regarding it. "Why will ye die?"

HE DIED FOR US.

1. That He might **deliver us from all iniquity**,	Titus 2. 14
2. That He might **bring us to God**,	1 Peter 3. 18
3. That He might deliver us from this **present evil world**,	Gal. 1. 4
4. That we might **receive the adoption of sons**,	Gal. 4 5

THE WILD ASS.

1. Man, **born like the wild ass**,	Job 11. 12
2. Man **lost** like the asses of Kish,	1 Sam. 9. 3
3. Man **snuffeth up** wind (vanity) like the wild ass,	Jer. 14. 6
4. Man, like the wild ass, used to the **wilderness**,	Jer. 2. 24
5. Man, like the ass, may be **redeemed**,	Exod. 13. 13
6. Man, like the ass, may have his **mouth opened** by God,	Num. 22. 28
7. Many, like the ass, may be **used** by the Lord,	Matt. 21. 3
8. Many, like the ass, may **know** his Master's crib (Bible),	Isa. 1. 3
9. Man's **jaw bone**, like the asses', may be a mighty weapon of victory,	Judg. 15. 16

YE MAY KNOW.
1 JOHN 5. 13.

IN this Epistle there are many things that *we* know.
We know—

1. That our sins are forgiven,	..	3. 5
2. That we have passed from death unto life,		3. 14
3. That we are of the Truth, ..	..	3. 19
4. That He is in us, ...	.. ...	4. 13
5 That we have eternal life,	..	5. 13
6. That He answers prayer,	..	5 15
7. That we have a new nature,	R.V.,	5. 18
8. That the whole world lieth in wickedness,		5. 19
9. That we have this knowledge from God,		5. 20
10. That we shall be like Him,	..	3. 2

THREEFOLD REST.
ISAIAH 14. 3.

I. The Need. "Bondage wherein thou wast made to serve." Slavery.

II. The Blessing. "Rest."

1. Rest from thy "Sorrow."
2. Rest from thy "Fear."
3. Rest from thy "Bondage."

III. The Blesser. "The *Lord* shall give."
"Come unto Me" (Matt. 11. 28).

FIND ME—FIND LIFE.
PROVERBS 8. 34-36.

1. A Proclamation. "Whoso findeth Me"—

(1) Findeth LIFE, and
(2) Shall obtain FAVOUR of the Lord. Satisfaction.

2. A Condition. "Hear, watch, wait."

3. A Warning. "He that sinneth against Me, wrongeth *his own* soul."

THE SURETY.
PROVERBS 11. 15.
"HE that is surety for a stranger shall smart for it."

1. The **Surety**, ...   The Christ.
2. The **Stranger**, ...   The Sinner.
3. The **Smarting**, ...   The Cross.

THE GRACE OF GOD.
TITUS 2. 11, 12.

1. **What the Grace of God Is**. It is not Law. It has nothing to do with human merit. It is the unmerited favour of God, in Almighty force.

2. **What the Grace of God Does**. It brings salvation. From the uttermost to the uttermost.

3. **To Whom this Grace of God Appears**. "To all men." Not to devils, but to *all* men, for that all have sinned.

4. **What this Grace of God Teaches**. To *deny* ungodliness and worldly lusts. To *live* soberly, righteously, and godly.

LIGHT FROM GOD.
JOHN 12. 35, 36.

1. The **Nature** of this Light. Christ Himself. "I am come a Light into the world" (v. 46).

2. The Evidence of being **Without the Light**. "He that walketh in darkness *knoweth not whither he goeth.*"

3. How this Light is to be **Enjoyed**. "*Believe* in the Light." Believe Him.

4. The Possibility of **Losing** this Light. "*While* ye have light, believe in it."

COULD NOT THIS MAN?
JOHN 11. 37.

THERE are many things Christ could not do, because He *would* not

1. Could He not have prevented **the Fall of Man**? Could, but did not.

2. Could He not **destroy the Devil**, as well as his works?   Could, but did not.

3. Could He not save men **without suffering** for them? Could, but did not.

4. Could He not save men **against their wills**?   Could, but will not.

5. Could He not bless us **without faith** and prayer? Could, but will not.

6. Could He not deliver from the **possibility of sinning**? Could, but does not.

THREE GREAT NECESSITIES.
LUKE 24. 46-49.

1. The Necessity laid upon the **Saviour**.   "To *suffer* and to rise from the dead. "

2. The Necessity laid upon the **Sinner**.   "Repentance. "

3. The Necessity laid upon the **Servant**.   "Witness. "

ATONEMENT.
2 CORINTHIANS 5. 14, 15.

1. Its **Nature**.   *"He* died. "

2. Its **Extent**.   "He died *for all.* "

3. Its **Need**.   "Then were *all dead.* "

4. Its **Purpose**.

(1) To Secure *Life.*   "They which live. "

(2) To Secure *a Consecrated* Life.   "Should not henceforth live unto themselves, but unto Him. "

BEHOLD THE MAN!
JOHN 19. 5.

1. The **God-sent Man**.   John 3. 16.

2. The **Sinless Man**.   "Which of you convinceth Me of sin?"

3. The **Sympathetic** Man. "Wept over Jerusalem."

4. The **Silent** Man. "Answered him (Pilate) nothing."

5. The **Suffering** Man. John 19 5.

6. The **Saving** Man. "Came to seek and to save" (Acts 15. 11).

THE LAMB OF GOD.
JOHN 1. 36, 37.

1. The **Testimony** of John. "Behold." A new Revelation.

2. The **Character** of Christ. "Lamb of God." He *belonged* to God; was *given* by God as a *Sacrifice* to God.

3. The **Mission** of Christ. "Take away the sin of the world" (v. 29).

4. The **Result** of Faith. "Followed Jesus."

SECRET SINS.
PSALM 19. 12.

BEWARE of living two lives—the secret and the public, the hidden and the revealed.

1. The **Burden** of this Prayer. Secret faults. Secret acts, thoughts, feelings.

2. The **Purpose** of this Prayer. "Cleansing." Without holiness no man seeth the Lord.

3. To **Whom** this Prayer was Made. "Thou." He looketh upon the heart.

4. The **Personality** of It. "Cleanse Thou *me*." Thou, me, with the cleansing Blood between (1 John 1. 7).

SOMETHING TO GLORY IN.
JEREMIAH 9. 23-24.

To glory in anything is to make it the chief delight.

I. **Some Things Men Glory In.**

1. WISDOM. "Let not the wise glory in their wisdom."

2. POWER.   "Neither let the mighty glory in his might."

3. WEALTH.   "Let not the rich glory in his riches."

II. Some Things Worth Glorying In.

1. THE KNOWLEDGE OF GOD. "Let him that glorieth, glory in this, that he *knoweth Me*."

2. The CHARACTER OF GOD. "Loving, Just, Righteous."

3. The WORD OF GOD. "In these things I delight, *saith the Lord*."

AN AWFUL TURNING.
PSALM 9. 17.

1. **Who?**   "The wicked."
2. **What?**   "Turned into Hell."
3. **Why?**   Because they "Forget God."

A GREAT DELIVERANCE.
PSALM 18. 16-20.

I. The Deliverer. See verse 2.

II. The Deliverance.

1. It was DIVINE. "He sent *from above*."
2. It was PERSONAL. "He took me."
3. It was COMPLETE. "He drew me *out*."
4. It was NEEDED. "Enemies too strong for me."
5. It was GRACIOUS. "Because He delighted in me."
6. It was BLESSED.   "He brought me into a large place" (v. 19).

"I AM THE DOOR."
JOHN 10. 9.

1. The **Blessing**. Salvation. "Shall be saved."
2. The **Way**. "By Me."
3. The **Condition**. "Enter in."
4. The **Offer**. "If any man."
5. The **Prospect**. "Shall go in and out and find pasture."

SPIRITUAL BLESSINGS
Ephesians 1. 3.
1. Their **Character**. "Spiritual. "
2. Their **Source**.   "In Christ. "
3. Their **Greatness**   "*All* spiritual blessings. "
4. Their **Giver**   "Father of our Lord Jesus Christ. "
5. Their **Effect**. "Blessed be God. .who has blessed us"

A CRY FOR THE AGES.
John 7. 37, 38.
This cry of Christ is a challenge to the ages.   It is the cry of—
1. **Almighty Fulness**. "Come unto Me. "
2. **Infinite Compassion**. "If *any* man. "
3. **Tenderest Pity**   "If any man *thirst*. "
4. **Pressing Invitation**.   "Let him *come* unto Me. "
5. **Assuring Promise**.   "Out of Him shall flow rivers of living water. "

"BEHOLD MY FEET. "
Luke 24. 39.
His feet are suggestive of—
1. **Suffering**   "They pierced My feet" (Psa. 22. 16).
2. **Mercy**. "She stood at His feet weeping" (Luke 7. 38).
3. **Power**.   "Lame, blind...cast at Jesus' feet, and He healed them all" (Matt. 15. 30)
4. **Rest**.   "Sitting at the feet of Jesus...in his right mind" (Luke 8. 35)
5. **Hope**.   "She came and fell at His feet" (Mark 7. 25; John 11 32).
6. **Teaching**   "Mary sat at His feet" (Luke 10. 39).
7 **Comfort**.   "Why are ye troubled?...Behold My feet" (Luke 24 38, 39)

8. **Service.** "Mary anointed the feet of Jesus...house filled" (John 12. 3).

9. **Worship.** "They held Him by the feet and worshipped Him" (Matt. 28. 9).

10. **Victory.** "Thou hast put all things under His feet" (Heb. 2. 8).

————

SALVATION CERTAINTIES.
2 TIMOTHY 1. 12.

1. **Revelation.** "I know *Him.*" "Jesus Christ, who hath abolished death" (v. 11).
2. **Faith** "I have believed."
3. **Surrender.** "I have committed."
4. **Assurance.** "I am persuaded."
5. **Confidence.** "HE *is* able."
6. **Experience.** "I know."
7. **Testimony.** "I am not ashamed "

————

AN UNFAILING REFUGE.
PROVERBS 18. 10.

1. Its **Nature.** "The *Name* of the Lord." His Name is His character.
2. Its **Strength.** "A strong tower."
3. Its **Acceptance.** "Righteous runneth into it and are safe—set aloft" (*margin*). The righteous are the *right-minded*.

————

THE BLOOD THAT SPEAKETH.
HEBREWS 12. 24.

THE blood of Abel speaks of vengeance (Gen. 4. 10). The Blood of Christ of *better things.* It speaks of—

1. **An Eternal Purpose,** .. .. Rev. 13. 8
2. **Forgiveness,** .. .. .. Col 1. 14

3. **Cleansing,** .. .. 1 John 1. 7
4. **Liberty,** .. .. Heb. 10. 19
5. **Peace,** .. .. Col. 1. 20
6. **Heaven,** .. .. Rev. 7. 14, 15

GRACE ALWAYS ALL SUFFICIENT.
2 CORINTHIANS 9. 8.

I. The Character of It.

1. It is "GRACE." Free favour of God. Not works.

2. It is "ALL Grace." Nothing but Grace all the way.

3. It is "All Grace ABOUNDING TOWARD YOU." For your own personal and eternal needs.

II. The Measure of It.

1. It is ALL-SUFFICIENT. As to its source.

2. It is All-sufficient ALWAYS. As to its outflow.

3. It is All-sufficient always IN ALL THINGS. As to its adaptability.

III. The Assurance of It. "God is able."

　　1. BELIEVE it.

　　2. EXPECT it.

　　3. THANK HIM for it.

IV. The Outcome of It. "May *abound in every good work.*"

SALVATION FOR ALL.
1 TIMOTHY 2. 3, 4.

1. An **Almighty Saviour.** "God our Saviour."

2. An **All-embracing Purpose.** "Who will have all men to be saved."

3. An **All-important Need.** "To come to a knowledge of the truth."

4. An **All-important End.** "This is acceptable in the sight of God."

AWAKE, AWAKE.
ISAIAH 52. 1, 2.

I. A Sorrowful Condition Suggested.

1. A State of INSENSIBILITY. "Awake, awake."

2. A State of UNCLEANNESS. "Shake thyself from the *dust.*"

3. A State of CAPTIVITY. "*Loose* thyself, O *captive* daughter."

II. An Arousing Call. The urgent call of God—

1. To AWAKE. To true consciousness.

2. To DECIDED ACTION. "Shake thyself."

3. To RECEIVE A GIFT. "*Put on* thy beautiful garments."

THE HEALING WATERS.
EZEKIEL 47. 1-12.

1. Their **Source.** "Threshold...of the sanctuary" (vv. 1-12).

2. Their **Course.** "Came down by the altar" (v. 1).

3. Their **Influence.** "Everything shall live whither the river cometh" (v. 9).

4. Their **Abundance.** "Waters to swim in" (v. 5).

HIMSELF FOR OUR SINS.
GALATIANS 1. 3-5.

HIMSELF for *our sins.* What a contrast! There are great deeps here.

1. **Revelation.** "Grace to you and peace from God the Father, and our Lord Jesus Christ."

2. **Substitution.** "Who gave Himself *for* our sins."

3. **Salvation.** "Deliver us from this present evil world."

4. **Explanation.** "According to the will of God our Father."

5. **Adoration.** "To whom be glory for ever and ever."

A CURE FOR CAREFULNESS.
PHILIPPIANS 4 6, 7.

1. The **Disease**   "Carefulness."
2. The **Remedy**   Prayerfulness.   "Let your requests be made known unto God."
3. The **Promise**   Blessfulness.   "The peace of God shall keep your hearts."

WHAT THINK YE OF CHRIST?
MATTHEW 22. 42.

1. As a **Teacher**
2. As a **Worker**
3. As a **Sufferer**.
4. As a **Saviour**

5 As a **Master**
6. As a **Friend**
7. As a **Judge**.

SOWING AND REAPING.
GALATIANS 4. 7, 8

1 **A Common Mistake**.   Self-deception.   "Be *not* deceived" by your own thoughts or feelings.
2. **A Solemn Reminder**   "God is not mocked." He will not be mocked by indifference, false promises, or professions.
3. **An Unfailing Law**.   "Whatsoever a man soweth, that shall he also reap."

FOUR TITLES OF CHRIST.
ZECHARIAH 10 4

1. The "**Corner**"   Christ our Foundation.
2. The "**Nail**"   Christ our Burden-bearer
3. The "**Battle-Bow**"   Christ our Defence
4. The "**Ruler**"   Christ our Lord (*margin*, R.V.).

THE POWER OF THE SON.
JOHN 5. 24.

1. The **Person Who Speaks.** "Verily, verily I say unto you."
2. The **Blessing Offered.** "Everlasting Life."
3. The **Promise Made.** "Shall not," "Hath."
4. The **Condition Mentioned.** He that "heareth" and "believeth."

THE SUN OF RIGHTEOUSNESS.
MALACHI. 4. 2.

As the Sun of Righteousness, Christ is—

1. The **Centre** of the New Creation. The law of attraction here is the law of love.
2. The **Glory** of the Spiritual World. His presence fills it.
3. The **Source** of all Spirit Blessings. Light, life, warmth, beauty, fruitfulness.
4. His **Movements** are Infallably Trustworthy. Never fails in His course of action.
5. His **Progress** is Irresistible. He cannot be hindered nor hurried.
6. His **Shining** is for the Good of All. No sunset for those who follow Him. Eternal gloom without Him.

ZACCHAEUS.
LUKE 19. 1-10.

THE story of his conversion. Note—

1. His **Anxiety.** "Sought to see Jesus."
2. His **Difficulties.** "*Chief* among the publicans and *little* of stature."
3. His **Earnestness.** "Ran...climbed."
4. His **Call.** "Come down."

5. His **Obedience.**   "He made haste. "

6. His **Acceptance.**   "Received Him gladly. "

7. His **Salvation.**   "This day is salvation come to this house. "

THE SINNER'S HOPE.
ISAIAH 59. 1, 2.

I. **Their Condition.**

1. SEPARATED from God.   "Your iniquities have separated you. "

2. UNFIT for God.   "Your sins have hidden His face. "

II. **Their Hope.**   In the fact that—

1. God's EAR is not Heavy.   Ever wide-awake to the cry of need.

2. God's HAND is not Shortened.   It takes a long arm to reach sinful men, and a strong hand to save them.

THE SAVIOUR.
1 TIMOTHY 2. 3-6.

1. The Saviour's **Power.**   *"God* our Saviour. "

2. The Saviour's **Purpose.**   "Who will have all men to be saved. "

3. The Saviour's **Provision.**   "Gave Himself a ransom for all. "

4. The Saviour's **Position.**   "Between God and men. "

SIRS, WE WOULD SEE JESUS.
JOHN 12. 21.

JESUS is a great attraction.

I. **Some Motives for Seeking Jesus.**

1. CURIOSITY.   "Saving Lazarus" (v. 9).

2. WORLDLY ADVANTAGE.   "Loaves and fishes. "

3. SOUL DISTRESS.   Woman in Simon's house.

II. **Where Jesus may be Seen.**

1 In BETHLEHEM   As the Lowly One.
2 In JERUSALEM   As the Merciful One (John 7 37).
3 In GETHSEMANE   As the Suffering One.
4 On THE CROSS   As the Redeeming One.
5 In THE RESURRECTION   As the Victorious One.
6 In THE HEAVENS.   As the Glorified One.

III **The Effect of Seeing Jesus.**

    1 CONFESSION.　　　　4. TRANSFORMATION.
    2 SALVATION　　　　　 5. GLORIFICATION.
    3 SATISFACTION.

THE VOICE OF THE BLOOD.
EXODUS 12 13, HEBREWS 12. 24.

"THE Blood that speaketh. "

1. Of **Sacrifice**   "Lamb slain. "

2 Of **Satisfaction.** Purpose of God accomplished through it

3 Of **Substitution.**   "Lamb slain" for the house. Christ for us.

4 Of **Submission** The sprinkled blood spoke of faith and obedience on the part of the household.

5. Of **Salvation**   Their safety depended on the blood.

CONVERSION.
MATTHEW 18. 3.

HERE are three reasons why it is needed.

1 Because by **nature** we are not now as "little children "

2 Because we are presently **unfit** for "the Kingdom of Heaven "

3. Because **Christ says.** "Except ye be converted ye cannot. " He knows

WHY NOT BELIEVE ME?
JOHN 8. 46.

"IF I say the truth, why do ye not believe me?" "I have told you the truth"—

1. About **My Character**, ...   **v 12**
2. About **My Mission**, ...   **v. 18**
3. About the **Awfulness of Sin**,   .   .   **v. 24**
4. About the **Conditions of Discipleship**, .   **v. 31**
5. About **Spiritual Freedom**,   .   **v. 36**
6 About **Your Own Condition**,   **vv. 42-44**
    "Why do you not believe Me?"

A CALL TO DECISION
2 SAMUEL 3. 17

1. **Whom** they sought. "They sought David."
2. **When** they sought him. "In times past."
3. **Why** they sought him. "To be king over them."
4. **"Now then, do it."** David is within your reach, and offered to you.

THE BLOOD OF CHRIST

I. **Its God-ward Aspect.**

1. Ground of ATONEMENT, ... Lev 17. 11
    A Covering.
2. Ground of REDEMPTION,   1 Pet 1 18, 19
    A Price.
3. Ground of PEACE, ...   Col 1 20
    A Purchase.

II **Its Man-ward Aspect.**

1 FORGIVENESS,   ..   . Col. 1. 14
2. CONTINUAL CLEANSING,   . 1 John 1 7
3. NEARNESS, ... Eph. 3. 13
4. BOLDNESS, ... Heb. 10. 19, 20

5. Holiness, ... Heb. 13. 12
6. Service, ... Heb. 9. 14
7. Victory, ... Rev. 12. 11

TWO CUPS.
John 18. 11; Psalm 116. 12, 13.

I. The Cup of Suffering offered to Christ (John 18. 11).

1. Its Contents. "Betrayal." False accusations, mockery, desertion, death, curse.
2. Its Nature "A cup." Not a well or spring.
3. The Giver. "My Father."
4. Its Acceptance. "Shall I not drink it?"

II. The Cup of Salvation offered to us (Psalm 116. 12, 13).

1. Its Contents. Pardon, peace, paradise, salvation.
2. Its Giver. "Gift of God."
3. Its Acceptance. "I *will take* the cup of salvation."

NEITHER MORE NOR LESS.
Exodus 30. 15.

Redemption is—

1. **Needed by All.** "Every man a ransom" (v. 12).
2. **Alike for All.** "Rich not give more, and the poor not less."
3. **Sufficient for All.** "Make an atonement for your souls."

LIFE AND DEATH.
Deuteronomy 30. 19, 20.

1. A **Responsibility.** "Life and death."
2. A **Privilege.** "I have set *before you* life."
3. An **Explanation.** "He is thy life."
4. An **Exhortation.** "Therefore choose life"
5. An **Encouragement.** "That both thou and thy seed may live."

A WISE CHOICE.
1 CHRONICLES 21. 13.

1. The **Difficulty.**   "I am in a great strait."
2. The **Alternative.**   "Between the Lord and...man."
3. The **Choice.**   "Let me fall into the hand of the Lord."
4. The **Reason.**   "For very great are His mercies."

———

WELL OR WOE.
ISAIAH 3. 10, 11.

1. Two **Classes.**   "Righteous...wicked."
2. Two **conditions.**   "Well. woe"
3. Two **Rewards.**   "Eat the fruit of their doings."
"The reward of his hands given him."

———

A GREAT LIGHT.
ISAIAH 9. 2.

I. **A Twofold Need.**
1. "WALKING in darkness."
2. "DWELLING in the shadow of death."

II. **A Twofold Privilege.**
1. "Have *seen* a GREAT LIGHT."
2. "UPON THEM hath the light shined."

———

THE PRODIGAL.
LUKE 15. 11-24.

1. He was **Bad** (v. 12).   3. He was **Sad** (v. 16).
2. He was **Mad** (v. 13).   4. He was **Glad** (v. 24).

———

WORKS OF GRACE.
PSALM 81. 6-16.

I. **The Infinite Grace of God.**   Seen in—
   1. REMOVING BURDENS, ...   **v** 6
   2. LIBERATING HANDS, ...   **v** 6

3. ANSWERING PRAYER, ... **v. 7**
4. TESTING FAITH, ... **v. 7**
5. ENCOURAGING HOPE, .. **vv 8, 9**
6. PROMISING SUFFICIENCY, .. **v. 10**

II. **The Base Ingratitude of Man.**
1. PRIDE MANIFESTED, ... *margin*, **v. 11**
2. SELF-WILL ASSERTED, ... **v. 12**
3. LOVE GRIEVED, ... **v 13**
4. PRIVILEGE LOST, ... **vv. 14-16**

THE BLESSED PEOPLE.
PSALM 89. 15-18.

1. What they **Know.** "The joyful sound."
2. Where they **Walk** "In the light of Thy countenance"
3. In what they **Rejoice.** "In Thy Name all the day."
4 How they are **Exalted.** "In Thy righteousness."
5. The Secret of their **Strength.** "Thou art "
6. The Sphere of their **Life.** "In Thy favour "
7. Their **Security.** "The Lord our Shield" (*margin*).

A GREAT SALVATION.
PSALM 106. 6-12.

I. **The Need of It.**
1. There was IGNORANCE of God's Wonders (v 7)
2. There was FORGETFULNESS of God's Mercies (v. 7).
3. There was REBELLION against God's Will (v. 7. R. V.).

II. **The Nature of It.** There was in it—
1. GRACE. "For His Name's sake."
2. PURPOSE. "That He might."
3. POWER. "Rebuked the Red Sea. "
4. GUIDANCE. "He led them "
5. PROTECTION. "He saved them from the enemy "
6. FAITH "They believed His words."
7. PRAISE. "They sang His praise "

A FIXED HEART.
PSALM 108. 1-6.

I. **The Heart Needs Fixing.**

II. **God only Can Properly Fix It.**

III. **The Characteristics of a Fixed Heart.** It is a —

1. CONFIDENT HEART. "O God, my heart is fixed."
2. HAPPY HEART. "I will sing praises."
3. WIDE-AWAKE HEARTS. "I will awake early."
4. FEARLESS HEART. "I will sing unto Thee *among the nations.*"
5. THANKFUL HEART. "Thy mercy is great."
6. GOD-HONOURING HEART. "Be Thou exalted."
7. PITIFUL HEART. "Save with Thy right hand."

THE BREAD FROM HEAVEN.
JOHN 6. 32-35.

1. Christ the **Bread of God** (v. 33). Meeting the need of God on our behalf.

2. Christ the **Living Bread** (v. 33). Meeting the world's need—dead in sins. He is the *Life-giving* Bread.

3. Christ the **Bread of Life** (v. 35). Meeting and sustaining the needs of His people. Eat, O friends.

SAUL'S CONVERSION.
ACTS 9. 1-20.

SEE him—

1. As a **Rebel.** "Yet breathing out threatenings" (see Acts 7. 58).
2. As a **Prisoner.** "He fell to the earth."
3. As an **Inquirer.** "Who art Thou, Lord?"
4. As a **Disciple.** "Lord, what wilt Thou have me to do?"
5. As a **Worshipper.** "Behold he prayeth."
6. As a **Witness.** "Straightway he preached Christ" (v. 20).

CONSIDER YOUR WAYS.
HAGGAI 1. 5, 6.
HAVE they not been disappointing? See how unsatisfying they have been.

1. "Ye have **sown much** and brought in *little.*"
2. "Ye **eat,** but ye have *not enough.*"
3. "Ye **drink,** but ye are *not filled* with drink."
4. "Ye **clothe** ye, but there is *no warmth.*"
5. Ye put "wages into **a bag with holes.**" No profit.

"CONSIDER YOUR WAYS."

A SURE FOUNDATION.
2 TIMOTHY 2. 19.

1. **There is a Foundation.** Men need not build on sand (Matt. 7 26)
2. **This Foundation is Laid by God.** "The foundation of God" (Isa. 28. 6).
3. **This Foundation is Immovable.** "Standeth sure."
4. **All who Build on it are Sealed for Him.** "Having this seal, the Lord knoweth them that are His."

THE POWER OF THE CROSS.
1 CORINTHIANS 1 18.

NOTE the place the Cross had in Paul's preaching (v. 17).

I. **What is Meant by the Cross?** The atoning death of the Lord Jesus Christ.

II. **What is Meant by the Preaching of the Cross?** Holding up Christ's death as the Divine remedy for the sins and souls of men. As Moses lifted up the serpent in the wilderness.

III. **What are the Effects of a Preached Cross?**

1. "FOOLISHNESS" to them that believe *not.*
2. "POWER OF GOD" to them that believe. Power to save and satisfy.

TRANSFORMING GRACE.
ZECHARIAH 3. 1-5.

1. A Sad **Condition**.   "Clothed with filthy garments."
2. A Strong **Opposition**.   "Satan standing to resist."
3. A Good **Position**.   "Standing before the angel."
Christ.
4. A Great **Transformation**.   "Filthy garments taken
away, and clothed with change of raiment."
5. A Perfect **Salvation**.   "Is not this a brand plucked
out of the fire?" (v. 2).

———

DEATH IN THE POT.

"THEN bring meal" (2 Kings 4. 41).   Overcome evil
with good.

1. There is death in the pot of **strong drink**.   Then
bring the "Water of Life."
2. There is death in the pot of **literature**.   Then bring
the "Word of God."
3. There is death in the pot of **worldly pleasure**.
Then bring the "Heavenly Treasures."
4. There is death in the pot of the **carnal mind**.   Then
bring the "Mind of Christ."
5. There is death in the pot of **false profession**.   Then
bring the "Gospel of Christ."

———

POTS v. HEARTS.
PSALM 68. 13.

1 A **Dangerous** Pot,	..	.. 2 Kings 4. 40
2. A **Boiling** Pot,	.. ..	.. Jer. 1. 13
3. A **Polluted** Pot,	.. ..	.. Ezek. 24. 6
4. A **Refining** Pot,	.. ..	.. Prov. 17. 3
5. An **Unfailing** Pot, ..	..	.. 2 Kings 4. 2
6. A **Golden** Pot,	.. ..	.. Heb. 9. 4
7. A **Consecrated** Pot,	..	.. Zech. 14. 20, 21

TWO KINDS OF BLINDNESS.
ISAIAH 42. 7-19.

I. Guilty Blindness. "To open the eyes of the blind" (v. 7).

1. Blind to THEIR OWN NEED.
2. Blind to the GOSPEL LIGHT (2 Cor. 4. 4).
3. Blindness of WILFUL IGNORANCE (Rom. 10. 3).

II. God-honouring Blindness. "Who is blind as the Lord's servant" (v. 19).

1. Blind to the ATTRACTIONS OF THE WORLD (1 John 2.16).
2. Blind to the TEMPTATIONS OF THE DEVIL (Matt. 4. 8).
3. Blind to SELF-EASE and PLEASURE.

FALSE FIRE.
ISAIAH 50. 10, 11.

LEARN here that—

I. The **difference** between the false and the true fire is real. The false is self-made. "Ye have kindled." The true is from above.

II. The **kindling** of a fire reveals a need felt. Implying darkness, danger.

III. The fire of man's kindling is **most uncertain**. Sparks, fitful, untrustworthy.

IV. Those who **walk in the light** of their own fire end in misery. "Lie down in sorrow."

V. The **way out** of darkness is very plain.

1. "TRUST in the Name of the Lord."
2. "STAY upon God."

GOD'S REMEDY FOR A WORLD'S WOES.
JOHN 3. 16.

I. The Object of God's Love. "The world." In all its darkness, guilt, hopelessness.

II. The Manifestation of God's Love. "Gave His Son." This the result of God's calculation of the world's need.

III. The Purpose of this Manifestation.
1. To Reveal HIS ATTITUDE TOWARDS ALL. "Loved."
2. To Make SALVATION POSSIBLE FOR ALL. "Whosoever believeth."
3. To Make SALVATION CERTAIN TO EVERY BELIEVER. "Not perish, but have."

LOVED AND LIFTED.
ISAIAH 38. 17.

I. A Miserable Condition. "In the pit of corruption." The pit, a place of darkness. Bondage.

II. A Sorrowful Experience. "For peace I had great bitterness." The bitterness of disappointment; the bitterness of a guilty conscience.

III. A Wonderful Deliverance.
1. The NATURE of It. "From the pit of corruption."
2. The COMFORT of It. "Thou hast cast all my sins behind Thy back."
3. The CAUSE of It. "In *love* to my soul."

THE LIGHT OF THE GOSPEL.
2 CORINTHIANS 4. 3, 4.

I. The Gospel. What is it? Good news. God's spell. Glory of Christ (R.V.).

II. Its Influence.
1. It is a LIGHT.
2. A Light that shines OUT OF DARKNESS (v. 6).
3. A Light that is to SHINE IN THE HEART.
4. A Light that REVEALS THE GLORY OF GOD in the face of Jesus Christ.

III. The Hiding of the Light. "If our Gospel be hid, " etc.

1. If hid, it is an evidence of UNBELIEF (v. 4).

2. If hid, an evidence of BONDAGE. "Satan hath blinded the mind. "

3. If hid, an evidence of BEING LOST. "If Gospel is hid—hid to them that are perishing" (R. V.).

A SAD CASE.
2 CHRONICLES 36. 16.

1. God's **Messengers** Mocked.
2. God's **Word** Despised.
3. God's **Prophets** Misused.
4. God's **Wrath** Aroused.
5. God's **Presence** Withdrawn. "No remedy. "

THE LAME MAN.
ACTS 3. 1-11.

1. He was **Helpless.** "Lame ..carried. "
2. He was **Hopeful.** "Look on us...and he gave heed unto them. "
3. He was **Helped.** "Took him by the hand and lifted him up. "
4. He was **Healed.** "He entered with them, leaping. "
5. He was **Happy.** "Praising God. "

CHRIST OUR PASSOVER.
1 Corinthians 5. 7.

SEE Exodus 12. 1-24. The Passover lamb—

1. Was **appointed** by God, ... John 1. 29
2. Was **subjected** to a time of testing, Luke 9. 35
   See Christ's whole public life.
3. Must be **without blemish,** .. 1 Peter. 18, 19
4. Must be **slain,** .. .. .. Luke 24. 26

5. Must **not break** its bones,   .. John 19. 36

6. Blood must be **sprinkled,**   .. Heb. 9. 21-23

7. Flesh must be eaten **roast with fire.** It is "Christ crucified" that satisfies.

THEY OVERCAME BY THE BLOOD.
REVELATION 12. 11.

1. The **Dragon's Character** and Downfall (v. 9).

2. The **Cause of his Downfall.** "Manchild enthroned" (v. 5).

3. The **Blessings Offered.** "Now is come salvation, strength, Kingdom of God, and the sovereignty of Christ."

4. The **Secret of Victory.** Threefold.

(1) By the "Blood of the Lamb."

(2) By the "Word of their Testimony."

(3) By "Loving *not* their lives unto the death." Self-surrender.

CHRIST'S SUFFERINGS AT THE HANDS OF MEN.
JOHN 18.

1. Betrayed by the **Hypocritical,**   ..   ..   v. 5

2. Defended by the **Passionate,**   ..   vv. 10-11

3. Smitten by the **Unreasonable,**   ..   vv. 21-23

4. Denied by the **Cowardly,**   ..   ..   v. 25

5. Shunned by the **Self-righteous,** ..   ..   v. 28

6. Questioned by the **Ambitious,** vv. 33-38; ch. 19. 1

7. Mocked by the **Frivolous,**   ..   vv. 19-23

THE SUN AND SHIELD.
PSALM 84. 11-12.

1. **Provision.** "The Lord is a Sun and Shield."

2. **Promise.** "He will give grace and glory."

3. **Prospect.** "No good thing will He withold."

4. **Privilege.** "Blessed is the man that trusteth in Thee."

THE JUBILEE GOSPEL.
LUKE 4. 18, 19.

1. **The Virtues of this Gospel.** It heals, delivers, recovers, liberates.

2. **The Authority of the Preacher.** "The *Spirit* of the Lord is upon *me*. He hath anointed me to preach."

3. **The Graciousness of the Offer.** "To the *poor*."

4. **The Time of Opportunity.** "The acceptable *year*." A limited time. "Behold, now is the accepted time."

THE BREAD OF LIFE.
JOHN 6. 51.

WHAT are its characteristics?

1. It "came down from Heaven." Divine.

2. It is the "Living Bread." Life-giving.

3. It was given "for the life of the world." All-sufficient.

4. He that eateth it will "live for ever." Eternal

5. It is to "any man." Universal.

THE SHIP WAS BROKEN.
ACTS 27. 40-44.

WE may learn from this shipwreck—

1. That there **are sunken rocks** in the course of life. Unbelief, neglect, love of world.

2. That our plans and purposes may be **suddenly broken up**. "Rich fool."

3. That unexpected trials and disappointments may be **for our good**. Paul.

4. That the sight of helplessness and suffering **calls forth** sympathy and self-sacrifice.

5. That in the presence of a great calamity **earthly things** lose their value. "Cargo overboard. "

6. That the **means of salvation** may be lightly esteemed. "Broken pieces of the ship. "

WISDOM'S CRY.
PROVERBS 1. 20-26.

IN this cry we hear the voice of Him who is the "Wisdom of God. " It is—

1. An **Open** Cry. "She crieth in the chief places of concourse. "

2. A **Pitiful** Cry. "How long, ye simple ones?"

3. A **Reproving** Cry. "How long will fools hate wisdom?"

4. An **Inviting** Cry. "Turn ye. "

5. A **Merciful** Cry. "Behold I will pour out my Spirit upon you, " etc.

6. A **Rejected** Cry. "I have called, and ye have refused. "

7. A **Mocking** Cry. "I will mock when your fear cometh. "

ARE YOU READY?
MATTHEW 25. 1-12.

I. The **Character of Christ**. "Behold, the *Bridegroom*. " One pledged to His own.

II. The **Church's Hope**. "Behold the Bridegroom *cometh*. "

III. The **Condition Revealed**. "Few wise and few foolish. " The real and the false

IV. The **Cry Made**. "There was a cry made "

1. It was made at an UNWELCOME hour. "Midnight. "

2. It was an AWAKENING cry. "All slumbered and slept."

3. It was a SEPARATING cry. "Come ye forth" (R.V.).

4. It was a SELF-SEARCHING cry. "They arose and trimmed their lamps."

V. The **Crisis Reached.** Then came the—

1. SECURITY of the Prepared. "They that were *ready* went in."

2. DOOM of the Unprepared. The *unready* were shut out (v. 10).

THEY HEARD HIM GLADLY.
MARK 12. 37.

REASONS why the common people, or the multitude, heard *Him* gladly.

1. Because He always **treated them respectfully.**

2. Because He **spoke plainly** and simply.

3. Because He **spoke sympathetically,** as one who loved them (8. 2).

4. Because He **showed no respect of persons.**

5. Because He **appealed to their deeper needs.**

6. Because "He **spake as one having authority.**"

7. Because His **life was in perfect accord** with His teaching.

MAN'S SEVENFOLD NEED DIVINELY MET IN JESUS CHRIST.
JOHN 1.

MAN's deepest need can be met by—

1. A Divine **Revelation of the Father.** Jesus Christ has declared Him, ... vv. 14-18

2. A Divine **Light** whereby we may see things as they really are in Christ the Light,   vv. 7-9

3. A Divine **Substitute** to atone for sin. Christ is the Lamb of God, ...   v. 29

4. A Divine **Right** to the Family of God.
Christ gives that right, ... **v. 12**
5. A Divine **Nature** to fit him for that holy
family. Christ by His Spirit gives that, .. **v. 13**
6. A Divine **Fulness** to satisfy that nature.
Christ has that, ... **v. 16**
7. A Divine **Power** for service. Christ
gives that, ... **v. 33**

SALVATION FACTS.
JOHN 3.

1. The **Character of God** (v. 16), .. Love.
2. The **Mission of Christ** (vv. 2, 17), Salvation.
3. The **Power of the Spirit** (v. 8), Life-giving.
4. The **Need of Man** (vv. 3, 19), .. Regeneration.
5. The **Condition of Life** (vv. 14, 15), Believing.
6. The **Consequence of Unbelief**
(vv. 18, 19), ... Condemnation.
7. The **Evidence of Faith** (v. 21), .. Works.

CHRIST DIED FOR US.
ROMANS 5. 6-11.

I. **The Object of His Death.**
  1. UNGODLY (v. 6).   3. ENEMIES (v. 10).
  2. SINNERS (v. 8).
II. **The Purpose of His Death.**
  1. TO SAVE (v. 9).   3. TO RECONCILE (v. 10)
  2. TO JUSTIFY (v. 9).   4. TO SATISFY (v. 11).

SEEK YE THE LORD.
ISAIAH 55. 6, 7.

1. The **Soul's Need.** "The Lord."
2. **How** the Lord is to be Found. "Seek ye."

3. **Encouragement** to Seek.
   (1) "He may be found."   (2) "He is near."
4. **The Time.** "While "
5. The **Manner**. "Let the wicked *forsake his way...* and *his* thoughts. "
6. The **Promised Blessings**. "He will *have mercy...* He will abundantly *pardon.* "

———

FORGIVENESS.
Acts 10. 43.

I, Of **Whom** the prophets witnessed. "To *Him.* "

II. Their **General** Testimony. "*All* the prophets. "

III. The **Nature** of their Testimony.

1. They testified to the "REMISSION of sins. "
2. That this remission was only "through HIS NAME. "
3. That this remission was given through "BELIEVING in Him. "
4. That this blessing was offered to "WHOSOEVER. "